Banking and Accounting Issues

Edited by Nizar Mohammad Alsharari

Published in London, United Kingdom

Banking and Accounting Issues
http://dx.doi.org/10.5772/intechopen.98048
Edited by Nizar Mohammad Alsharari

Contributors
Lucky Nugroho, Maria Bengtsson, Rim Khemiri, Nadia Ben Farhat-Toumi, Nouha Ben Arfa, Mahfud Sholihin, Dian Andari, Carmem Leal, Maria Elisabete Duarte Neves, Diogo Rocha, Rosaria Cerrone, Rui Jorge Rodrigues Silva, Bernardo Cardoso, José Vale, Rúben Nunes, Rogério Bessa, Joana Monteiro, Pattarake Sarajoti, Pattanaporn Chatjuthamard, Suwongrat Papangkorn, Nizar Mohammad Alsharari

First published in London, United Kingdom, 2022 by IntechOpen
IntechOpen is the global imprint of INTECHOPEN LIMITED, registered in England and Wales, registration number: 11086078, 5 Princes Gate Court, London, SW7 2QJ, United Kingdom

British Library Cataloguing-in-Publication Data
A catalogue record for this book is available from the British Library

Additional hard and PDF copies can be obtained from orders@intechopen.com

Banking and Accounting Issues
Edited by Nizar Mohammad Alsharari
p. cm.
Print ISBN 978-1-80355-771-7
Online ISBN 978-1-80355-772-4
eBook (PDF) ISBN 978-1-80355-773-1

For EU product safety concerns:
IN TECH d.o.o., Prolaz Marije Krucifikse Kozulić 3, 51000 Rijeka, Croatia,
info@intechopen.com or visit our website at intechopen.com.

Meet the editor

Dr. Nizar Mohammad Alsharari is an Associate Professor of Accounting and Finance, and Ph.D. supervisor at the Department of Accounting, Finance, and Entrepreneurship, College of Business, Jackson State University, USA. He obtained his Ph.D. in Accounting and Finance from Durham University, UK. Dr. Alsharari has more than twenty years of experience in public sector management and academia. He has published more than forty articles in high-ranking journals emphasizing management accounting, institutional approach, and public sector management. Dr. Alsharari is a certified expert in QuickBooks Accounting and IMA Data Analytics and has good experience in artificial intelligence and cloud computing. He is also interested in studying accounting innovations, cloud accounting, budgeting, and government accounting. He has authored many peer-reviewed scientific papers and chapters and edited and reviewed several books and articles from international publishers.

Contents

Preface

Banking and Accounting Issues provides business users, government leaders, academics, students, and practitioners with the most contemporary, relevant, and reliable financial and non-financial information. Topics are selected in such a way so as to cover various needs and demands of the international business community and academic environment.

The constantly changing landscape of banking and accounting challenges experts and practitioners to stay informed of the field's most up-to-date research. This book will empower students, researchers, and academicians with a strong understanding of critical issues within banking and accounting by providing both broad and detailed perspectives on cutting-edge theories and developments in the field. It presents general information on conceptual, methodological, organizational, and managerial issues as well as insights into emerging trends and future opportunities within the discipline.

The growing complications of modern business have put substantial demands on the banking and accounting fields. This book introduces new research issues about financial reporting, financial analysis, energy products, Islamic banking, Islamic accounting, banking regulations, banking profitability, financial assets, financial performance, working capital management, accounting policy, accounting standards, and associated issues. Banking and accounting challenges require new concepts in the preparation and presentation of financial reports for various stakeholders. The banking and accounting issues focus on how effectively the business works, transforming business administration and creating business process improvements, cultural shifts, and new ways of doing things. The editor would like to thank all the authors for their valuable contributions. A warm thanks to the publication staff at IntechOpen and all anonymous reviewers for their support in this book's production.

Nizar M. Alsharari, Ph.D.
Associate Professor of Accounting,
Department of Accounting, Finance, and Entrepreneurship,
College of Business,
Jackson State University,
Jackson, Mississippi, United States of America

Section 1

Financial Reporting and Analysis

Chapter 1

Financial Reporting and Analysis of Tesla Green Technology in the United States Market

Nizar Mohammad Alsharari

Abstract

This study aims to discuss and analyze the financial position and performance of the US Tesla green technology company in the United States. This study uses a case study approach, financial data, and website methodologies to collect and analyze the research data. The case study is Tesla, Inc., which is a US electric vehicle and clean energy company based in Austin, Texas. Tesla is a green technology company that produces and designs electric cars, battery energy storage from home to grid-scale, solar roof tiles and solar panels, and related products and services. Tesla is growing fastly by introducing new green products, and it is now one of the world's most valuable enterprises. It has a high market capitalization of almost US$1 trillion to become the world's most valuable automaker. This study concludes that Tesla has changed their strategy to become the most worldwide sales of purely battery electric vehicles, capturing 23% of the market and 16% of the plug-in electric battery in the market for 2020. It has also developed a significant installer of photovoltaic systems through its subsidiary Tesla Energy in the United States. One of the largest global battery energy-storage systems suppliers is Tesla Energy, with 3.99 gigawatt-hours installed in 2021.

Keywords: financial reporting, financial analysis, tesla, manufacturing company, United States

1. Introduction

Global business has become more competitive than before. The technology and dynamic life increase the opportunities and risks for several firms. Accordingly, financial statements and financial analysis must be developed to assess the company's performance relative to its past performance or relative to its industrial competitors [1–6]. The financial statements are annual reports containing essential information about the firm, including income, cash flows, and current financial condition, illustrating the assets, liabilities, and owners' equity. However, if the financial information is not analyzed well, it will not help the company's success and management decision-making. In addition, a firm should be prepared for the uncertainties and opportunities in the future; therefore, the financial analysis can support oversight of the future business [3, 7, 8].

The financial analysis uses financial statements to evaluate the firm's overall performance, assess the equity securities, value opportunities, and risk, grow company earnings, and increase the cash flow. This study discusses financial statements, the difference and similarities between US GAAP and IFRS, financial data collection, research methodology, and analysis. In addition, a case study of one of the recent international companies, which is Tesla Motors, will be explained, and financial analysis and results will be applied to it [9, 10].

The used financial analysis method is financial ratios analysis. In this research, the profitability ratio, liquidity ratio, leverage ratio, and activity ratio will be applied to the financial statement of Tesla Motors. This study aims to evaluate the financial position of Tesla Motors through ratios and formulas to analyze the efficiency and business risk of the enterprise.

2. Literature review

2.1 Financial statements overview

A financial statement consists three main statements that provide essential details and information about the company's performance—income statements, balance sheets, and cash flow statements. The statements are analyzed annually using financial analysis techniques to continuously compare the firm effectiveness with previous years and compare it with the competitors from the same industry [11–13].

2.1.1 Income statement

The income statement is defined as the profit and loss statements representing the cost of sales, total operating expenses, net profit to the net sales over a certain period, and earnings per share. The cost of sales contains the cost of merchandise, production, materials purchase expenses, research and development costs, and total operating expenses, including administrative and distribution expenses. To increase the net profit of the firm, expenses must be decreased, and sales have to be increased. The return of investment, financial flexibility, operating capabilities, and risk are essential information gathered from the income statement. The firm's overall performance is measured by the return of investment, where the enterprise's ability to adapt to consequences and opportunities is defined as financial flexibility. Moreover, the ability to maintain operations at the desired level is considered the operating capability, and risk is defined as the uncertainty related to the firm's future. In summary, an Income statement supports the stakeholders and managers in evaluating the past performance, predicting future performance, and reducing the risk and uncertainty in achieving future cash flows [14].

2.1.2 Balance sheet

The balance sheet statement is referred to as the statement of financial position. The primary role of the balance sheet is to report the firm's assets, "economic resources," liabilities, "economic obligations," and equity over a particular period where total assets should be equal to total liabilities and equity "residual claims of owners." The assets are shown concerning its cash liquidity, and the liabilities are related to its maturity date. The balance sheet can be measured by several values based on the relevance and reliability of desired attributes—a one-time cost, present cost, present market value, net realizable value, and the current value of future cash flows. At a specific balance sheet date, the current or present cost is the cash required to attain the asset, whereas the current market value is the amount of cash gained from selling the asset. In addition, the net realizable value is represented as the cash obtained from the sale of a future asset. The benefit of the balance sheet is to gather information and data about obligations, resources, and net resources equity. As well as it supports predicting the time, cost amounts, potential, and uncertainty of future cash flows [14].

2.1.3 Statement of cash flow

The cash flow statement is a classification of cash payments and cash receipts issued by financing, operating, and investing activities. Each firm prepares the cash flow statement annually and compares the current year with previous years to evaluate the overall performance and plan the organization's expenditures. The information and details provided by the cash flow statement report to stakeholders, lenders, and investors are cash that comes from or is used in operating and financing activities and the change of cash, whether increasing or decreasing in a particular period. In addition, the statement of cash flow support making economic decisions about the firm. The financing activities related to a firm are treasury stock, which describes the reacquisition of earlier issued shares, stock issuance, dividends payment to stakeholders, debt financing, and debt repayment. Investing activities contain fixed assets, debt sale or purchase, and equity securities of entities. Additionally, the operating activities are related to manufacturing companies and the sale of goods [14].

The above three statements can be prepared in accordance with two types of the conceptual framework, which are The International Financial Reporting Standards (IFRS), which is used the worldwide, and the United States Generally Accepted Accounting Principles (US GAAP), which was used in the US but recently it has been used by some firms in the UK and India. Both representations have similarities and differences in finance and account aspects. Some differences and similarities in financial aspects are illustrated in the table below (Similarities and Differences A comparison of IFRS, US GAAP, and UK GAAP*, 2005) (see **Table 1**).

2.2 Financial analysis techniques

To evaluate firm performance, it is complimentary to analyze the presented data and compare it with historical data or/and other competitors from the same industry. Thus, the basis and elements of comparison must be clarified to ensure an entity's excellent performance and effectiveness. Analytical techniques can assess the firm's capabilities to generate and grow the cash flow and earnings. Additionally, it supports identifying the cash flow and earnings risks for current and future times.

For example, one of the main aspects of comparison is the firm profitability compared with other companies. In most cases, there will be differences between the companies in the firm size, presenting financial information or/and the currency of financial data. Therefore, comparing the firms based on the net income will provide the right and valuable results. An alternative methodology was created, a ratio analysis

Financial Statement	IFRS	US GAAP
Income statement	1. No standard format. 2. Present in one of two formats, either function or nature. 3. Prohibits extraordinary items category.	1. Use single-step or multistep format. 2. Allow extraordinary items category.
Balance sheet	1. No particular format. 2. Liquidity presentation of assets & liabilities. 3. Present current and non-current assets and current and non-current liabilities.	1. Current assets, liabilities, and equity and decreasing the order of liquidity. 2. Public companies should follow SEC guidelines.
Cash flow statements	1. Use direct or indirect methods. 2. Limit flexibility of content. 3. Overdrafts cash and cash equivalent with short-term maturity. 4. No exemptions.	1. Use direct or indirect methods. 2. More guidance for each specific category. 3. Cash includes equivalent but excludes overdrafts. 4. Limited exemptions for specific investment firms.

Sources: The Author.

Table 1.
IFRS and US GAAP conceptual frameworks: Similarities and differences in financial statements preparation.

technique that expresses one value concerning another value that enables more sufficient and accurate comparison and results. Furthermore, performing the standard size of financial statements eliminate the size factor, which provides improper results.

Regarding the issue of currency differences that appear from comparing international companies, an alternative method rather than using ratio analysis is using global exchange rates and unifying the currency in financial status at the end of a particular period. In addition to that, the enterprise compares its performance over time. Using the ratio analysis, which is horizontal financial statements that compare the current year to a based year and implement the results as a graph, shows the significant changes in the firm's effectiveness and performance [14].

The primary objectives of using ratio analysis are as follows:

1. Assess the past performance, evaluate the current financial position, and predict future opportunities and risks.

2. Support analysis to determine earnings and free cash flow.

3. Examine the firm's financial flexibility and ability to provide the cash needed to grow the firm and meet the obligations in normal or unexpected circumstances.

4. Improve management's ability to make better decisions related to enterprise growth (Henry, Robinson, and Van Greuning, n.d.).

Types of ratio Analysis:

1. **Profitability ratio.** It concentrates on the enterprise's effectiveness in using resources and operating processes to earn and increase income.

2. **Liquidity ratio.** It evaluates the organization's ability to meet financial obligations in the short term.

3. **Leverage ratio.** The leverage ratio provides the data on long-term solvency in an enterprise.

4. **Activity ratio.** It implements to assess the firm of using its assets.

5. **Market test ratio.** It provides measurements of market strength.

6. **Cash flow ratio.** It measures the cash adequacy and cash flow return (Analysis and Use of Financial Statements, 2004).

3. Case study: financial analysis of tesla motors

3.1 Automobile industry overview

The automobile industry is the producer of electric, hybrid, and gasoline-powered vehicles and one of the largest industries that affect the economy and culture of the world. Moreover, it opened a broader market area for many businesses and commerce by using vehicles in transporting people and goods. Based on the worldwide statistics, the leading countries for the production of passenger cars in 2018 are represented in the figure below. The total global sales of passenger cars reached 62 million vehicles in 2018, and the United States produced around 2.8 million vehicles. Accordingly, the US is considered one of the largest automobile markets in production and sales.

The most produced and selling brands of vehicles in the US automobile industry are Ford, Volkswagen, Toyota, Hyundai, and Chevrolet. All mentioned models are fuel-based vehicles where a new generation of alternative energy resources was developed in the US to produce and sell hybrid and electric vehicles. One of the leading global producers of electric cars is Tesla Motors. This research discusses an overview of Tesla Motors, methodology, and analysis of Tesla's financial statements (see **Figure 1**) [16].

3.2 Company background: tesla motors

Tesla Motors is an international manufacturing automotive and energy company founded in 2003 and based in California, US. The company is founded by Martin Eberhard, Marc Tarpenning, Elon Musk, J. B. Straubel, and Ian Wright. The organization aims to establish a sustainable energy eco-system by creating affordable vehicles and building unique energy solutions like solar roofs, power walls, and power packs. Tesla's automotive and energy solution enables the consumers to manage the generation, consumption, and storage of renewable energy. Tesla Motors achieved a financial turnover of around 21.5 billion US dollars in the fiscal year of 2018 and 45,000 employees in 30 worldwide branches.

Due to the massive competition in the automotive industry, the global economy affecting the business, and the competitive prices, Tesla Motors added a unique value to its customers by alternating fuel-based vehicles with electric vehicles. Although Tesla avoids the risk of increasing the oil prices, technological and political environments significantly impact Tesla vehicle prices. Therefore, the financial and

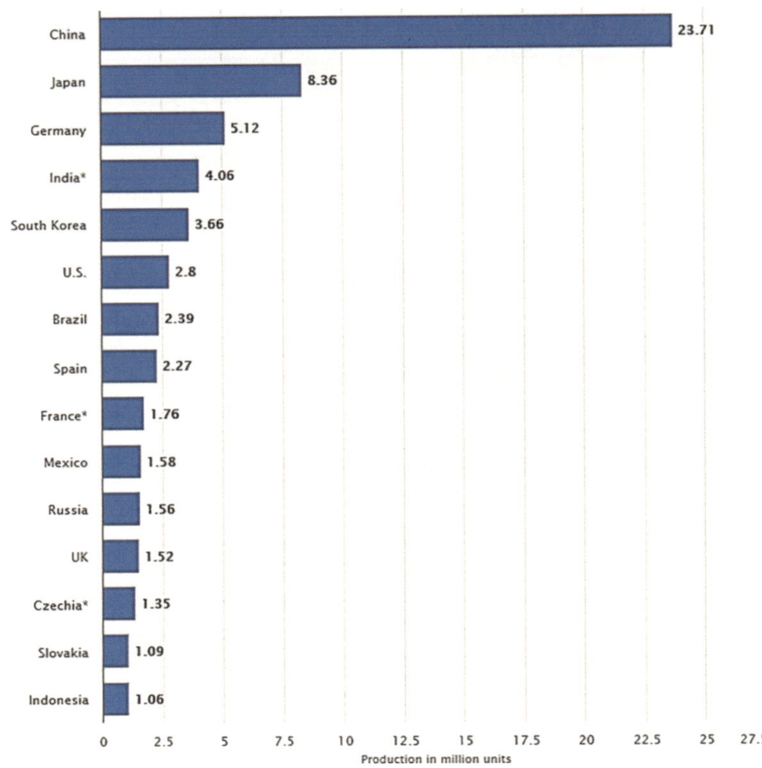

Figure 1.
Leading countries for the production of cars in 2018 [15].

non-financial performance of Tesla should be analyzed carefully to support in making critical decisions and to determine the future risk and potential of the company [17].

4. Research methodology

The historical financial information and data of Tesla Motors provide a better understanding of its financial position and cash flow forecast. Moreover, by comparing the annual financial reports, the created value of Tesla and performance relative to peers can be examined. The financial information contains annual reports of Tesla's income statement, balance sheet, and cash flow. Those financial details are authenticated and published by Tesla Motors company. In this research, the financial data duration will be analyzed, including the years from 2015 to 2018. A copy of detailed Tesla financial statements is attached in appendix A. Furthermore, the model used to evaluate Tesla's financial performance is described in (**Figure 2**).

The financial technique used in this research is the ratios analysis technique, which provides financial measurements and results to indicate the performance of Tesla Motors. The main four ratios for financial data analysis are liquidity ratios, assets management ratios, profitability ratios, and debt management ratios (Appendix B). Each ratio contains various formulas that describe an essential principle of finance and account, represented in the table below (see **Table 2**).

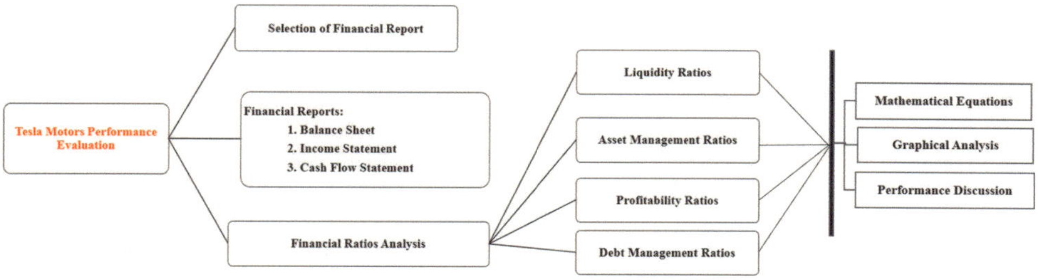

Figure 2.
The research methodology.

Liquidity Ratios	Asset Management Ratios	Profitability Ratios	Debt Management Ratios
1. Current Ratio	1. Accounts Receivable Turnover	1. Net Profit Margin	1. Debt Ratio
2. Quick Ratio	2. Inventory Turnover Ratio	2. Gross Profit Margin Ratio	2. Time Interest Earned
3. Cash Ratio	3. Accounts Payable Turnover	3. Operating Profit Margin	

Table 2.
Financial ratios analysis.

5. Financial analysis and results

5.1 Liquidity ratios

The liquidity ratio indicates the strong ability to use its asset to cover its short-term debts. The three liquidity ratios used in this research are current ratio, quick ratio, acid test, and cash ratio.

5.1.1 Current ratio

The current ratio formula is performed by dividing the current assets by the current liabilities for the same year. The current asset consists of cash and cash equivalents, restricted cash, net accounts receivable, inventory, prepaid expenses, and other current assets, where current liability includes Accounts payable, accrued liabilities, deferred revenue, resale value guarantee, customer deposits, current portion of long-term debt and capital leases (see **Table 3** and **Figure 3**).

Analysis: As observed from the above table and graph, the current ratio exceeded only in 2016, when the firm used its assets correctly and paid the creditor back. On the other hand, for 2017 and 2018, the current ratio decreased, indicating that the firm could not meet its short-term obligations. The liquidity position of General Motors has been reducing negatively for the past two years. Accordingly, the firm can increase its current liabilities compared to its current assets by increasing inventory sales, resulting in increasing the cash. Moreover, the average current ratio of the automobile industry is 1.01 for 2018, which means that General Motors is less than the average current ratio of 17.69%.

Category/Year	2018	2017	2016	2015
Current Assets	$ 8,306,308	$ 6,570,520	$ 6,259,796	$ 2,782,006
Current Liability	$ 9,992,136	$ 7,674,670	$ 5,827,005	$ 2,811,035
Current Ratio	0.8313	0.8561	1.0743	0.9897

Table 3.
Current ratio analysis.

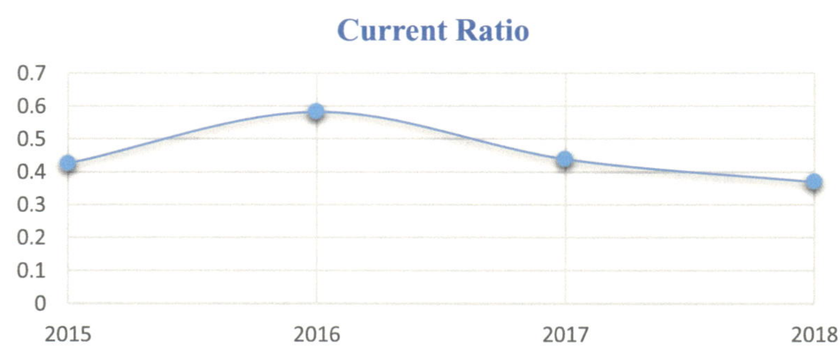

Figure 3.
Current ratio graph.

5.1.2 Acid test ratio

The acid test or quick ratio is calculated by eliminating the inventories from current assets and dividing them by current liabilities (see **Table 4** and **Figure 4**).

Analysis: it is obtained that General Motors has poor liquidity since its liquid assets are low and cannot pay off and cover its entire current liability.

Category/Year	2018	2017	2016	2015
(Current Assets-Inventories)	$ 5,192,862	$ 4,306,983	$ 4,192,342	$ 1,594,168
Current Liability	$ 9,992,136	$ 7,674,670	$ 5,827,005	$ 2,811,035
Acid Test Ratio	0.5197	0.5612	0.7195	0.5671

Table 4.
Acid test ratio.

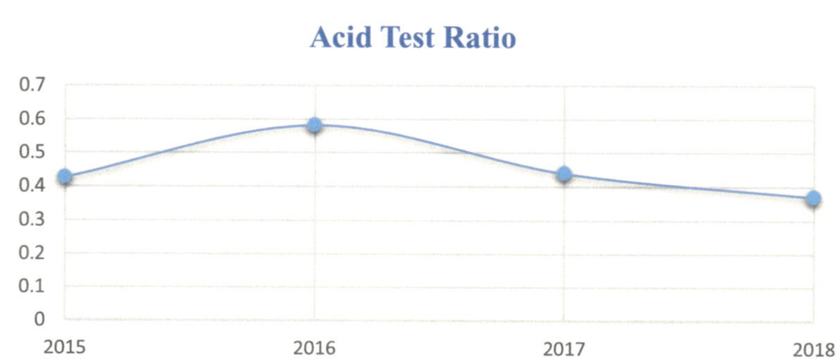

Figure 4.
Acid test ratio graph.

5.1.3 Cash ratio

A cash ratio is a type of measurement, which evaluates the strong ability to cover its current liability by only its cash and cash equivalent (see **Table 5** and **Figure 5**).

Analysis: Although the cash and cash equivalent increased from the year 2015 to 2018 except between 2016 and 2017, there was a slight reduction, but the company failed to cover its liabilities. Thus, it should increase its investments to increase its cash and cover the current liabilities.

Category/Year	2018	2017	2016	2015
Cash and Cash Equivalent	$ 3,685,618	$ 3,367,914	$ 3,393,216	$ 1,196,908
Current Liability	$ 9,992,136	$ 7,674,670	$ 5,827,005	$ 2,811,035
Cash Ratio	0.3689	0.4388	0.5823	0.4258

Table 5.
Cash ratio.

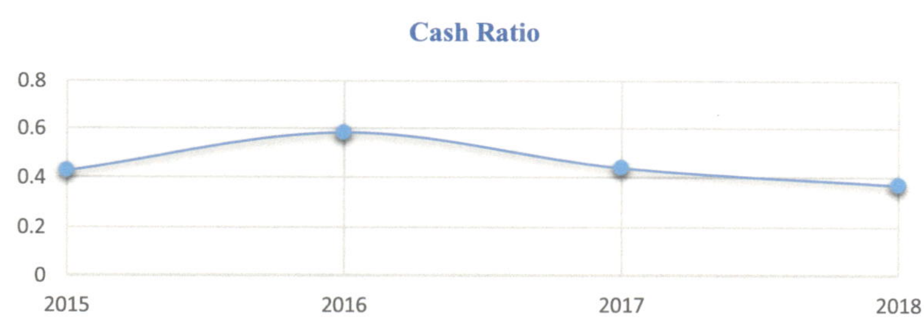

Figure 5.
Cash ratio graph.

5.2 Asset management ratios

The most important financial ratios for the manufacturing company are asset management because it effectively measures the enterprise usage and control of its assets. It consists many ratios, but in this research, the accounts receivable turnover, inventory turnover, accounts Payable turnover, and total asset turnover will be implemented on General Motors' financial statements.

5.2.1 Accounts receivable turnover ratio

The accounts receivable turnover measures the number of cash collection times during a particular period, and it is calculated by dividing the sales by the average account receivable (see **Table 6** and **Figure 6**).

Category/Year	2018	2017	2016	2015
Sales	$ 21,461,268	$ 11,758,751	$ 7,000,132	$ 4,046,025
Average Accounts Receivable	$ 949,022	$ 515,381	$ 499,142	$ 168,965
Accounts Receivable Turnover Ratio	22.61	22.82	14.02	23.95

Table 6.
Accounts receivable turnover ratio.

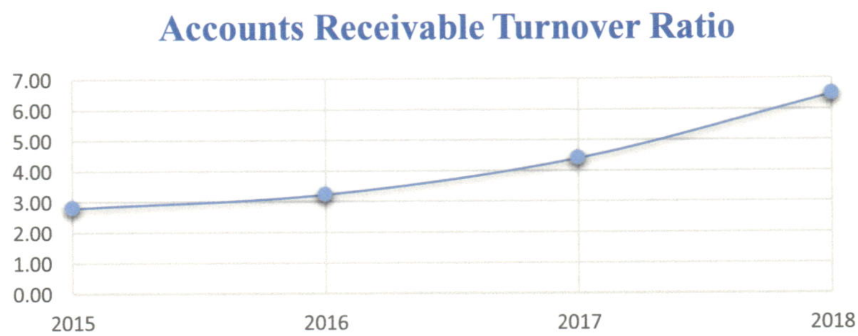

Figure 6.
Accounts receivable turnover ratio graph.

Analysis: Based on collected data, the accounts receivable turnover ratio decreased at the end of 2016 and increased in 2017 and 2018. The graph indicates that Tesla Motors is doing well in collecting its cash annually.

5.2.2 Inventory turnover ratio

This ratio is calculated several times inventories are sold and restocked yearly. All manufacturers have Inventories to keep unsold stocks which cost them significant value until the materials are sold out. It is measured by dividing the cost of goods sold over the average inventories (see **Table** 7 and **Figure** 7).

Analysis: The inventory turnover ratio indicates that Tesla Motors has improved over four years, wherein in 2018, the firm renewed its total inventory about 6.48 times a year.

Category/Year	2018	2017	2016	2015
Cost of Goods Sold	$ 17,419,247	$ 9,536,264	$ 5,400,875	$ 3,122,522
Average Inventories	$ 2,688,491	$ 2,165,495	$ 1,672,646	$ 1,115,756
Inventory Turnover Ratio	6.48	4.40	3.23	2.80

Table 7.
Inventory turnover ratio.

Figure 7.
Inventory turnover ratio graph.

5.2.3 Accounts payable turnover ratio

Since raw materials are considered the main expenses of manufacturing firms, the accounts payable turnover measures the speed of paying the purchasing of raw materials or inventories on the account. The account payable turnover is calculated by dividing the purchases over average accounts payable. The below formula calculates the value of the purchase (see **Table 8** and **Figure 8**).

Category/Year	2018	2017	2016	2015
Purchases	$ 18,269,156	$ 9,732,347	$ 6,190,491	$ 3,446,685
Average Accounts Payable	$ 3,404,451	$ 2,390,250	$ 1,860,341	$ 916,148
Accounts Payable Turnover Ratio	5.366	4.072	3.328	3.762

Table 8.
Accounts payable turnover ratio.

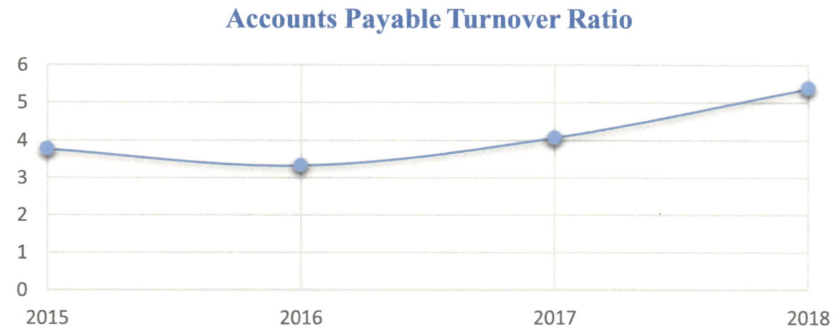

Figure 8.
Accounts payable turnover ratio graph.

Purchases = Cost of goods sold + [(Ending inventory) – (Beginning inventory)].

Analysis: It has been observed that Tesla Motors can pay its purchases on time 5.366 times in 2018, which is improved compared to previous years.

5.3 Profitability ratios

The company's overall efficiency and performance are evaluated by the profitability ratio, where it concentrates on measuring the assets and controlling the expenses to generate a reasonable rate of return. In addition, it analyses the firm current operational performance compared to previous years. The net profit margin, gross profit margin ratio, and operating profit margin ratio will be performed on the financial statements of Tesla Motors.

5.3.1 Net profit margin

The net profit margin is calculated by dividing the net profit after tax over the net sales. For any automotive company, the higher the net profit margin, the better the performance (see **Table 9** and **Figure 9**).

Category/Year	2018	2017	2016	2015
Net Profit after Tax	$ 1,062,582	$ 2,240,578	$ 773,046	$ 888,663
Sales	$ 21,461,268	$ 11,758,751	$ 7,000,132	$ 4,046,025
Net Profit Margin (Percentage)	4.951%	19.055%	11.043%	21.964%

Table 9.
Net profit margin.

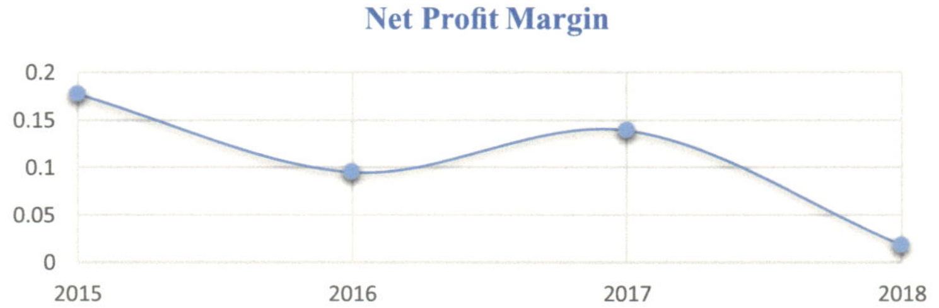

Figure 9.
Net profit margin graph.

Analysis: As observed from previous data, the net profit margin significantly decreased in 2018 compared to previous years, where the most profitable year is 2015 and the second most profitable year is 2017.

5.3.2 Gross profit margin ratio

A gross profit margin serves as the source of paying additional expenses and savings for the future to assess financial health. The gross profit margin ratio is calculated by dividing the gross profit over sales (see **Table 10** and **Figure 10**).

Category/Year	2018	2017	2016	2015
Gross Profit Margin	$ 1,004,745	$ 2,209,032	$ 746,348	$ 875,624
Sales	$ 21,461,268	$ 11,758,751	$ 7,000,132	$ 4,046,025
Gross Profit Margin Ratio (Percentage)	4.682%	18.786%	10.662%	21.642%

Table 10.
Gross profit margin ratio.

Figure 10.
Gross profit margin ratio graph.

Analysis: From 2015 to 2018, the gross profit margins are positive, which indicates that the firm is profitable.

5.3.3 Operating profit margin ratio

This ratio is calculated by dividing the operating profits over sales (see **Table 11** and **Figure 11**).

Analysis: The operating margin of Tesla Motors is dramatically decreased in 2018 compared to previous years, which indicates that the firm is earning less per dollar of sales. The low operating profit margin is due to high fixed production costs or high sales volume.

Category/Year	2018	2017	2016	2015
Operating Profits	$ 388,073	$ 1,632,086	$ 667,340	$ 716,629
Sales	$ 21,461,268	$ 11,758,751	$ 7,000,132	$ 4,046,025
Operating Profit Margin Ratio	0.018	0.139	0.095	0.177

Table 11.
Operating profit margin ratio.

Figure 11.
Operating profit margin ratio figure.

5.4 Debt management ratios

The degree of safety afforded to creditors is financial leverage or debt financing. There are two methods to obtain the enterprise debt by determining the borrowed funds used to finance assets on the balance sheet. The other is by obtaining the fixed charges covered by the operating profits in the income statement.

5.4.1 Debt ratio

The debt ratio is calculated by dividing total debt over total assets, where total debt contains current liabilities and long-term debt (see **Table 12** and **Figure 12**).

Analysis: The debt ratio is less than one, which indicates that a higher amount of the firm's assets is financed by its equity, not by its liability.

Category/Year	2018	2017	2016	2015
Total Debt	$ 13,433,874	$ 15,348,310	$ 10,923,162	$ 4,125,915
Total Assets	$ 29,739,614	$ 28,655,372	$ 22,664,076	$ 8,067,939
Debt Ratio	0.452	0.536	0.482	0.511

Table 12.
Debt ratio.

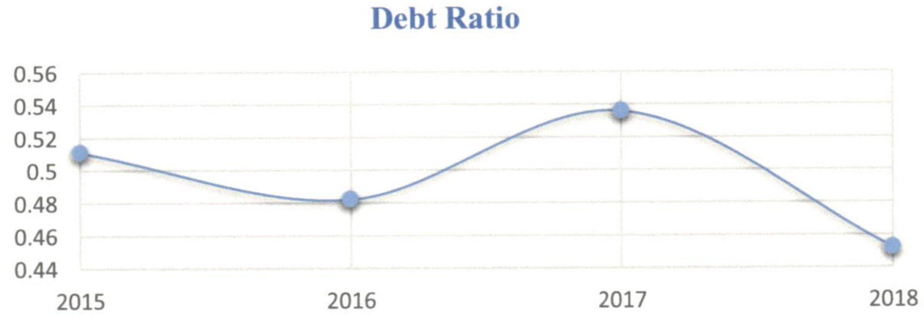

Figure 12.
Debt ratio graph.

5.4.2 Time interest earned ratio

The time interest earned is measured by dividing the earnings "EBIT" before interest tax by the interest charged. The ratio indicates the enterprise's ability to meet the interest payment (see **Table 13** and **Figure 13**).

Analysis: As observed, the company can pay for the interest. The higher the ratio is, the better since it indicates that the firm covers the interest from its earnings.

Category/Year	2018	2017	2016	2015
EBIT	$ 4,340,986	$ 2,208,596	$ 1,600,685	$ 917,671
Interest Charges	$ 663,071	$ 471,259	$ 198,810	$ 118,851
Time Interest Earned Ratio	6.547	4.687	8.051	7.721

Table 13.
Time interest earned ratio.

Figure 13.
Time interest earned graph.

6. The conclusions

An overview of financial statements, financial presentation methods, and financial analysis was discussed. A real-life case study on Tesla Motors was implemented to perform the financial analysis and concluded the results of its financial statements and analyses to evaluate its performance.

This study concludes that Tesla Motors continuously suffers from losses. Tesla Motors has a high value of assets since they concentrate on adding value to the customers and inventing unique electric vehicles. In addition, the automobile industry is too competitive where vehicle manufacturers compete to drive the attention of various stakeholders in the market. Furthermore, the new idea of shifting from fuel-based vehicles to electric-based vehicles needs significant duration to convince stakeholders to purchase the developed electric cars. However, this research proves that Tesla Motors made low gross profits where it decreased from 21.642% in 2015 to 4.682% in 2018. The decrement is due to high maintenance costs, research and development cost, selling expenses, and administrative expenses. Furthermore, the interest percentage is too high where Tesla Motors is accumulating the losses, which leads to increasing the interest expenses of the current year. The financial ratios support Tesla Motors to highlight the current firm position and provide the potential threats and opportunities in the future.

This study concludes that Tesla has changed their strategy to become the most worldwide sales of purely battery electric vehicles, capturing 23% of the market and 16% of the plug-in electric battery in the market for 2020. It has also developed a significant installer of photovoltaic systems through its subsidiary Tesla Energy in the United States. One of the largest global battery energy-storage systems suppliers is Tesla Energy, with 3.99 gigawatt-hours (GWh) installed in 2021.

This study also concludes that Tesla has changed its production strategy over time. It started to produce its first car model, the Roadster sports car, in 2009, which was followed by the Model S sedan in 2012, the Model X SUV in 2015, the Model 3 sedan in 2017, and the Model Y crossover in 2020. However, the Model 3 is the best-selling plug-in electric car in the global market, and, in the mid of 2021, it became the first electric car sale with 1 million units globally. The sale strategy thus has been developed. The global sales of Tesla increased to 936,222 cars in 2021, with an 87% increase over the previous year, and cumulative sales for all years totaled 2.3 million cars at the end of 2021. By the end of 2021, The market capitalization of Tesla reached $1 trillion to hold the rank 6 in US market history.

Appendix A

- The year 2017–2018

	December 31, 2018	December 31, 2017
Assets		
Current assets		
Cash and cash equivalents	$ 3,685,618	$ 3,367,914
Restricted cash	192,551	155,323
Accounts receivable, net	949,022	515,381
Inventory	3,113,446	2,263,537
Prepaid expenses and other current assets	365,671	268,365
Total current assets	8,306,308	6,570,520
Operating lease vehicles, net	2,089,758	4,116,604
Solar energy systems, leased and to be leased, net	6,271,396	6,347,490
Property, plant and equipment, net	11,330,077	10,027,522
Goodwill and intangible assets, net	350,651	421,739
MyPower customer notes receivable, net of current portion	421,548	456,652
Restricted cash, net of current portion	398,219	441,722
Other assets	571,657	273,123
Total assets	$ 29,739,614	$ 28,655,372
Liabilities and Equity		
Current liabilities		
Accounts payable	$ 3,404,451	$ 2,390,250
Accrued liabilities and other	2,094,253	1,731,366
Deferred revenue	630,292	1,015,253
Resale value guarantees	502,840	787,333
Customer deposits	792,601	853,919
Current portion of long-term debt and capital leases (1)	2,567,699	896,549
Total current liabilities	9,992,136	7,674,670
Long-term debt and capital leases, net of current portion (1)	9,403,672	9,418,319
Deferred revenue, net of current portion	990,873	1,177,799
Resale value guarantees, net of current portion	328,926	2,309,222
Other long-term liabilities	2,710,403	2,442,970
Total liabilities	23,426,010	23,022,980
Redeemable noncontrolling interests in subsidiaries	555,964	397,734
Convertible senior notes (1)	-	70
Total stockholders' equity	4,923,243	4,237,242
Noncontrolling interests in subsidiaries	834,397	997,346
Total liabilities and equity	$ 29,739,614	$ 28,655,372

	Three Months Ended			Year Ended	
	December 31, 2018	September 30, 2018	December 31, 2017	December 31, 2018	December 31, 2017
Revenues					
Automotive sales	$ 6,073,471	$ 5,878,305	$ 2,409,109	$ 17,631,522	$ 8,534,752
Automotive leasing	249,748	220,461	293,086	883,461	1,106,548
Total automotive revenue	6,323,219	6,098,766	2,702,195	18,514,983	9,641,300
Energy generation and storage	371,497	399,317	298,037	1,555,244	1,116,266
Services and other	531,157	326,330	288,017	1,391,041	1,001,185
Total revenues	7,225,873	6,824,413	3,288,249	21,461,268	11,758,751
Cost of revenues					
Automotive sales	4,658,517	4,405,919	1,999,631	13,685,572	6,724,480
Automotive leasing	127,731	119,283	191,541	488,425	708,224
Total automotive cost of revenues	4,786,248	4,525,202	2,191,172	14,173,997	7,432,704
Energy generation and storage	328,706	330,554	281,715	1,364,896	874,538
Services and other	668,019	444,992	376,576	1,880,354	1,229,022
Total cost of revenues	5,782,973	5,300,748	2,849,463	17,419,247	9,536,264
Gross profit	1,442,900	1,523,665	438,786	4,042,021	2,222,487
Operating expenses					
Research and development	356,297	350,848	354,637	1,460,370	1,378,073
Selling, general and administrative	667,452	729,876	682,290	2,834,491	2,476,500
Restructuring and other	5,615	26,184	-	135,233	-
Total operating expenses	1,029,364	1,106,908	1,036,927	4,430,094	3,854,573
Income (loss) from operations	413,536	416,757	(598,141)	(388,073)	(1,632,086)
Interest income	7,348	6,907	6,280	24,533	19,686
Interest expense	(174,723)	(175,220)	(146,363)	(663,071)	(471,259)
Other (expense) income, net	(14,205)	22,876	(41,677)	21,866	(125,373)
Income (loss) before income taxes	231,956	271,320	(779,901)	(1,004,745)	(2,209,032)
Provision (benefit) for income taxes	21,878	16,647	(9,094)	57,837	31,546
Net income (loss)	210,078	254,673	(770,807)	(1,062,582)	(2,240,578)
Net income (loss) attributable to noncontrolling interests and redeemable noncontrolling interests	70,595	(56,843)	(95,457)	(86,491)	(279,178)
Net income (loss) attributable to common stockholders	$ 139,483	$ 311,516	$ (675,350)	$ (976,091)	$ (1,961,400)

	Three Months Ended			Year Ended	
	December 31, 2018	September 30, 2018	December 31, 2017	December 31, 2018	December 31, 2017
Cash Flows from Operating Activities					
Net income (loss)	$ 210,078	$ 254,673	$ (770,807)	$ (1,062,582)	$ (2,240,578)
Adjustments to reconcile net income (loss) to net cash provided by (used in) operating activities:					
Depreciation, amortization and impairment	496,737	502,825	469,606	1,901,050	1,636,003
Stock-based compensation	205,313	204,728	134,348	749,024	466,760
Losses related to the SolarCity acquisition	–	–	27,950	–	57,746
Other	123,385	77,737	151,756	452,359	516,018
Changes in operating assets and liabilities, net of effect of business combinations	199,048	351,318	497,038	57,951	(496,603)
Net cash provided by (used in) operating activities	1,234,561	1,391,281	509,891	2,097,802	(60,654)
Cash Flows from Investing Activities					
Capital expenditures	(324,978)	(510,271)	(786,688)	(2,100,724)	(3,414,814)
Payments for the cost of solar energy systems, leased and to be leased	(28,923)	(49,494)	(119,455)	(218,792)	(666,540)
Business combinations, net of cash acquired	(11,108)	(1,200)	(5,376)	(17,912)	(114,523)
Net cash used in investing activities	(365,009)	(560,965)	(911,519)	(2,337,428)	(4,195,877)
Cash Flows from Financing Activities					
Net cash flows from debt activities	(184,099)	(195,760)	28,056	37,202	2,414,896
Collateralized lease (repayments) borrowings	(216,081)	(142,568)	94,894	(559,167)	511,321
Net borrowings under Warehouse Agreements and automotive asset-backed notes	193,086	114,942	116,820	596,125	283,811
Net cash flows from noncontrolling interests - Auto	37,575	17,224	31,763	111,753	43,417
Net cash flows from noncontrolling interests - Solar	(18,567)	27,070	(5,479)	92,120	484,070
Proceeds from issuances of common stock in public offerings	–	–	–	–	400,175
Other	75,777	94,874	19,788	295,722	277,174
Net cash (used in) provided by financing activities	(112,309)	(84,218)	285,842	573,755	4,414,864
Effect of exchange rate changes on cash and cash equivalents and restricted cash	(3,821)	(6,370)	3,990	(22,700)	39,726
Net increase (decrease) in cash and cash equivalents and restricted cash	753,422	739,728	(111,796)	311,429	198,059
Cash and cash equivalents and restricted cash at beginning of period	3,522,966	2,783,238	4,076,755	3,964,959	3,766,900
Cash and cash equivalents and restricted cash at end of period	$ 4,276,388	$ 3,522,966	$ 3,964,959	$ 4,276,388	$ 3,964,959

- The year 2017–2016

	December 31, 2017	December 31, 2016
Assets		
Current assets		
Cash and cash equivalents	$ 3,367,914	$ 3,393,216
Restricted cash	155,323	105,519
Accounts receivable, net	515,381	499,142
Inventory	2,263,537	2,067,454
Prepaid expenses and other current assets	268,365	194,465
Total current assets	6,570,520	6,259,796
Operating lease vehicles, net	4,116,604	3,134,080
Solar energy systems, leased and to be leased, net	6,347,490	5,919,880
Property, plant and equipment, net	10,027,522	5,982,957
Goodwill and intangible assets, net	421,739	376,145
MyPower customer notes receivable, net of current portion	456,652	506,302
Restricted cash, net of current portion	441,722	268,165
Other assets	273,123	216,751
Total assets	$ 28,655,372	$ 22,664,076
Liabilities and Equity		
Current liabilities		
Accounts payable	$ 2,390,250	$ 1,860,341
Accrued liabilities and other	1,731,366	1,210,028
Deferred revenue	1,015,253	763,126
Resale value guarantees	787,333	179,504
Customer deposits	853,919	663,859
Current portion of long-term debt and capital leases (1)	858,026	1,150,147
Total current liabilities	7,636,147	5,827,005
Long-term debt and capital leases, net of current portion (1)	9,456,842	5,969,500
Deferred revenue, net of current portion	1,177,799	851,790
Resale value guarantees, net of current portion	2,309,222	2,210,423
Other long-term liabilities	2,442,970	1,891,449
Total liabilities	23,022,980	16,750,167
Redeemable noncontrolling interests in subsidiaries	397,734	367,039
Convertible senior notes (1)(2)	70	8,784
Total stockholders' equity	4,237,242	4,752,911
Noncontrolling interests in subsidiaries	997,346	785,175
Total liabilities and equity	$ 28,655,372	$ 22,664,076

	Three Months Ended			Year Ended	
	December 31, 2017	September 30, 2017	December 31, 2016	December 31, 2017	December 31, 2016
Revenues					
Automotive sales	$ 2,409,109	$ 2,076,731	$ 1,739,449	$ 8,534,752	$ 5,589,007
Automotive leasing	293,086	286,158	254,674	1,106,548	761,759
Total automotive revenue	2,702,195	2,362,889	1,994,123	9,641,300	6,350,766
Energy generation and storage	298,037	317,505	131,385	1,116,266	181,394
Services and other	288,017	304,281	159,123	1,001,185	467,972
Total revenues	3,288,249	2,984,675	2,284,631	11,758,751	7,000,132
Cost of revenues					
Automotive sales	1,999,631	1,755,622	1,372,604	6,724,480	4,268,087
Automotive leasing	191,541	175,224	171,818	708,224	481,994
Total automotive cost of revenues	2,191,172	1,930,846	1,544,422	7,432,704	4,750,081
Energy generation and storage	281,715	237,288	127,779	874,538	178,332
Services and other	376,576	367,401	177,152	1,229,022	472,462
Total cost of revenues (1)	2,849,463	2,535,535	1,849,353	9,536,264	5,400,875
Gross profit	438,786	449,140	435,278	2,222,487	1,599,257
Operating expenses					
Research and development (1)	354,637	331,622	245,960	1,378,073	834,408
Selling, general and administrative (1)	682,290	652,998	456,016	2,476,500	1,432,189
Total operating expenses	1,036,927	984,620	701,976	3,854,573	2,266,597
Loss from operations	(598,141)	(535,480)	(266,698)	(1,632,086)	(667,340)
Interest income	6,280	5,531	2,179	19,686	8,530
Interest expense (2)(3)	(146,363)	(117,109)	(65,104)	(471,259)	(198,810)
Other (expense) income, net	(41,677)	(24,390)	121,224	(125,373)	111,272
Loss before income taxes	(779,901)	(671,448)	(208,399)	(2,209,032)	(746,348)
(Benefit) provision for income taxes	(9,094)	(285)	11,070	31,546	26,698
Net loss	(770,807)	(671,163)	(219,469)	(2,240,578)	(773,046)
Net loss attributable to noncontrolling interests and redeemable noncontrolling interests	(95,457)	(51,787)	(98,132)	(279,178)	(98,132)
Net loss attributable to common stockholders	$ (675,350)	$ (619,376)	$ (121,337)	$ (1,961,400)	$ (674,914)

	Three Months Ended			Year Ended	
	December 31, 2017	September 30, 2017	December 31, 2016	December 31, 2017	December 31, 2016
Cash Flows from Operating Activities					
Net loss	$ (770,807)	$ (671,163)	$ (219,469)	$ (2,240,578)	$ (773,046)
Adjustments to reconcile net loss to net cash provided by (used in) operating activities:					
Depreciation and amortization	469,606	400,624	326,939	1,636,003	947,099
Stock-based compensation	134,348	112,653	87,711	466,760	334,225
Losses (gains) related to the SolarCity acquisition	27,950	18,225	(88,727)	57,746	(88,727)
Other	151,756	88,867	(8,068)	516,018	150,481
Changes in operating assets and liabilities, net of effect of business combinations	497,038	(249,768)	(546,595)	(496,603)	(693,861)
Net cash provided by (used in) operating activities	509,891	(300,562)	(448,209)	(60,654)	(123,829)
Cash Flows from Investing Activities					
Capital expenditures	(786,688)	(1,116,434)	(521,612)	(3,414,814)	(1,280,802)
Payments for the cost of solar energy systems, leased and to be leased	(119,455)	(128,293)	(159,669)	(666,540)	(159,669)
Business combinations, net of cash acquired	(5,376)	-	213,523	(114,523)	213,523
Maturities of short-term marketable securities	-	-	-	-	16,667
Changes in restricted cash and other	(50,357)	(70,205)	(126,993)	(223,090)	(206,149)
Net cash used in investing activities	(961,876)	(1,314,932)	(594,751)	(4,418,967)	(1,416,430)
Cash Flows from Financing Activities					
Net cash flows from debt activities	28,056	1,820,399	880,154	2,414,896	538,439
Collateralized lease borrowings	94,894	80,752	212,040	511,321	769,709
Net borrowings under warehouse facilities	116,820	78,297	90,000	283,811	390,000
Net cash flows from noncontrolling interests	26,284	41,643	180,277	527,487	180,277
Proceeds from issuances of common stock in public offerings	-	-	-	400,175	1,701,734
Other	19,788	80,415	10,356	277,174	163,817
Net cash provided by financing activities	285,842	2,101,506	1,372,827	4,414,864	3,743,976
Effect of exchange rate changes on cash and cash equivalents	4,027	8,094	(20,908)	39,455	(7,409)
Net (decrease) increase in cash and cash equivalents	(162,116)	494,106	308,959	(25,302)	2,196,308
Cash and cash equivalents at beginning of period	3,530,030	3,035,924	3,084,257	3,393,216	1,196,908
Cash and cash equivalents at end of period	$ 3,367,914	$ 3,530,030	$ 3,393,216	$ 3,367,914	$ 3,393,216

- The year 2016–2015

	Dec 31, 2016	Dec 31, 2015
Assets		
Current assets		
Cash and cash equivalents	$ 3,393,216	$ 1,196,908
Restricted cash and marketable securities - current	105,519	22,628
Accounts receivable	499,142	168,965
Inventory	2,067,454	1,277,838
Prepaid expenses and other current assets	194,465	115,667
Total current assets	6,259,796	2,782,006
Operating lease vehicles, net	3,134,080	1,791,403
Solar energy systems, leased and to be leased, net	5,919,880	-
Property, plant and equipment, net	5,982,957	3,403,334
Intangible assets, net	376,145	12,574
MyPower customer notes receivable, net of current portion	506,302	-
Restricted cash, net of current portion	268,165	31,522
Other assets	216,751	47,100
Total assets	$ 22,664,076	$ 8,067,939
Liabilities and Stockholders' Equity		
Current liabilities		
Accounts payable	$ 1,860,341	$ 916,148
Accrued and other current liabilities	1,210,028	422,798
Deferred revenue	763,126	423,961
Resale value guarantees	179,504	136,831
Customer deposits	663,859	283,370
Current portion of long-term debt and capital leases (1)	1,150,147	627,927
Total current liabilities	5,827,005	2,811,035
Long-term debt and capital leases, net of current portion (1)	5,969,500	2,021,093
Deferred revenue, net of current portion	851,790	446,105
Resale value guarantees, net of current portion	2,210,423	1,293,741
Other long-term liabilities	1,891,449	364,976
Total liabilities	16,750,167	6,936,950
Redeemable noncontrolling interests in subsidiaries	367,039	-
Convertible senior notes (1)(2)	8,784	47,285
Stockholders' equity	4,752,911	1,083,704
Noncontrolling interests in subsidiaries	785,175	-
Total liabilities and equity	$ 22,664,076	$ 8,067,939

	Three Months Ended			Year Ended	
	Dec 31, 2016	Sep 30, 2016	Dec 31, 2015	Dec 31, 2016	Dec 31, 2015
Revenue					
Automotive	$ 1,739,449	$ 1,917,442	$ 1,014,337	$ 5,589,007	$ 3,431,586
Automotive leasing	254,674	231,285	102,670	761,759	309,387
Total automotive revenue	$ 1,994,123	$ 2,148,727	$ 1,117,007	$ 6,350,766	$ 3,740,973
Energy generation and storage	131,385	23,334	11,494	181,394	14,477
Services and other	159,123	126,375	85,878	467,972	290,575
Total revenue	$ 2,284,631	$ 2,298,436	$ 1,214,379	$ 7,000,132	$ 4,046,025
Cost of revenue					
Automotive	1,372,604	1,355,102	831,349	4,268,087	2,639,927
Automotive leasing	171,818	161,959	65,092	481,994	183,375
Total automotive cost of revenue	$ 1,544,422	$ 1,517,061	$ 896,441	$ 4,750,081	2,823,302
Energy generation and storage	127,779	24,281	10,134	178,332	12,287
Services and other	177,152	120,359	89,240	472,462	286,933
Total cost of revenue (1)	$ 1,849,353	$ 1,661,701	$ 995,815	$ 5,400,875	$ 3,122,522
Gross profit	$ 435,278	$ 636,735	$ 218,564	$ 1,599,257	$ 923,503
Operating expenses					
Research and development (1)	$ 245,960	$ 214,302	$ 190,243	$ 834,408	$ 717,900
Selling, general and administrative (1)	456,016	336,811	288,654	1,432,189	922,232
Total operating expenses	$ 701,976	$ 551,113	$ 478,897	$ 2,266,597	$ 1,640,132
Income (loss) from operations	(266,698)	85,622	(260,333)	(667,340)	(716,629)
Interest income	2,179	2,858	750	8,530	1,508
Interest expense (2)(3)	(65,104)	(46,713)	(38,617)	(198,810)	(118,851)
Other income (expense), net (4)	121,224	(11,756)	(17,149)	111,272	(41,652)
Income (loss) before income taxes	$ (208,399)	$ 30,011	$ (315,349)	$ (746,348)	$ (875,624)
Provision for income taxes	11,070	8,133	5,048	26,698	13,039
Net income (loss)	$ (219,469)	$ 21,878	$ (320,397)	$ (773,046)	$ (888,663)
Net income (loss) attributable to noncontrolling interests and redeemable noncontrolling interest	(98,132)	$ -	$ -	(98,132)	$ -
Net income (loss) attributable to common stockholders	$ (121,337)	$ 21,878	$ (320,397)	$ (674,914)	$ (888,663)

	Three Months Ended			Year Ended	
	Dec 31, 2016	Sep 30, 2016	Dec 31, 2015	Dec 31, 2016	Dec 31, 2015
Cash flows from operating activities					
Net loss	$ (219,469)	$ 21,878	$ (320,397)	$ (773,046)	$ (888,663)
Adjustments to reconcile net loss to net cash provided by (used in) operating activities:					
Depreciation and amortization	326,939	280,469	143,723	947,099	422,590
Stock-based compensation	87,711	89,543	55,605	334,225	197,999
Gain on acquisition of SolarCity	(88,727)	-	-	(88,727)	-
Other	(8,068)	67,481	106,826	150,481	236,864
Change in operating assets and liabilities, net of impact of business combination					
Accounts receivable	(106,055)	(109,084)	(32,106)	(216,565)	46,267
Inventory and operating lease vehicles	(667,489)	(580,283)	(482,478)	(2,465,703)	(1,573,860)
Accounts payable and accrued liabilities	53,112	484,579	174,107	750,640	263,345
Deferred revenue	126,775	91,043	135,948	382,962	322,203
Customer deposits	(20,778)	10,584	16,407	388,361	36,721
Other	67,840	67,440	172,516	466,444	412,035
Cash provided by (used in) operating activities	(448,209)	423,650	(29,849)	(123,829)	(524,499)
Cash flows from investing activities					
Capital expenditures	(521,612)	(247,611)	(411,222)	(1,280,802)	(1,634,850)
Payments for the cost of solar energy systems, leased and to be leased	(159,669)	-	-	(159,669)	-
Cash acquired through (used in) business combination	213,523	-	-	213,523	(12,260)
Change in restricted cash and other	(126,993)	(20,395)	(3,058)	(189,482)	(26,441)
Cash used in investing activities	(594,751)	(268,006)	(414,280)	(1,416,430)	(1,673,551)
Cash flows from financing activities					
Proceeds (repayments) from debt activities, net	968,613	(522,513)	135,000	975,417	318,972
Collateralized borrowing	212,040	173,144	208,794	769,709	568,745
Net cash flows from noncontrolling interests	180,277	-	-	180,277	-
Proceeds from issuance of common stock in a public offering	-	-	(20,000)	1,701,734	730,000
Other	11,897	28,499	(98,756)	116,839	(94,194)
Cash provided by (used in) financing activities	1,372,827	(320,870)	225,038	3,743,976	1,523,523
Effect of foreign exchange rates on cash and cash equivalents	(20,908)	3,182	(10,037)	(7,409)	(34,278)
Net increase (decrease) in cash and cash equivalents	308,959	(162,044)	(229,128)	2,196,308	(708,805)
Cash at the beginning of the period	3,084,257	3,246,301	1,426,036	1,196,908	1,905,713
Cash at the end of the period	$ 3,393,216	$ 3,084,257	$ 1,196,908	$ 3,393,216	$ 1,196,908

Appendix B

Liquidity ratios

Current Ratio:
Current Ratio = Current assets /Current liabilities -------------------- **(1)**
Quick Ratio:
Quick Ratio= (Current Assets-Inventories)/Current Liabilities --------------------- **(2)**
Cash Ratio:
Cash Ratio = Cash / Current Liabilities -------------------- **(3)**

Asset management ratios

Accounts receivable turnover:
Accounts receivable turnover = Sales /Average Accounts receivable ------------------- **(4)**
Average collection period:
Average collection period = 360 days / Accounts receivable turnover ----------------- **(5)**
Inventory Turnover Ratio:
Inventory Turnover Ratio = Cost of Goods Sold / Average Inventory ----------------- **(6)**
Accounts Payable turnover:
Accounts Payable turnover = Purchases / Average Accounts Payable ------------------ **(7)**
Accounts Payable turnover in days:
Accounts Payable turnover in days = 360 / Accounts Payable turnover -------------- **(8)**
Fixed asset turnover:
Fixed asset turnover = Sales / Average Net fixed asset --------------- **(9)**
Total asset turnover :
Total asset turnover = Sales / Average Total asset --------------- **(10)**

Profitability Ratio

Net Profit margin:
Net Profit margin = Net profit after tax/sales -------------------- **(11)**
Gross Profit margin ratio:
Gross Profit margin ratio= Gross profit/sales -------------------- **(12)**
Return on Total Assets:
Return on Total Assets = (Net income+ (1-T) Interest expenses+ Minority interests) / Average total assets -------------------- **(13)**
Return on common stock equity:
Return on common stock equity = (Net income – Preferred dividends) / Average Common stockholders' equity------- **(14)**
Operating Profit Margin:
Operating Profit Margin = Operating profits / Sales -------------- **(15)**

Debt coverage ratio

Debt Ratio:
Debt Ratio =Total liabilities / Total assets -------------- **(16)**
Time interest earned:
Time interest earned = EBIT / Interest charged ------------- **(17)**

Author details

Nizar Mohammad Alsharari
Department of Accounting, Finance, and Entrepreneurship, Jackson State University, College of Business, United States

*Address all correspondence to: nizaralsharari@gmail.com

References

[1] Alsharari NM. Management accounting and organizational change: Alternative perspectives. International Journal of Organizational Analysis. 2019a (Accepted Manuscript)

[2] Alsharari NM. A comparative analysis of taxation and revenue trends in the Middle East and North Africa (MENA) region. Pacific Accounting Review. 2019b (just-accepted)

[3] Alsharari NM. Accounting changes and beyond budgeting principles (BBP) in the public sector. International Journal of Public Sector Management. 2019c (just-accepted)

[4] Alsharari NM. Internationalization market and higher education field: Institutional perspectives. International Journal of Educational Management. 2019d (just-accepted)

[5] Alsharari NM. Institutional change of cloud ERP implementation in the public sector. International Journal of Disruptive Innovation in Government. 2021

[6] Alsharari NM, Al-Shboul M, Alteneiji S. Implementation of cloud ERP in the SME: Evidence from UAE. Journal of Small Business and Enterprise Development. 2020

[7] Alsharari NM. Results based costing (RBC) system: Questioning the unit of analysis in ABC. Corporate Ownership and Control. 2016a;**13**(2):587-603

[8] Alsharari NM. The diffusion of accounting innovations in the new public sector as influenced by IMF reforms: Actor-network theory. International Journal of Actor-Network Theory and Technological Innovation (IJANTTI). 2016b;**8**(4):26-51

[9] Alsharari NM. The development of accounting education and practice in an environment of socio-economic transformation in the Middle East: The case of Jordan. International Journal of Educational Management. 2017a;**31**(6): 736-751

[10] Alsharari NM. Institutional logics and ERP implementation in public sector agency. The Journal of Developing Areas. 2017b;**51**(2):417-425

[11] Alsharari, N. M. Management accounting relevance: Practice, variance and current research agenda. UOS Journal for Humanities and Social Sciences, University of Sharjah. 2016

[12] Alsharari NM. Internationalization of the higher education system: An interpretive analysis. International Journal of Educational Management. 2018a;**32**(3):359-381

[13] Alsharari NM. Multilevel institutional analysis of accounting change in public management. International Journal of Organizational Analysis. 2018b;**26**(1):91-106

[14] White G, Sondhi A, Fried D. The Analysis and Use of Financial Statements. Hoboken, NJ: Wiley; 2003

[15] Rejeb A. Financial Analysis of Automotive Industry: Evidence from General Motors and Honda Motor, LTD. 2015

[16] Statista. (2019). Passenger Car Production by Country 2018 | Statista. [online] Available at: https://www.statista.com/statistics/226032/light-vehicle-producing-countries/ [Accessed August 25, 2019].

[17] Sehested P. Valuation of Tesla Motors Inc. Master Thesis. Copenhagen Business School; 2014

Section 2

Islamic Accounting and Islamic Banking

Chapter 2

The Concept of Accounting in Islamic Bank (Indonesia Empirical Cases)

Lucky Nugroho

Abstract

This chapter aims to explain the implementation of accounting in Islamic banks industries. Moreover, the research question will include the following: (i) What are the principles of Islamic banking? (ii) How is the implementation of Islamic accounting in Islamic banks? (iii) What is meant by Islamic ethical principles? (iv) What is meant by Islamic financial transactions? (v) What is meant by Islamic financial statements?. Furthermore, based on the formulation of the problem, this chapter aims to understand the implementation of understanding the accounting process for Islamic banking institutions according to Islamic Accounting Standards. In addition, the implication of this chapter is to provide a scientific repertoire in the field of Islamic accounting, especially related to the Islamic banking industry.

Keywords: Islamic bank, accounting, Islamic accounting, Islamic principles, Islamic financial transactions

1. Introduction

The historical background of establishing Islamic banks in various countries has differences in the year of establishment and the motivation for establishing Islamic banks in these countries. Moreover, the background and motivation for the establishment of Islamic banks in several countries are as follows:

- In 1950, the first Islamic bank was established in Pakistan. The Muslim community of fund owners founded the Islamic bank. The bank implements interest-free for savers and borrowers. This bank aims to provide loans to poor farmers to use for agricultural improvement on their land. However, banks still charge low administrative fees for borrowers to cover the bank's administrative costs [1, 2].

- On July 25, 1963, the first Islamic bank in Egypt was established under Mith-Ghamr Islamic Savings Bank. The bank was founded by El-Naggar, who is an academic. In addition, the establishment at Mith-Ghamr was an experimental bank that imitated the savings bank in Germany, which was then implemented in rural areas in Egypt. However, the purpose of this bank is different from the savings bank in Germany, where the purpose of the Mith-Ghamr Islamic Savings

Bank is to mobilize funds from the public in Egypt by applying Islamic principles to provide customers with a halal income. The objectives of establishing the Mith-Ghamr Islamic savings bank are as follows: (i) as an institution that mobilizes funds in rural Egyptian communities so that people who have excess funds can be appropriately allocated to people who need capital; (ii) as an educational center to manage the finances of the Egyptian people so that people have the habit of saving and saving to improve their welfare; (iii) helping to mobilize idle funds in Egyptian rural communities so that idle funds in the community can be used as capital for productive activities. The development of this bank was quite successful and was accepted by the people in Egypt. However, after the Mith-Ghamr Islamic Savings Bank developed quite widely in the community for approximately 3 years, this bank was closed in 1967 by the government due to political reasons [3, 4].

- In the same year (1963), with the establishment of the Islamic Savings Bank, in Malaysia, a Hajj Savings Bank was also established. The objectives of establishing a Hajj Savings Bank by the Malaysian government are (i) to accommodate savings from the people who are going for Hajj so that they can carry out the pilgrimage and also have material provisions when carrying out Hajj; (ii) empowering Malaysian Muslim community funds to participate in financing development projects in Malaysia that are under Islamic principles; (iii) in addition, with the existence of this Hajj bank, pilgrims in Malaysia can carry out their Hajj journey more safely and comfortably due to the adequate facilities and services of this Malaysian Hajj Savings Bank [5, 6].

- Meanwhile, in 1982, the first Islamic Bank in Europe was established in Copenhagen, Denmark. The background to the widespread existence of Islamic banks in continental Europe was that there was a phenomenon that investors from countries from the Middle East would bring or transfer petrodollars funds from conventional banks in Europe to Islamic banks in the European country. Therefore, in anticipation of the repatriation of these funds, governments in European countries support the strategy of conventional banking to keep investors from the Middle East by providing incentives and convenience to open Islamic banking services to conventional banks in Europe (dual-banking) [2, 7].

- The year 1992 was a milestone in developing Islamic banking in Indonesia. This was marked by the establishment of Bank Muamalat Indonesia (BMI) on the idea of the Indonesian Ulema Council (MUI) and the Indonesian Muslim Intellectuals Association (ICMI). However, at that time, BMI had not given any color to the growth of Islamic banking in Indonesia because of its relatively small assets. The Islamic banking industry in Indonesia only developed after 1999 after issuing Law No. 10 of 1998 concerning banking, so in Indonesia, there are two forms of Islamic banking, namely Islamic Commercial Banks (BUS) and Islamic Business Units (UUS) [4, 8].

Referring to the statement from [9, 10], the economic and financial crises that occurred in the world were caused by greed from humans, so they took action that maximizes profits without paying attention to environmental sustainability, social problems, and the next generation. Furthermore, the country's economic growth also depends on the financial sector, which functions to drive the real sector in the form of business activities such as production, processing, manufacturing, and so on that contribute directly to the economy as the locomotive of the financial sector in the banking industry [11, 12]. Therefore, if the banking industry experiences a shock or disturbance, it will impact the economic crisis. For example, this happened in the period 2007–2008 where banks in America failed to distribute housing loan products, which resulted in the bankruptcy of several of these financial institutions [13, 14]. The impact of the shock on the financial sector impacts is increasing unemployment and increasing inflation, which leads to a crisis in the country [15, 16]. Therefore, according to better function of the financial sector, one of which is the banking industry as the locomotive of the financial sector, it will have implications for economic growth, which will also get better [17, 18].

In addition, according to [19, 20], the development of the number of Islamic financial institutions in the Middle East and Indonesia is as follows:

Based on **Table 1**, it is known that the number of Islamic financial institutions in Middle Eastern countries is 248. However, the number of Islamic banks is 52, and Islamic window banking is 32. Therefore, there is a potential for 84 Islamic bank financial institutions that will use Islamic banking accounting in Middle Eastern countries. In addition, according to **Table 2**, there are also 34 Islamic banks and 168 Islamic rural banks in Indonesia, so there is a potential for 202 Islamic banking financial institutions to use Islamic banking accounting. Thus the existence of Islamic accounting for banking institutions becomes a necessity.

Therefore, based on the phenomenon of the existence of Islamic banks and the urgency of the existence of Islamic banks to improve welfare for the community, it is necessary to apply an Islamic accounting system to record, acknowledge, and disclose

Countries in the Middle East	Islamic bank	Financial and investment companies	Islamic banking windows	Takaful companies	Islamic insurance windows	Total	Share (%)
Bahrain	27	5	10	10	0	52	20.97
Saudi Arabia	6	21	8	28	2	65	26.21
Kuwait	5	54	2	12	1	74	29.84
Qatar	6	5	5	4	2	22	8.87
United Arab Emirates	8	10	7	10	0	35	14.11
Total	52	95	32	64	5	248	100.00
Share (%)	20.97	38.31	12.90	25.81	2.02	100	

Table 1.
Islamic financial institution development in Middle East countries.

Country	Islamic bank	Financial and investment companies	Takaful companies	Islamic rural bank	Islamic microfinance institution	Total
Indonesia	34	58	7	163	4500	4762
Share (%)	0.71	1.22	0.15	3.42	94.50	100.00

Table 2.
Islamic financial institution development in Indonesia.

transactions based on Islamic principles. Thus, the formulation of the problems that will be discussed in this chapter of this book includes the following:

- What is meant by Islamic accounting?
- What is meant by Islamic ethical principles?
- What is meant by Islamic financial transactions?
- What is meant by Islamic financial statements?

Furthermore, based on the formulation of the problem, this chapter aims to understand the accounting process for Islamic banking institutions under Islamic Accounting Standards. In addition, the implication of this chapter is to provide scientific references in the field of Islamic accounting, especially related to the Islamic banking industry.

2. Discussion

Furthermore, before we discuss what Islamic accounting means, we must understand the concept of Islamic finance. The theory presented by a () states that the company's activities running its business must understand that it must be based on the Tawhid String Relationship (TSR). Where TSR is a theory that states that all human activities, including earning a living, must be based on the Qur'an and Hadith, and other Islamic laws; however, according to [19, 20], the application of Islamic laws must also be accompanied by knowledge, so that science in Islam has an important role, therefore, in maqasid sharia (sharia goals) reason must be maintained. Sharia maqasid, according to [21–23] includes the following: *hifdz al-din* (religion protection), *hifdz al-nafs* (protection of the soul), *hifdz al-'aql* (protection of the intellect), *hifdz al-nasl* (hereditary/family protection), and *hifdz al-maal* (property ownership protection). Furthermore, the sharia maqasid is implemented in daily human life in meeting basic needs (daruriyyat), secondary needs (hajiyyat), and tertiary needs (tahsiniyyat). Thus, Islamic banking as a bank that applies sharia principles should apply Islamic accounting in every transaction.

2.1 Islamic accounting

The Islamic banking industry in the world has such rapid growth that an accounting system following Islamic principles must support it. According to [24], the definition of Islamic accounting based on etymology (origin of the word) comes from the Arabic language, namely *Muhasabah* (*mashdar hassaba-yuhasibu*), which means to count, measure, or add up based on Islamic principles. In addition, according to [25], *Muhasabah* is closely related to *Hisab* where *Hisab* is one of the processes of calculating charity during human life in the world by Allah. Therefore, for every action and activity in *muamalah* (human social activity), such as trade transactions, then every Muslim must always be in a state of trust, honesty and have a high commitment to keep his promises. The development of the word *Hisab* in Arabic refers to the word *Al-Hisbah*. This public institution has existed in Islamic society since the beginning of the Islamic period until the period of Western occupation that conducts inspections of trade activities. The person conducting the inspection is called the *Muhtasib*, whose function is to carry out the following tasks:

- Ensuring communities have the right to appropriate scales and correct measurements;
- Monitor and provide sanctions for business fraud, such as concealing damage and submitting incorrect information related to the goods being transacted;
- Conduct inspections on contracts that are not by Islamic principles that contain *MAGHRIB* activities (*Maysir*-gambling, *Gharar*-uncertainty activities, and *Riba*-interest rate) as well as activities that Allah and the Messenger prohibit;
- Maintain the implementation of the free market society;
- Preventing hoarding of goods that are needed by the community.

Furthermore, referring to the definition of Islamic accounting, according to [26], the purpose of Islamic accounting is to provide benefits for humanity. This is because the legal basis for implementing Islamic accounting comes from the Qur'an and Hadith, as well as other sources of Islamic law such as *Ijma*, *Qiyas*, and *Ijtihad*. Some references to verses of the Qur'an that make the legal basis of Islamic accounting are as follows:

- Al Baqarah verse 282, which means:

> *O you who have believed, when you contract (i.e. when you have or contract a debt) a debt one upon another for a stated term, then write it down. And let a writer write it down between you with justice, and let not any writer refuse to write it down, as Allah has taught him. So let him write and let the one upon whom is the truthful duty of payment (i.e. the debtor) dictate, and let him be pious to Allah his Lord and not depreciate anything therein. So, in case the one upon whom is the truthful duty is foolish, or weak, or unable to dictate himself, then let his patron dictate with justice. And call in to witness two witnesses of your men; yet, in case the two are not two men, then one man and two women from among the witnesses you are satisfied with, so that (in case) one of the two women should err, then either of the two should remind the other, and let the witnesses not refuse whenever they are called (upon). And be not too loath to write it down, (whether) it is small or great, with (Literally: to is term) its term. That is more equitable in the Providence of Allah, and more upright for testimony, and likelier that you will not be suspicious. Except (when) it is commerce present that you transact among yourselves, then it shall be no fault in you if you do not write it down. And take witnesses when you sell one to another, and let not either writer or witness be harmed, and in case you perform (that), then that is evident immorality in you. And be pious to Allah, and Allah teaches you; and Allah is Ever-Knowing of everything.*

Therefore, related to the verse above, Muslims have instructions to record or write related to debt and receivable transactions. Furthermore, if the parties making the debts and receivables cannot record, they can use a third party to be a witness to carry out the transaction reasonably. Thus, if interpreted from the perspective of Islamic accounting, the implementation of Islamic accounting must be based on the principles of justice.

2.2 Islamic ethical principles

According to [27–29], Muslim activities must refer to the concept of the Tawhid String Relationship (TSR), where all activities and activities in the lives of Muslims must follow and obey the sources of Islamic law, namely Al-Qur'an, hadith, and other legal sources that apply. Therefore, referring to the legal basis of Islamic accounting, namely QS, Al Baqarah verse 282, then there are important things that include:

1. In the implementation of every activity with good intentions, in any case, including accounts payable, who must carry out documentation by writing it down or recording it. Thus, if there is a dispute in its implementation, there is evidence as a standard reference to resolve it fairly;

2. In addition, those who are appointed or assigned as witnesses who write or record transactions may not refuse. Allah SWT has essentially given him the knowledge and ability to write. Furthermore, the witness who writes or who records the transaction must record the transaction correctly and precisely following what is in the transaction or who is informed according to the actual incident not reduced or exaggerated;

3. Furthermore, in *muamalah*, it is obligatory to have and present two witnesses who will be asked to testify at any time when needed. Furthermore, the two witnesses must be male with the conditions that they must be adults who are reasonable and not a slave and have good morals. If a dispute occurs in the future, the testimonies of these witnesses can be additional evidence so that it is not only written documents that serve as guidelines in making decisions in the dispute. Therefore, with a witness mechanism, it is hoped to realize justice in *muamalah*;

4. In addition, if the debtor is a person who is weak in mind or weak in condition and does not have the ability because he is still tiny so he is unable to act on his own, as is the case with foreigners who do not understand the local language. Thus, the debtor can appoint a guardian or representative in this *muamalah* process. In addition, the guardian or representative appointed must have an honest and trustworthy attitude in carrying out his duties as a guardian in such activities;

5. Furthermore, if two males or male witnesses cannot be fulfilled, they can be replaced by one male and two females. This reflects that Islamic law is flexible and provides a solution that does not fulfill two male witnesses.

The implementation of Islamic accounting must be under the objectives and based on Islamic laws (shari'ah). Therefore, the application or implementation of Islamic accounting must meet the principles of Islamic ethics, which include:

1. Accountability, the essence of accountability, is related to trust, where trust is a responsibility in human transactions with Allah SWT. The purpose of humans being created on this earth is as a caliph where later they will be held account-

able. Therefore, if implemented in accounting, it can be realized in accounting reporting;

2. Brotherhood (*ukhuwah*), the principle of brotherhood (*ukhuwa*h), is essentially a universal value that regulates social interaction and harmonization of the parties' interests for the public benefit in the spirit of mutual help. Brotherhood in Islamic transactions based on the principles of knowing each other (*ta'aruf*), mutual understanding (*tafahum*), mutual assistance (*ta'awun*), mutual guarantees (*takaful*), mutual synergy, and alliances (*tahaluf*);

3. Justice, the essence of the principle of justice, is to put something in its place and give something only to those who have the right and treat things according to their position. The implementation of justice in business activities is in the form of the principle of *muamalah*, which prohibits the existence of elements: usury (the element of interest in all its forms and types, both usury *nasiah* and *fadh*l); tyranny (elements that harm oneself, others, and the environment); *maisyir* (gambling elements and speculative nature); *gharar* (element of obscurity); and *haram* (*haram* elements in both goods and services and related operational activities);

4. Truth, the principle of truth, has a relationship with justice. Therefore, the principle of justice and truth become an inseparable unit. Furthermore, the accounting process is constantly faced with the issue of measurement, recognition, and reporting. These activities will produce good grades if they are based on truth values;

5. Benefit (*maslahah*), the principle of beneficence (*maslahah*), is essentially all forms of goodness and benefits worldly and hereafter dimensions, material and spiritual, as well as individual and collective. Shari'ah transactions that are considered beneficial must fulfill all the elements that are the objectives of shari'ah provisions (*maqasid shari'ah*), namely in the form of maintaining: aqidah, faith, and piety (*deen*); intellectual (*aql*); lineage (*nasl*); soul and salvation (*nafs*); and property (*mall*);

6. Balance (*tawazun*), the principle of balance (*tawazun*), essentially includes the balance of material and spiritual aspects, private and public aspects, financial sector and the real sector, business and social, and balance of utilization and preservation aspects. Islamic transactions do not emphasize the maximization of company profits solely for the benefit of the owners (shareholders). So that the benefits obtained do not only focus on shareholders but on all parties who can feel the existence of economic activity;

7. Universalism (*syumuliyah*), the principle of universalism (*syumuliyah*), can essentially be carried out with and for all interested parties (stakeholders) without distinction of ethnicity, religion, race, and class, following the spirit of universal mercy (*rahmatan lil alamin*).

2.3 Islamic financial transactions

The transaction is an activity carried out by someone that causes changes to the assets or finances owned, whether it is increased or decreased—for example, selling property, buying goods, paying debts, and paying the various expenses to meet the necessities of life [30, 31]. In the transaction, there is transaction administration. As for what is meant by the administration here, it is an activity to record changes in the finances of a person or organization, which is carried out carefully and using specific methods. Whereas in an economic system based on Islamic principles, transactions must always be based on the rules of Islamic law (shari'ah), because transactions are a manifestation of human charity that has the value of worship before Allah SWT, so that in Islamic accounting transactions can be grouped into two: (i) halal transactions; (ii) illegal transactions (*haram*) [31].

Furthermore, the transaction involves a contract (*akad*). *Akad* is a written agreement between the parties that contains the rights and obligations of each party, the agreed terms, and conditions under the provisions of shari'ah and applicable law. Furthermore, when viewed from a language perspective, the pronunciation of the contract comes from the Arabic pronunciation of al-acid, which means the engagement, agreement, or consensus all-ittifaq. In fiqh terminology, the contract is defined as the ties of *ijab* (statement by making a bond) and qabul (statement of accepting a bond) by the will of the Shari'ah, which affects the object of the engagement. So, the contract is an engagement, an agreement marked by a statement of binding (*ijab*), and a statement of accepting a bond (qabul) following Islamic shari'ah, which affects the object that the engagement factor binds. From this understanding, in the contract, at least two parties will carry out the engagement, then the object of the engagement and accompanied by consent and qabul for the implementation of the engagement.

In the Islamic economic system, contracts are generally divided into the *tabarru'* contract and the *tijarah* contract. *Tabarru's* contract is an agreement/contract that does not seek material gain. So, it is pure virtue and only hopes for a reward from Allah SWT, while the tijarah contract is an agreement/contract whose purpose is to seek business profits. The following is an explanation of the two types of contracts. In essence, the *tabarru'* contract is a contract of doing good that expects a reply from Allah SWT alone. That is why this contract is not intended to seek commercial gain. The logical consequence is that if the *tabarru'* contract is carried out by taking commercial profits, it is no longer a tabarru' contract. Instead, it will be a tijarah contract. If he wants to remain a tabarru' contract, he may not take advantage (commercial profits) from the tabarru' contract. Of course, he is not obliged to bear the costs of implementing the *tabarru'* contract. That is, he may ask for a replacement for the costs incurred in carrying out the *tabarru'* contract. Furthermore, the difference between tabarru' and tijarah contracts is shown in **Table 3** below:

Tabarru'	*Tijarah*
Not-Profit-Oriented	Profit-Transaction-Oriented
The purpose of the transaction is to help.	The purpose of the transaction is to seek commercial profits.
The party providing the kindness may ask for a fee to the beneficiary to cover operational costs. However, it is forbidden to take profit from tabarru transactions.	The *tijarah* transaction contract can be converted into a tabarru contract with the agreement of the owner of the funds or goods to release his rights to cancel the obligations of the party who has not fulfilled his obligations.
The *tabarru'* contract cannot be converted into a *tijarah* contract unless followed by prior approval.	*Tijarah* contract can be divided into natural certainty return and natural uncertainty return.

Source: [32].

Table 3.
Difference between Tabaru' and Tijarah.

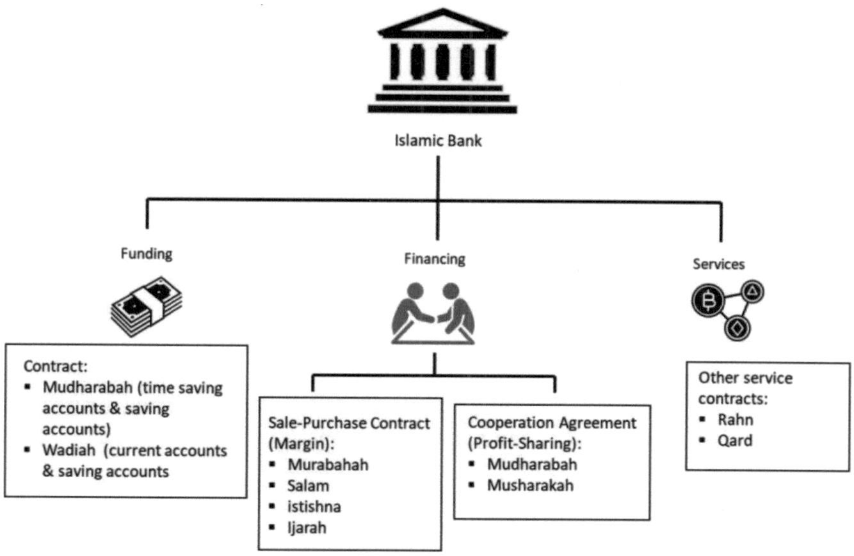

Figure 1.
The contracts on Islamic bank. Sumber: [11].

Therefore, transactions in Islamic banks must be based on contracts that are tailored to the needs and objectives, as shown in **Figure 1** as follows:

Referring to **Figure 1** above, Islamic banks have different contracts tailored to each transaction's purpose. Therefore, the products at Islamic banks are divided into 3 (three), namely (i) funding, (ii) financing, and (iii) services. Funding contracts (giro, savings, and time deposits) are divided into:

- Mudharabah (cooperation agreement) for savings and time deposits;
- Wadiah (deposit contract) for current accounts and savings.

Financing products are divided into 2 (two) principles, namely buying and selling, which generate margin and cooperation based on the principle of profit sharing. The distribution of sale and purchase financing contracts at Islamic banks includes:

- Murabahah is a pure sale and purchase contract between the delivery of goods and payment;
- Salam is a sale and purchase contract where the delivery of goods purchased at a later date or commonly called a purchase with an order, but the payment has been received in advance by the seller;
- Istishna is a sale and purchase contract based on orders with specific payment terms with a payment system based on the progress of manufacture.

Meanwhile, the financing contract based on the principle of cooperation includes:

- Mudharabah is a cooperation agreement in which the bank owns capital. The customer is the owner of the skills or expertise, divided based on the agreed ratio.

- Musyarakah is a cooperation agreement in which the bank participates in part of the capital so that both parties, both the bank and the customer, contribute funds or capital.

Furthermore, other contracts at Islamic banks include:

- *Rahn, rahn* is a pawn agreement that is pledging its assets to get financing;

- *Qardh, qardh* contract is a bailout or financing that requires no reward.

2.4 Islamic bank financial statements

Furthermore, Islamic financial reports consist of financial statements for commercial activities and financial reports for social activities consisting of:

- Activities financial report

  a. Balance sheet (statement of financial position)

  b. Income statement

  c. Statement of changes in equity

  d. Cash flow statement

- Social activities financial report

  a. Report on the source and use of zakat funds;

  b. Report on sources and uses of social funds.

In addition, financial reports have two functions, namely as a recording tool and as a tool for analyzing. Therefore, in principle, the financial statements are the same for small and giant businesses. The only difference is the nominal in it and the number of activities or activities covered by the entity. Users need financial reports at any time because financial statements can provide information regarding the following matters:

- Stakeholders must be aware of past, present, and projected financial conditions;

- Supervise company activities because financial performance can be manipulated through financial reports.

Islamic banks are financial institutions with an intermediary function in the community, collecting and distributing them back to the community following Islamic principles. Referring to **Figure 1** above, the sources of funds from Islamic banks consist of:

- Wadiah Current Account;

- Wadiah Savings;

- Mudharabah Savings;
- Mudharabah Deposits.

Furthermore, the sources of funds are channeled by Islamic banks with the following financing contracts:

- Sale and Purchase (Murabahah, Istishna, & Salam);
- Profit Sharing (Mudharabah and Musyarakah);
- Rent (Ijarah);
- Other Disbursement of Funds (Rahn and Qardh).

The results of the distribution of financing to the community generate income, which includes:

- Margin Revenue;
- Revenue Sharing;
- Rental/Ujrah Income;
- Other Disbursement Income.
- In addition to running their operations, Islamic banks need operational costs such as labor, promotion, and general and administrative costs.

In addition, the financial statements of Islamic banks that are prepared and responsible for the management have a purpose for the users and stakeholders of Islamic banks. In more detail, the objectives of the Islamic bank financial statements include the following:

- Provide information for users of financial statements;
- Bank accountability report to investors;
- Improve bank compliance with Islamic principles;
- Provide information on bank compliance with Islamic principles;
- Bank accountability report in securing funds and investing at a reasonable rate of return;
- Provide information on the level of investment returns;
- Provide information for the fulfillment of social function obligations.

Furthermore, the components of the financial statements of Islamic banks that differentiate them from conventional banks include:

- Statement of financial position
- Statements of income and other comprehensive income;
- Revenue and profit-sharing reconciliation reports;
- Reports on sources and uses of benevolent funds;
- Report on sources and distribution of zakat funds.

3. Conclusions

The development of Islamic banking financial institutions in the world is a necessity. Therefore, there is great potential for using Islamic accounting in these institutions. Furthermore, based on this, in the implementation of Islamic accounting in banking, several things need to be considered, which include::

- The application of Islamic accounting refers to the Al-Quran Surah Al-Baqarah verse 282;
- The application of Islamic Ethical principles of Islamic accounting must consider the principles of (i) Accountability; (ii) Brotherhood; (iii) Justice; (iv) Truth; (v) Benefits; (vi) Balance; (vii) Universalism.
- The implementation of Islamic bank financial statements generally consists of activities financial reports and social activities financial reports.

Author details

Lucky Nugroho
Mercu Buana University, Jakarta, Indonesia

*Address all correspondence to: lucky.nugroho@mercubuana.ac.id

References

[1] Chachi A. Origin and development of commercial and islamic banking operations. ournal of King Abdulaziz University: Islamic Economics. 2008;**21**(2):29-66

[2] Labetubun MAH, Maulida AZ, Triwardhani D, Bagenda C, Nugroho L, Hargyatni T, et al. Lembaga Keuangan Bank & Non Bank (Sebuah Tinjauan Teori dan Praktis). Penerbit Widina. 2021

[3] Nugroho L, Utami W, Sukmadilaga C, Fitrijanti T. The urgency of allignment Islamic bank to increasing the outreach (Indonesia evidence). International Journal of Economics and Financial Issues. 2017;**7**(4):283-291

[4] Diantanti NP et al.. Pengantar Bisnis Islam (Tinjauan Konsep dan Praktis). Bandung: Widina Bhakti Persada Bandung; 2021

[5] Nugroho L, Husnadi TC, Utami W, Hidayah N. Maslahah and strategy to establish a single state-owned Islamic bank in Indonesia. Tazkia Islamic Finance and Business Review. 2017;**10**(1):17-33

[6] Nugroho L. Konsep Ekonomi dan Perbankan dalam Islam. In: Pengantar Perbankan Syariah. 1st ed. Vol. 1. Widina Bhakti Persada bandung; 2020. pp. 1-26

[7] Bilal M, Abbas S. Comparison of Islamic banking and conventional banking: an empirical review. Studies. 2015;**4**(1):39-43

[8] Izhar H, Asutay M. Estimating the profitability of Islamic banking: Evidence from bank Muamalat Indonesia. Review of Islamic Economics. 2007;**11**(2):17-29

[9] Nugroho L, Badawi A, Hidayah N, Ahmad NH. Snapshot in customer deposit of islamic bank religion, age, and gender as the reflection of pancasila five principles of Indonesia nation. Journal of Business Research. 2020;**5**(1):74-95

[10] Mukminin K. How close islamic banks are to global fraud- learnings from Dubai Islamic bank in the time of sub-prime crisis. European Journal of Islamic Finance. 2018;**10**:1-9

[11] Nugroho L et al.. Pengantar Perbankan Syariah. Bandung: Widina Bhakti Persada Bandung; 2020

[12] Nugroho L, Bararah HN. Pengaruh good corporate governance dan biaya operasional dan pendapatan operasional (BOPO) terhadap stabilitas keuangan bank umum syariah di Indonesia Tahun 2012-2017. Inovbiz: Jurnal Inovasi Bisnis. 2018;**6**(2):160-169

[13] Sudarsono H. Dampak krisis keuangan global terhadap perbankan di Indonesia: Perbandingan antara Bank Konvensional dan Bank Syariah. La_Riba. 2009;**3**(1):12-23

[14] Masyita D. Why do people see a financial system as a whole very important? Journal of Islamic Monetary Economics and Finance. 2015;**1**(1):79-106

[15] Nezky M. Pengaruh Krisis Ekonomi Amerika Serikat Terhadap Bursa Saham Dan Perdagangan Indonesia. Buletin Ekonomi Moneter dan Perbankan. 2013;**15**(3):89-103

[16] Nugroho L, Anisa N. Pengaruh manajemen bank induk, kualitas aset, dan efisiensi terhadap stabilitas bank syariah di indonesia (periode tahun 2013-2017). Inovbiz: Jurnal Inovasi Bisnis. 2018;**6**(2):114-122

[17] Borio CEV, White WR. Whither Monetary and Financial Stability? The

Implications of Evolving Policy Regimes. SSRN Electron. J; 2011

[18] Soekapdjo S, Tribudhi DA, Nugroho L. Pengaruh fundamental ekonomi dan kinerja keuangan terhadap kredit bermasalah pada bank syariah di Indonesia. Ekonika: Jurnal Ekonomi Universitas Kadiri. 2019;**4**(2):126

[19] Ihwanudin N, Maulida S, Fatriansyah AIA, Rahayu SS, Nugroho L, Harnovinsah H, et al. Pengantar perbankan syariah (konsep, regulasi & praktis). Widina Bhakti Persada Bandung. 2020

[20] Novikov V, Britikova E, Yarushkina E, Kovalenko L. Islamic banking in the global financial system: current situation and global environment. In: 5th International Conference on Economics, Management, Law and Education (EMLE 2019). Vol. 110. 2020. pp. 138-143

[21] Arafah W, Nugroho L. Maqhashid sharia in clean water financing business model at islamic bank. Online. 2016

[22] Nugraha E, Nugroho L, Lindra C, Sukiati W. Maqashid sharia implementation in indonesia and Bahrain. Etikonomi. 2020;**19**(1):155-168

[23] Nugroho L, Utami W, Doktoralina CM. Ekosistem bisnis wisata halal dalam perspektif maqasid syariah. Perisai: Islamic Banking and Finance Journal. 2019;**3**(2):84-92

[24] Darma S, Mukhlis. Urgensi pembukuan transaksi ditinjau dari perspektif syariah. AT-Tasiri'iy. 2019;**2**(2):17-39

[25] Batubara Z. Akuntansi dalam pandangan islam. JAS (Jurnal Akunt. Syariah). 2019;**3**(1):66-77

[26] Aziz LH et al.. Akuntansi Syariah (Sebuah Tinjauan Teori Dan Praktis), First. Bandung: Penerbit Widina Bhakti Persada Bandung; 2021

[27] Choudhury MA. Islamic perspective of socioeconomic development. Journal of Islamic Economics, Banking and Finance. 2010;**6**(3):37-54

[28] Nugroho L, Mariyanti T. Discourses of Islamic performance ratio based on tawhid string relationship. Journal of Islamic Economics & Social Science. 2021;**2**(1):44-52

[29] Nugroho L, Meiwanto Doktoralina C, Indriawati F, Safira S, Yahaya S. Microeconomics and tawhid string relation concept (TSR). International Journal of Economics and Business Administration. 2020;**8**(3):293-306

[30] Labetubun MAH et al.. Sistem Ekonomi Indonesia. Bandung: Widina Bhakti Persada Bandung; 2021

[31] Foley CF, Manova K. International trade, multinational activity, and corporate finance. Economics. 2015;**7**(1):119-146

[32] Sukmadilaga C, Nugroho L. Pengantar Akuntansi Perbankan Syariah Prinsip, Praktik dan Kinerja., First., no. 1. Pusaka Media: Lampung; 2017

Chapter 3

Islamic Banking and Islamic Accounting in Indonesia: History and Recent Development

Mahfud Sholihin and Dian Andari

Abstract

Islamic banks (IBs) have distinctive characteristics compared with the conventional ones. IBs only perform permissible (*halal*) financial transactions viewed from Islamic perspective and avoid usury (*riba*) and overspeculation (*gharar*). Consequently, IBs require special accounting to accommodate their nature. In terms of accounting, Indonesia is unique, as it has two accounting (for business organizations) standard setters: Financial Accounting Standard Board (*Dewan Standar Akuntansi Keuangan*-DSAK) and Sharia Financial Accounting Standard Board (*Dewan Standar Akuntansi Keuangan Syariah*-DSAS). This chapter discusses the development of IBs in Indonesia, a country with majority of its citizens being Muslim. Further, it explains the development of Islamic Financial Accounting Standards (IFAS) including how the standards are developed (the due processes). Finally, this chapter describes whether Islamic financial accounting standards developed in Indonesia has sufficiently fulfilled the accounting standards needed by Islamic banks in Indonesia.

Keywords: Dewan Standar Akuntansi Syariah (DSAS), Institute of Indonesia Chartered Accountants (IAI), Indonesia, Islamic accounting, Islamic banking

1. Introduction

This chapter discusses Islamic banking and Islamic accounting development and implementation in Indonesia. The first part of this chapter elaborates on the emergence and development of Islamic banks (IBs) in Indonesia. Then, the next part discusses the history and role of Islamic accounting in Indonesia. The chapter intended to develop understanding related to Indonesia Islamic banking and accounting as a unique case of Islamic finance state of the art.

As the most Muslim populous country in the world, the development of Islamic banking in Indonesia is not without challenges. The emergence of Islamic banks in Indonesia was triggered by internal and external factors. The growth of demand in permissible (*halal*) financial services started in the Middle East encouraged Indonesia to join the opportunity to pave its way in the banking sector after the formation of Islamic financial institutions at the grassroot level [1–3]. PT. Bank Muamalat

Indonesia (BMI) was the first Islamic bank in Indonesia established in 1990 in Jakarta, Indonesia. The stagnant development in its first years led to the enactment of the Indonesian Law No. 21 of 2008 about Islamic banking (or Sharia Banking) that set the definition and legal foundation for Islamic banks to grow in Indonesia.

Upon the establishment, the development of Islamic banks became more steady and apparent over time. In 2020 itself, the growth of Islamic banking (yoy) had double-digit increment for 13.11 percent (yoy). Even though the Islamic banking industry growth is increasing, the inferior competitive advantage only contributes to less than 10 percent of national banking assets [4]. Hence, in 2021, the ministry of state-owned enterprise combined three state-owned Islamic banks (PT. Bank Syariah Mandiri, PT. Bank Negara Indonesia Syariah, and PT. Bank Rakyat Indonesia Syariah) into PT. Bank Syariah Indonesia (BSI) through merger. This merger resulted in the improvement of the competitive advantage of BSI to its conventional counterparts [4]. This momentum marked the commitment of the government and stakeholders to boost the development of Islamic banking in Indonesia.

Accountability is important to ensure the relevance and reliability of information in Islamic banks. It can be said that the development of Islamic accounting in Indonesia is driven by the growth of Islamic banking and finance [5]. There is a demand to accommodate accounting standards for Islamic transactions; hence, reliable information can be used by users for making a sound decision. *Dewan Standar Akuntansi Syariah Ikatan Akuntan Indonesia* or Sharia Financial Accounting Standard Board of the Institute of Indonesia Chartered Accountants (DSAS IAI) was formed to review, to study, and to issue accounting standards for Islamic financial transactions. The standard must be embedded with Islamic values and norms; hence, the process also demands knowledge in Islamic law, accounting, and business.

Until today, the Islamic or Sharia accounting in Indonesia has developed to myriad activities and transactions performed by Islamic banks (i.e. *mudarabah* (investment), *murabaha* (cost-plus), and *ijarah* (leases),). Islamic-based transactions also encompass social or charitable activities that need guidance and standard to operate accountably. Accounting standards for Islamic social or charitable activities such as zakah (Islamic compulsory alms), sadaqah, and waqf (charity) were set to allow both nonprofit and profit organizations to perform a systematic financial reporting. Indeed, these activities are also committed by Islamic banks and other Islamic profit-oriented organizations as manifestations of their Islamic ethical identity. Therefore, it is expected that Islamic accounting is able to fulfill its goal to assist Islamic Banks to be accountable to their stakeholders and God by being fair and transparent in business.

2. Islamic banks (IBs) in Indonesia

2.1 Islamic banking emergence in Indonesia

The history of Islamic banks in Indonesia cannot be detached from the Islamic banking as a global phenomenon. The early concept of Islamic financial institutions was established by the idea of a bank with a profit-sharing system [1, 2]. In the 1940s, a Pakistan bank specifically set up to manage Hajj (pilgrimage) funds was founded but failed to prevail. The establishment of Mit Ghamr Local Saving Bank in Egypt marked as a breakthrough of modern Islamic banking in 1963. By 1967, the National Bank of Egypt and the Central Bank of Egypt took over Mit Ghamr operation due to declining performance during political turmoil. With this acquisition, Mit Ghamr's interest-free principle has been abandoned, and banks are once again functioning on an interest basis. In 1971, the concept of interest-free was finally reinvented during the Sadat administration with the establishment of the Nacelle Social Bank. The purpose of the bank is to continue its business according to the concepts practiced by Mit Ghamr. The growth of economy also drove more Muslim countries to facilitate Islamic principle-based banks. Dubai Islamic Bank in 1971, the first bank initiated by private institutions, indicated growing interest in the Islamic financial facilities. In 1975, Faysal Islamic Bank started to operate in Sudan and Egypt, and at the same time, the Kuwait government established Kuwait Finance House. Finally, the Islamic Development Bank (IsDB) was formed in October 1975, which consisted of 22 founding Islamic countries. IsDB provides financial assistance for the development of its member countries, helping them to establish Islamic banks in their respective countries and playing an important role in research in Islamic economics, banking, and finance. Now, IsDB, based in Jeddah-Saudi Arabia, continues to operate with more than 56 member countries. Subsequently, the efforts to establish Islamic banks began to spread in many countries. Some countries such as Pakistan, Iran, and Sudan decided to change their financial system by adopting an interest-free system. In other Islamic and Muslim majority countries such as Malaysia and Indonesia, interest-free banks operate side by side with conventional banks.

Despite the grassroot Islamic microfinance in Indonesia already prevailing, the contemporary Islamic banking development was marked in the 1980s. Expecting efficiency and economic strengthening, the Indonesian government implemented deregulation allowing banks to set interest rates in 1983 [3, 4]. "Pakto 88," a monetary policy package as part of deregulation, was promulgated to support liberalization of Indonesia banking system encouraging the emergence of banks. Along with, grass-root developing Islamic financial institutions, named BMT Salman ITB in Bandung and Koperasi Ridho Gusti in Jakarta, paved a way to be a pilot model for Islamic banks in Indonesia. In 1990, the Indonesia Ulema Council (Majelis Ulama Indonesia a.k.a. MUI) formed a task force to establish the first Islamic bank in Indonesia, PT. Bank Muamalat Indonesia (BMI). Initially, the bank received less recognition from the public due to lack of legal foundation to operate. The legal basis for banking under the Sharia system was only in one of the paragraphs of "banks with a profit-sharing system" in Law no. 7 of 1992, without details on the basis of Sharia law and the types of businesses that are allowed. In 1998, Law No. 7/1992 became Law No. 10 of 1998, clearly stating that there are two banking systems (dual-banking system) in the country, the conventional banking system and the Islamic banking system. This law encouraged the establishment of several other Islamic banks or Islamic windows, namely Bank IFI, Bank Syariah Mandiri, Bank Niaga, Bank BTN, Bank Mega, Bank BRI, Bank Bukopin, BPD Jabar, and BPD Aceh.

2.2 Islamic banking in Indonesia: Theory and practice

The dual-banking system in Indonesia allows conventional banks and Islamic banks to operate. The operationalization of both banking in parallel is called the dual-banking system. According to Indonesian Law No. 21 of 2008 about Islamic banking (or Sharia Banking) [5],

> *"Islamic Banks are banks that carry out business activities based on Islamic law (Sharia) principles, or Islamic legal principles regulated in the Islamic legal opinion (fatwa) of the Indonesian Ulema Council (Indonesian: Majelis Ulama Indonesia a.k.a. MUI) such as*

> *the principles of justice and balance ('adl wa tawazun), benefit (maslahah), universalism (alamiyah), and does not involve excessive speculation (gharar), gambling (maysir), usury (riba), exploitation (zalim) and unlawful (haram) objects." (translated)*

In addition, the law also mandates Islamic banks to perform social functions by facilitating collection of Islamic alms and charities and distributing it through Islamic charitable institutions. There are three categories of Islamic bank entities operating in Indonesia: Islamic commercial banks, Islamic-windowed banks, and Islamic rural banks. Islamic commercial banks are full-fledged Islamic banks that offer only Islamic financial products and operate under Islamic principles. Islamic-windowed banks, however, are business units or divisions of a conventional commercial bank (CCB). This business unit offers Islamic financial products. Meanwhile, Islamic rural banks are banks that operate in certain regions and only offer a more limited type of product compared with Islamic commercial and Islamic-windowed banks. Usually, the size of Islamic rural banks is significantly smaller than Islamic commercial banks. All these banks must comply with Islamic banking regulation.

Substantially, Islamic banks must nurture their identity as value-based institutions. Islamic bank's ethical identity explains how Islamic value is followed by the institution to stakeholders as a distinguishing characteristic from conventional banking practices [1–3]. There are five main traits of Islamic banks identity, namely: underlying philosophy and values; provision of interest-free products and services; restriction to Islamically acceptable deals; focus on developmental and social goals; and subjection to additional reviews by the Sharia Supervisory Board (SSB) [6]. The traits are broken down into several indices such as commitment to Sharia, existence of SSB, contribution to alms and charity (zakat and shadaqah), commitment to employees, and so on. While Belal et al. [7] conducted a longitudinal study to Islami Bank Bangladesh Limited (IBBL), a panel study of Islamic Identity Index measurement that was conducted by Zaki et al. [8] compares communicated and ideal ethical identities similar to those in Haniffa and Hudaib [9] but targeted Islamic banks in Asia. The result shows that three out of seven banks show value above the average, while the remaining have wide disparity. It indicates that not all Islamic banks in Asia have shared identity as Islamic banks. From the research, it is interesting that Indonesia Islamic bank's ethical identity index outperforms other Islamic banks in Asia even compared with Middle Eastern banks. It suggests that there is more consideration in the institutionalization of Islamic banks in Indonesia so that it can represent the Islamic norms and values in the banking industry.

The implementation of the regulatory and supervisory functions of Islamic banking from the aspect of implementing prudential principles and good governance is carried out by the Financial Services Authority (Indonesian: Otoritas Jasa Keuangan a.k.a. OJK) as is the case with conventional banking, but with a regulation and supervision system that is adjusted to the peculiarities of the Islamic banking operational system. The problem of fulfilling Sharia principles is unique for Islamic banks, because essentially Islamic banks are banks that offer products that comply with Islamic principles.

As prudential institutions, banks bear responsibility to manage its risk accordingly. As the distinction between conventional and Islamic banks, all stakeholders demand Islamic compliance as the foundational value of Islamic banks. The uniqueness of Islamic Banks (IB) entails consequence on risk exposing the bank [4]. Salem [5] argues that credit risk in IBs is higher than that in Conventional Banks (CBs) due to potential moral hazard triggered by asymmetric information embedded in Profit-Loss Sharing (PLS) contracts. However, deliberate negligence or misconduct committed by the *mudharib* or *musyarakah*'s management partner is proven, IBs can switch the contract to debt-like financing and impose penalties to the violating party [6, 9, 10]. IBs are claimed to have higher liquidity risk compared with conventional counterparts. The lack of liquid Sharia-compliant instruments causes inflexibility in securitization and diversification [11–13]. Accessibility to the capital market is impeded as there is less or even none of the interbank market for IBs [7, 8, 14]. Moreover, unlike conventional banking, the "last resort for lender" function happened to be complicated due to the injunction of usury, which is naturally prohibited by Shari'ah [11]. Sharia compliance, legal and fiduciary risk. Sharia noncompliance risk arises when IB violates Sharia law principles [15]. Failure in complying to Sharia can disturb or even fail the completion of contract, contributing to fiduciary risk due to poor due diligence and misconduct by IB [16]. The Islamic values and norms must be manifested and hence followed in Islamic banks, contributing complexity in Islamic banks that is unique compared to conventional banking.

Systems to ensure sharia compliance are important in Islamic banking. Therefore, the existence of Sharia Supervisory Board (SSB) in Indonesia Islamic Banking is mandatory. According to Law No. 21 of 2008 about Sharia Banking, the National Sharia Board of Indonesian Ulema Council (Indonesian: Dewan Standar Nasional Majelis Ulama Indonesia a.k.a. DSN MUI) issues Islamic legal guidance (fatwa) on lawfulness of Islamic bank's products and then SSBs guard its implementation in IBs. Additionally, OJK stipulates that all Islamic banking products may only be offered to the public after the bank has received a fatwa from the DSN-MUI and obtained permission from the OJK. At the operational level, each Islamic bank is also required to have a Sharia Supervisory Board (SSB), which has two functions, the first is the sharia supervisory function and the second is an advisory function when banks are faced with questions about whether an activity is sharia-compliant or not, as well as in the process of developing a product that will be submitted to DSN to obtain a fatwa. In addition to these functions, Sharia Banking is also directed to have an internal audit function that focuses on monitoring sharia compliance to assist DPS, and in carrying out external audits used by sharia banks are auditors who have qualifications and competencies in Islamic law subjects.

2.3 Recent development of Islamic banking in Indonesia

OJK categorizes institutions in Islamic financial industry into three subsectors, namely Islamic banks, Islamic non-banking financial institutions (Islamic NBFI), and Islamic capital market with a total capitalization of assets for IDR 1801.40 trillion or USD 127,71 billion (excluding Islamic stocks) in 2020 [17]. Islamic capital market contributes the largest proportion for IDR 1076.22, then Islamic banking for IDR 608.90, and the least, Islamic financial non-banking institutions for IDR 116.28 trillion (USD 1 = IDR 14,050). Since its establishment, the growth of Islamic financial industry in Indonesia has been growing. Regardless of its contribution to national market share that only counts for 9.95 percent in 2020, the growth of Islamic financial assets recorded 22.71 percent (yoy) consisting of the growth of Islamic capital market, Islamic banks, and Islamic NBFI for 30.58, 13.11, and 10.15, in sequence. From the banking industry, Sharia commercial banks dominate the growth proportion followed by Sharia business units and Sharia rural banks (**Figures 1** and **2**).

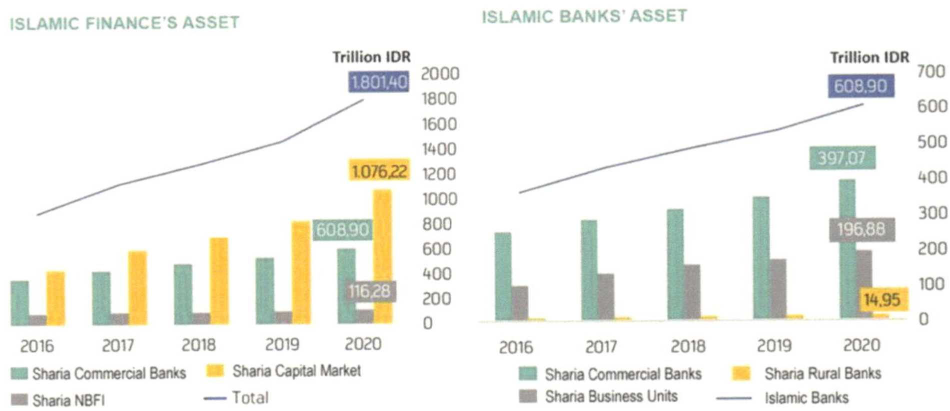

Figure 1.
The growth of Islamic finance and banking assets in Indonesia from 2016 to 2020. Source: Financial service authority (OJK), 2021.

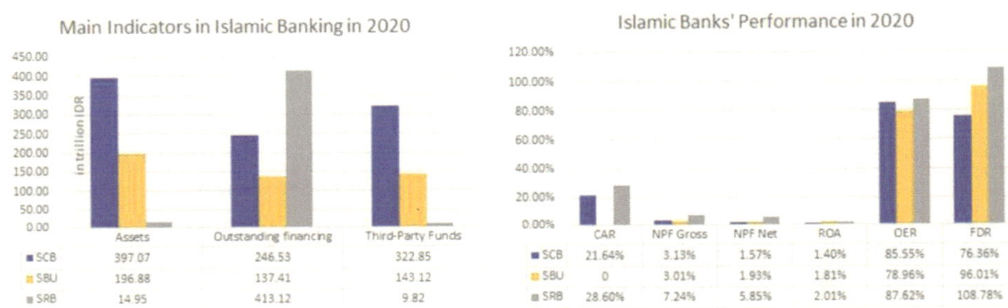

Figure 2.
Islamic banks' main indicators and performance in 2020. Source: Financial service authority (OJK), 2021.

The future of Islamic banking in Indonesia is promising if stakeholders, especially the government, commit to the development of the industry. The dual-banking system put Islamic banking in a competition with conventional banking. As a "newcomer" in the financial industry, Islamic banking market capitalization is far below conventional banking. The size of Islamic banks is significantly low compared with its counterparts, leading to the low capacity of lending. Nationally, the market share of the banking industry in terms of assets shows the dominance of several banks in BUKU 4[1], while most banks still have a small business scale and market share, including Islamic banks. Structurally, both conventional commercial banks (CCBs) and Sharia commercial banks (SCBs), the majority of banks are in BUKU 2 with 58 BUK (*Bank Umum Konvensional*, Conventional General Bank) and 7 BUS (*Bank Umum Syariah*, Sharia General Bank), respectively. In terms of BUK, there are already seven banks that are in BUKU 4, while there is not one BUS that is included in BUKU 4 and only a small part is included in BUKU 3 (**Figures 3** and **4**).

The Financial Services Authority (OJK) encourages banking consolidation policies and strengthens bank capital in Indonesia as stated in POJK No. 12/POJK.03/2020 concerning Commercial Bank Consolidation. In 2021, the Ministry of State-Owned

[1] BUKU is categorization of banks in Indonesia. Bank BUKU 4 is the biggest bank in Indonesia with capital more than IDR30 billions.

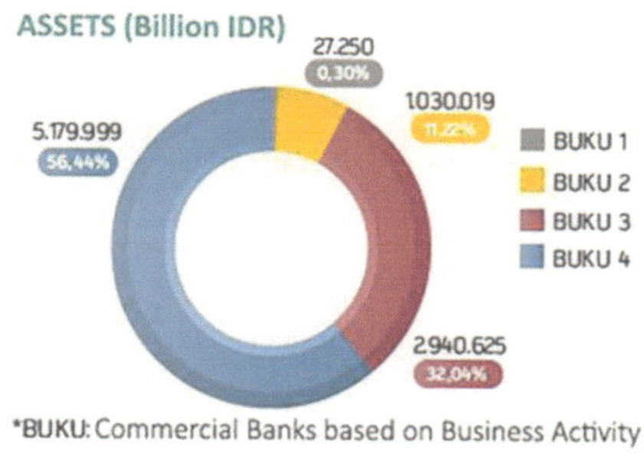

Number of Conventional Banks and Islamic Banks based on BUKU

Conventional Commercial Banks		Sharia Commercial Banks	
BUKU 1	4 banks	BUKU 1	3 banks
BUKU 2	58 banks	BUKU 2	7 banks
BUKU 3	26 banks	BUKU 3	4 banks
BUKU 4	7 banks		

Figure 3.
Classification of commercial banks based on business activity in Indonesia in 2020. Source: Financial service authority (OJK), 2020.

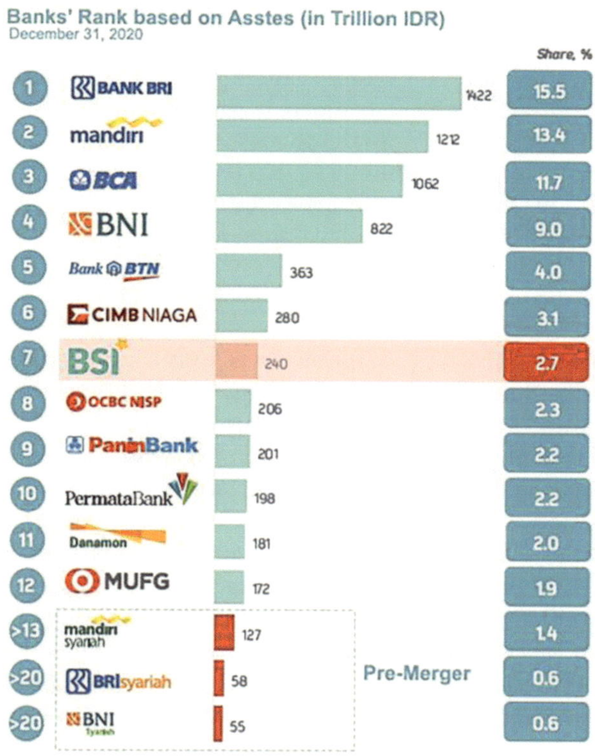

Figure 4.
Bank's rank based on assets in Indonesian, 2020. Sources: Financial service authority (OJK), 2020.

Company of Indonesia finalized the merger of three state-owned Islamic banks. PT. Bank Syariah Mandiri, PT. Bank Negara Indonesia Syariah, and PT. Bank Rakyat Indonesia Syariah were merged into PT. Bank Syariah Indonesia. By the end of 2021, there are 12 operating Sharia commercial banks in Indonesia from [16] the prior of the merger (**Table 1**) [12]. This merger has brought three largest Sharia commercial banks, which were previously excluded from the top 10 of the biggest operating commercial banks nationally, up the ranks to the seventh position with 2.7 percent of the

Year	Sharia commercial banks	Sharia business units	Sharia rural banks
2014	12	22	163
2015	12	22	163
2016	13	21	166
2017	13	21	167
2018	14	20	167
2019	14	20	164
2020	14	20	164
Oct-21	12	20	163

Sources: Financial service authority (OJK), 2020.

Table 1.
The number of Islamic banks in Indonesia according to classification.

national market share of the banking industry. The Islamic bank merger is an important consolidation momentum for Islamic banking to be able to present Islamic Banks that are strong in capital and able to compete in the national banking industry. In addition, the "new" bank, Bank Syariah Indonesia, has the opportunity to join BUKU 4 by increasing the scale of the economy so that it can contribute significantly to the national economy. This merger manifested as the commitment of the Indonesian government to support Islamic bank's development.

2.4 Indonesia Islamic banking way forward

The growth of Islamic banking in Indonesia is promising. During the 2020 pandemic, Islamic banks still maintained their growth and robustness through the crisis. The bank should keep innovating to capture larger market share. If Indonesian Islamic banks fail to capture the potential benefit from Muslim demography, the industry might not develop [1]. Islamic banks must maintain their identity by balancing the social function and communicating its value to the users. Reputational risks remain the vital issue in Islamic banks. Muslim community is diverse, many interpret Islamic law differently according to schools or teachings. Sharia governance may offer solutions for a systematic Sharia compliance guarantor that bridge different opinions among Sharia scholars and build public trust to the permissibility *(halal)* value in Islamic banking. At the implementation level, the government must take the Sharia audit into account as there are loopholes in the process. It must be understood that Sharia audit differs from audit for Sharia/Islamic financial institutions. This leads to the human capital issue. It is understandable that due to the small size of institutions, the labor market for Islamic banking is not as strong as the conventional counterparts.

A recent opportunity to be captured by Islamic banks is the digitalization of banking services. Young adults in their productive age dominate Indonesia populations. This generation has high literature in digital technology, especially the internet. Financial technology has emerged as the institution offers digital-based financial services. The easy, timeless, and reliable platform has captured the young generation to use financial services from start-up companies. Albeit becoming a new competitor for conventional banking, this institution may not replace the role of conventional banking later in the future due to the fundamental role and robustness of banking institutions that are supported by other supporting prudential institutions. The

Islamic banks must capture the momentum to invest in technology. First, branding is important to capture the new market by making Islamic financial transactions user-friendly and easy to access. This branding also involves the strategy to increase awareness and literacy on Islamic banking that has been lacking in the society. Second, the bank should maintain its security as the number of cyberattacks increases, ranging from identity theft, skimming, to phishing, and banks must mitigate this risk appropriately to protect the customers.

3. Islamic accounting in Indonesia

3.1 History

As previously mentioned, the development of Islamic accounting in Indonesia cannot be separated from the establishment of the first Islamic Bank in Indonesia, namely Bank Muamalat Indonesia (BMI) in 1991 and the existence of Law No. 7 of 1992 concerning banking, which is further detailed in Government Regulation 72 of 1992, Law no. 10 of 1998 and Law no. 23 of 1999. After BMI was established, there was a problem because BMI was an Islamic Bank but the financial statements made were not based on Sharia accounting. In addition, the existence of this Islamic bank also requires supervision and auditing of Islamic bank products. These factors encourage the importance of developing Islamic accounting.

In 2002, IAI through the Financial Accounting Standards Board (DSAK) ratified PSAK No. 59, Islamic Banking Accounting, which became effective in January 2003. Another thing that contributed to the development of Islamic accounting was the emergence of the IAI Sharia Accounting Committee in 2005. In 2010, IAI decided to transform the institution by establishing a Sharia Financial Accounting Standards Board (DSAS), which is authorized to formulate Islamic Financial Accounting Standards (IFAS). Islamic accounting, in Indonesia is often called as Sharia accounting, is accounting based on an Islamic (teachings) paradigm. It is an instrument or subsystem to implement Islamic teachings, especially in business. Therefore, the objectives of Islamic accounting must be consistent with the objectives of Islamic teachings (*maqaasid shari'ah*), namely to achieve happiness of human beings, both materially and spiritually.

To achieve the above objectives, Islamic accounting relies on various principles: (1) brotherhood (*ukhuwah*), which upholds the value of togetherness in obtaining benefits (sharing economy); (2) justice (*'adalah*), which does not tolerate usury, injustice, gambling and speculation (*maysir*), excessive uncertainty (*gharar*), and does not perform unacceptable (*haram*) goods or services; (3) beneficial (*maslahah*) in an effort to protect the objectives of sharia (protecting faith, reason, descent, life, and property); (4) balance (*tawazun*) of material and spiritual aspects, private and public, financial and real sectors, and utilization and conservation (for example, natural resources); and (5) universalism (*syumuliyah*), which considers various stakeholders to realize the welfare of the universe (*rahmatan lil alamin*). Thus, the benefits of Islamic accounting are not only for Muslims, but also for all mankind, even for the universe [18].

In general, the model or approach to develope Islamic accounting can look like **Figure 5**. From **Figure 5**, there are two approaches in developing Islamic accounting [19]. The first approach is often called the "ideal" approach. In this approach, the development of Islamic accounting begins with the search for sharia sources and then

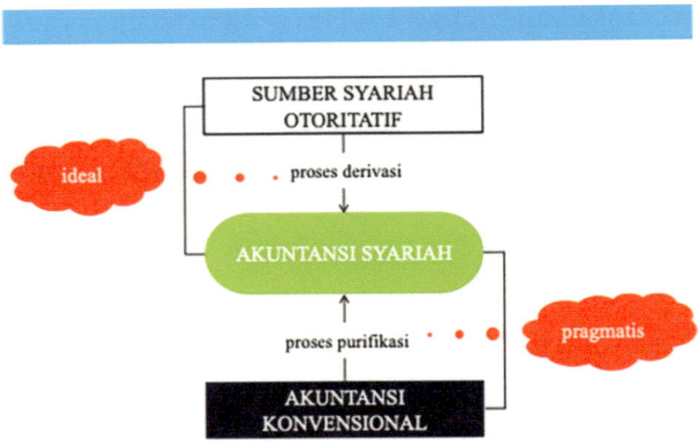

Figure 5.
Approaches in Islamic accounting development. Source: Sholihin [19].

is derived into Sharia accounting standards. The second approach is often referred to as the "pragmatic" approach. This approach starts from conventional accounting, then the purification process is carried out. Conventional accounting that is not in accordance with sharia is abandoned and which is not contrary to sharia remains. Islamic Financial Accounting Standard Board (*Dewan Standar Akuntansi Syariah*-DSAS) of the Institute of Indonesia Chartered Accountants (IAI) uses the second approach. In this case, to assess the compliance with Sharia, DSAS IAI relies on the fatwas of the National Sharia Council of the Indonesian Ulema Council (DSN MUI). Even in the DSAS membership, there are representatives/ex-officio of DSN MUI.

In developing Islamic Financial Accounting Standards (IFAS), DSAS IAI is very careful and follows a very strict due process. The due process adopted in the preparation of Islamic financial accounting standards are: (1) identifying the issues (and consulting with the Consultative Board of IAI if necessary), (2) conducting research related to the issues that have been identified, (3) discussing the material, (4) ratifying and publishing the exposure draft, (5) conducting public hearings and if necessary conducting limited hearings, (6) discussing public input, and (7) ratifying standards. In the discussion, the first thing to discuss is the aspect of transaction clarity from a sharia perspective. Even though during the discussion, there were already members of DSAS IAI from DSN MUI who became members, institutionally DSAS IAI again proposed the standards that had been ratified to DSN MUI to be checked/reviewed again for compliance with Sharia. So, Sharia accounting standards in Indonesia are developed by starting from the clarity of sharia aspects and ending with checking again the conformity of the standards with sharia. This procedure is intended to achieve the blessing of the ratified Islamic accounting standards and not to conflict with sharia.

3.2 Recent development

To date (December 2021), several Statements of Islamic Financial Accounting Standards (SIFAS) have been published by DSAS. In addition to PSAK 59 (Islamic Banking Accounting), DSAS have published SIFAS 101 (Sharia

DOI: http://dx.doi.org/10.5772/intechopen.103654

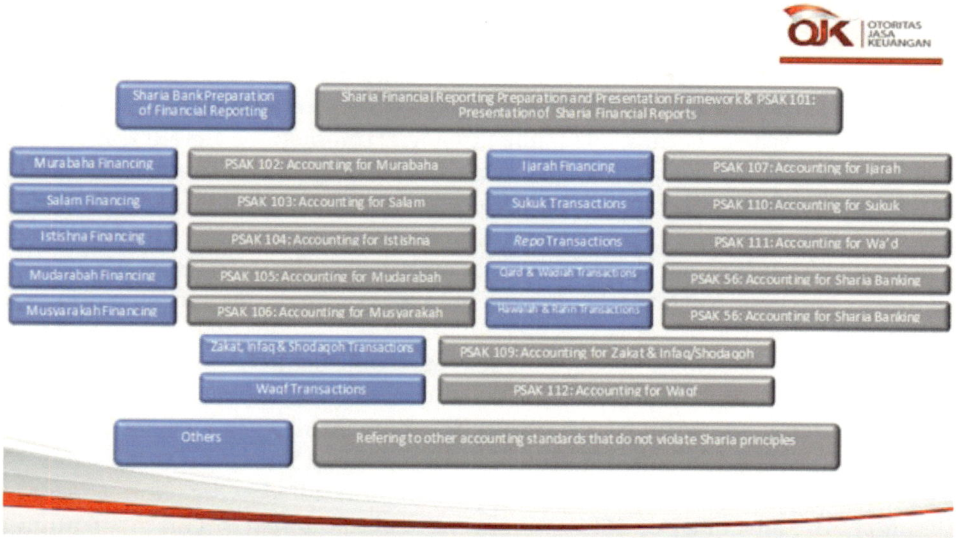

Figure 6.
Mapping between transactions in Islamic Bank (in blue) and the accounting standard (in gray). Source: Hendarsyah [20].

Financial Statement Presentation), SIFAS 102 (Accounting for *Murabaha*), SIFAS 103 (Accounting for *Salam*), SIFAS 104 (Accounting for *Istishna'*), SIFAS 105 (Accounting for *Mudharabah*), SIFAS 106 (Accounting for *Musyarakah*), SIFAS 107 (Accounting for *Ijarah*), SIFAS 108 (Accounting for Sharia Insurance Transactions), SIFAS 109 (Accounting for Zakat and Infaq/Alms), SIFAS 110 (Accounting for *Sukuk*), SIFAS 111 (Accounting for *Wa'd*), and the last is SIFAS 112 (Accounting for Waqf). In addition, DSAS has also issued Interpretation of Financial Accounting Standards (ISAK) 101 concerning Recognition of Deferred *Murabaha* Revenues Without Significant Risk Related to Inventory Ownership and ISAK 102 about Impairment of *Murabaha* Receivables has also been issued.

Until now, DSAS continues to work to develop various accounting standards to support the development of Islamic economics and finance. DSAS IAI in developing standards uses a transaction-based approach, not an accounting approach for certain institutions, even though the first Islamic accounting standard that appears is Islamic Banking Accounting (PSAK 59).

From the SIFAS above, it can be seen that the DSAS IAI does not only focus on accounting standards for commercial activities. However, DSAS IAI also pays great attention to the aspects of social finance (Social Islamic Finance), namely the issuance of SIFAS 109 and SIFAS 112. SIFAS 109 is currently being reviewed due to the development of various programs and social activities in the distribution of zakat, infaq, and alms for community empowerment.

The mapping of transactions used by Islamic banking and how the match between those transactions and the IFAS can be seen in **Figure 6** [20].

4. Conslusion

This chapter discusses the development of IBs in Indonesia and explains the development of Islamic financial accounting standards including how the standards are developed (the due processes). This chapter also describes whether Islamic financial accounting standards developed in Indonesia have sufficiently fulfilled the accounting standards needed by Islamic banks in Indonesia.

Islamic banks (IBs) have distinctive characteristics compared to the conventional ones. IBs only perform permissible (*halal*) financial transactions viewed from Islamic perspective and avoid usury (riba) and overspeculation (*gharar*). The growth of demand in permissible (*halal*) financial services started in the Middle East encouraged Indonesia to join the opportunity to pave its way in the banking sector after the formation of Islamic financial institutions at the grassroot level. PT. Bank Muamalat Indonesia (BMI) was the first Islamic bank in Indonesia established in 1990 in Jakarta, Indonesia.

Upon the establishment, the development of Islamic banks became more steady and apparent over time. Hence, in 2021, the ministry of state-owned enterprise combined three state-owned Islamic banks (PT. Bank Syariah Mandiri, PT. Bank Negara Indonesia Syariah, and PT. Bank Rakyat Indonesia Syariah) into PT. Bank Syariah Indonesia (BSI) through merger. This merger resulted in the improvement of the competitive advantage of BSI to its conventional counterparts. This momentum marked the commitment of the government and stakeholders to boost the development of Islamic banking in Indonesia.

Accountability is important to ensure the relevance and reliability of information in Islamic banks. Consequently, there is a demand to accommodate accounting standards for Islamic transactions to provide reliable information for users for making a sound decision. *Dewan Standar Akuntansi Syariah Ikatan Akuntan Indonesia* or Sharia Financial Accounting Standard Board of the Institute of Indonesia Chartered Accountants (DSAS IAI) was formed to review, to study, and to issue accounting standards for Islamic financial transactions. The standard must be embedded with Islamic values and norms; hence, the process also demands knowledge in Islamic law, accounting, and business, and it is called as Sharia Financial Accounting Standard.

Until December 2021, several Statements of Islamic Financial Accounting Standards (SIFAS) have been published by DSAS IAI. In addition to PSAK 59 (Islamic Banking Accounting), DSAS have published SIFAS 101 (Sharia Financial Statement Presentation), SIFAS 102 (Accounting for *Murabaha*), SIFAS 103 (Accounting for *Salam*), SIFAS 104 (Accounting for *Istishna'*), SIFAS 105 (Accounting for *Mudharabah*), SIFAS 106 (Accounting for *Musyarakah*), SIFAS 107 (Accounting for *Ijarah*), SIFAS 108 (Accounting for Sharia Insurance Transactions), SIFAS 109 (Accounting for Zakat and Infaq/Alms), SIFAS 110 (Accounting for *Sukuk*), SIFAS 111 (Accounting for *Wa'd*), and the last is SIFAS 112 (Accounting for Waqf). In addition, DSAS has also issued Interpretation of Financial Accounting Standards (ISAK) 101 concerning Recognition of Deferred *Murabaha* Revenues Without Significant Risk Related to Inventory Ownership and ISAK 102 about Impairment of *Murabaha* Receivables has also been issued. It is expected that Islamic accounting is able to fulfill its goal to assist Islamic Banks to be accountable to their stakeholders and God by being fair and transparent in business.

Author details

Mahfud Sholihin* and Dian Andari
Department of Accounting, Gadjah Mada University, Yogyakarta, Indonesia

*Address all correspondence to: mahfud@ugm.ac.id

References

[1] Iqbal M, Molyneux P. Thirty Years of Islamic Banking: History, Performance and Prospects. London: Palgrave Macmillan; 2005

[2] Waemustafa W. The emergence of Islamic banking: Development, trends, and challenges. IOSR Journal of Business and Management. 2013;**7**(2):67

[3] Otoritas Jasa Keuangan. Sejarah Perbankan Syariah. 2021. Available from: https://www.ojk.go.id/id/kanal/syariah/tentang-syariah/pages/sejarah-perbankan-syariah.aspx

[4] Otoritas Jasa Keuangan. Laporan Perkembangan Syariah Indonesia. 2020. Available from: https://www.ojk.go.id/id/kanal/syariah/data-dan-statistik/laporan-perkembangan-keuangan-syariah-indonesia/Pages/Laporan-Perkembangan-Keuangan-Syariah-Indonesia-2020.aspx

[5] Sulaiman M. The influence of Riba and zakat on Islamic accounting. Indonesian Management and Accounting Review. 2003;**2**(2):149-167

[6] Haniffa R, Hudaib M. Exploring the ethical identity of Islamic banks via communication in annual reports. Journal of Business Ethics. 2007;**76**:97-116

[7] Belal AR, Abdelsalam O, Nizamee SS. Ethical Reporting in Islamic Bank Bangladesh Limited (1983-2010). Journal of Business Ethics. 2015;**129**(4):769-784. DOI: 10.1007/s10551-014-2133-8

[8] Zaki A, Sholihin M, Barokah Z. The association of Islamic bank ethical identity and financial performance: Evidence from Asia. Asian Journal of Business Ethics. 2014;**3**:97-110

[9] Abduh M, Azmi OM. Islamic banking and economic growth: The Indonesian experience. International Journal of Islamic and Middle Eastern Finance and Management. 2012;**5**(1):35-47. DOI: 10.1108/17538391211216811

[10] Indonesian Law No. 21 of 2008 about Islamic Banking

[11] Salem RA. Risk Management for Islamic Banks. Edinburgh: Edinburgh University Press; 2013

[12] Ariffin NM. Liquidity risk management and financial performance in Malaysia: Empirircal evidence from Islamic banks. Aceh International Journal of Social Science. 2012;**1**(2):77-84

[13] Siddiqui A. Financial contracts, risk adn performance of Islamic Bankingd. Managerial Finance. 2008;**34**(10):680-694

[14] Ariffin NM, Archer S, Karim RAA. Risks in Islamic banks: Evidence from empirical research. Journal of Banking Regulation. 2009;**10**(2):153-163. DOI: 10.0.4.33/jbr.2008.27

[15] van Greuning H, Iqbal Z. Risk Analysis for Islamic Banks. Washington DC: The World Bank; 2007

[16] Sundararajan V. Risk measurement and Disclosure in Islamic finance and the implications of profit sharing investment accounts. In: Iqbal M, Ali S.S, Muljawan, D, editors. Advances in Islamic Economics and Finance. Vol. 1. Jeddah: Islamic Research and Training Institute; 2007. pp. 121-152

[17] Martson D, Sundararajan V. Unique risks of Islamic banks: Implications for systemic stability. In: Tariqullah K,

Muljawan D, editors. Islamic Financial Architecture: Risk Management and Financial Stability. Jeddah: Islamic Research and Training Institute; 2006

[18] Institute of Indonesia Chartered Accountants, Pernyataan Standar Akuntansi Keuangan Syariah, 2020

[19] Sholihin M. Menggapai Berkah dengan Akuntansi Syariah. In: IAI Peduli Covid-19: Percepatan Penanganan Covid-19 dari Perspektif Akuntan. Jakarta: IAI; 2021

[20] Hendarsyah DF. Arah Pengembangan Perbankan Syariah: Peluang dan Tantangan Akuntansi Syariah. Materials presented at Islamic Accounting Seminar, MAKSI, FEB UGM. 2020

Section 3

Banking Regulation and Risks

Chapter 4

Banking Regulation for ESG Principles and Climate Risk

Rosaria Cerrone

Abstract

Nowadays banking activity is greatly influenced by environmental and social conditions. For this reason, regulators have been committed to defining Environment, Social, and Governance (ESG) principles. In addition, climate change has shown the relevance of climate risks that have relevant implications in the new risk management process. The 2030 Agenda for Sustainable Development is based on the 17 SDGs that are, in the next future, the main challenge for the worldwide economy as they will be the basis for real sustainable activities. In this context, banks play a very relevant role as they have the power to lead this new challenge and are able to facilitate businesses to run toward a sustainable green economy. For this reason, banks' activity is now oriented to increase and allocate credit and investment to more sustainable sectors. As climate risk is, at the same time, cause and effect for a socially responsible activity, regulators have been considering the role of banks for the green and ecological transition, which is necessary to face this new risk. The chapter is an overview of rules, regulations, and guidelines for banks referred to ESG principles and their adoption in a global perspective; it also refers to climate risk that, due to its components, may require further capital to preserve banks' stability.

Keywords: climate risk, climate change, ESG, environmental sustainability, sustainability risk, sustainable finance

1. Introduction

The chapter describes the change of banking regulation toward governance and environmental sustainability challenges. It shows that it has not been fully understood how these new types of environmental and social risks affect differently banking activity. As risks are global and systemic, it is necessary regulatory coordination. The main international and European initiative to assess the relevance of environmental climate risks for banking regulation considers some banking policy recommendations for countries to coordinate their regulatory actions. This is due to the fact that banks play a crucial role in providing credit and financial resources that can be used to mitigate the negative effects of environmental risks enabling the economy to become more resilient.

Regulators are now aware that there are linkages between natural disasters and financial market instability. In fact, climate change could potentially threaten financial resilience in general and economic prosperity over the longer term.

In recent times, the frequency and intensity of natural disasters have increased, causing much greater damage to economies. The negative effects are not only physical and material, but they can lead to high loan losses and provisioning for banks located in those areas with hard difficulties.

The main environmental risks create potentially negative externalities for the banking sector and for this reason banks are analyzing these risks and are putting them into their risk management models and governance frameworks.

By affording these challenges, banks also play an important role in supporting the economy's adaptation to environmental changes and in creating financial resilience to environmental risks. For this reason, new loan policies are devoted to reallocating credit to more sustainable sectors of the economy; by doing so banks contribute to reducing environmental sustainability risks, mitigating their impact.

Banks are facing these risks by adopting different types of green banking practices. These practices are referred to as the option of the ESG guidelines with a particular focus on risk management in the area of project finance and the allocation of credit to renewable energy resources. Other practices are specifically positioned to mobilize capital to the green economy, including renewable and clean energy projects by making loans and investments, and structuring specialized transactions [1].

Banks are facing new challenges. For this reason the European regulatory framework for sustainable finance has greatly developed. European leadership in sustainable finance has given rise to several regulations. In particular, banks will consider the CRR Pillar 3 and EU taxonomy disclosures, also because EBA is also aligning its position to this view.

The structural shift toward the green transition and the climate crisis is exposing banks to physical and transition risks, which they need to be ready to manage. Banks will need to strengthen their risk management frameworks and reassess their business strategies. A recent ECB assessment shows that banks have made some progress in adapting their practices to manage these risks, but none are close to meeting the supervisory expectations [2]. For this reason, supervisors have already planned a number of specific measures for next years and beyond, including a thematic review of banks' environmental risk management practices and a stress test on climate-related risks. Many of the proposed regulatory changes actually stem from research conducted by the European Banking Authority and the ECB and are focused on issues identified in the use of internal models by European banks. The chapter is structured with paragraph 2 that describes the relevance of ESG principles in the banking and financial sector and the source of ESG risks, with particular relevance for climate-related risk; paragraph 3 focuses on the difficulties of regulators to define so new rules and guidelines to define new strategies to control these new risks; paragraph 4 concludes the chapter pointing out the main policy implications of this new era for banks and financial institutions.

2. ESG principle in the financial sector

During the last years banking and financial sector has been involved in a great change, which has been characterized by the introduction of the new principles of Environmental Social and Governance (ESG). These principles are forcing banks toward an innovative vision of management both internal and external. It is known that there is a wide interpretation of the meaning of the ESG principles. In general, banks are becoming more and more active in investment and asset allocation, and in new business models as well. The attention to the environment and its exploitation, to the reduction of pollution or carbon emissions, are influencing their choices and strategies. New attention to social justice and social principles are very relevant so new governmental bodies are under control. The final goal is a more sustainable framework for financial activity with a selection of assets and sectors to finance.

The first step toward sustainable finance was the Action Plan of Financing Sustainable Growth, which was published in 2018 by the European Commission. The regulatory framework began to be defined to give banks and financial institutions a new scheme that granted the real development of innovative strategies about the introduction of sustainability principles as the basis for new growth of the financial system.

Beyond EC's Action Plan there was EBA's Plan which gave other guidelines to banks and rules about the adoption of ESG principles. In particular, it became necessary for regulators to implement ESG principles in their rules for the financial sector.

The definition of a complete framework of ESG principles is very important but it is still long to be completed; anyway it is important to reach a full acceptance and a full change toward sustainable finance.

The ESG principles are tied with the 2030 United Nations Sustainable Development Goals (SDG) agenda that considers environmental challenges, including climate change, as a major concern to the stability of the global economy. The most important step toward the control of the climate risk was the Paris Agreement was adopted in 2015 to strengthen the global response to the threat of climate change. Financial policy and regulation are increasingly recognized as important for managing the transition toward a more environmentally sustainable economy. The evolution to a more sustainable economy requires the adoption of new paradigms and the green guidelines in lending activity to reach a better selection of economic activities to finance [1]. At the same time, governmental or regulatory intervention is necessary to guide the banking sector in allocating more credit and investment to sustainable activity and in protecting the economy against related financial risks. The role of financial regulation in supporting the transition to a more sustainable economic path has been deemed critical by international organizations. The definition of ESG factors is not simple or easy also because there are a number of guidelines and rules formulated by various institutions. **Table 1** presents the existing frameworks currently used by international institutions.

In **Table 1**, if one considers the frameworks addressing ESG factors, it can be noticed that the idea to have a wider vision of the factors different from the economic and financial ones, begins in 2003 with the Equator Principles that induce banks to consider and measure environmental and social risks in lending activity. The most recent Principles of UNEP FI are specifically devoted to the adoption of SDGs and the Paris Agreement in banking activity.

Guidelines, frameworks, and principles try to offer a multi-layer dimension of ESG factors. This effort is due to regulators' position to recognize the relevance of these aspects for banks and to induce their choices and managerial strategies.

As concerns the environmental factors international institutions and authorities are working in recent times. It consists of guidelines and best practices proposed as suggestions to banks and financial institutions. These guidelines are important because they are the first step to having a uniform discipline about sustainable finance and green financial assets. On the basis of these initial definitions, banks and financial institutions must face new risks deriving from these factors that should be considered in financial management and the financial markets.

Framework	Year	Content
Frameworks addressing ESG factors		
Equator Principles	2003	Guidelines used to identify, assess and manage environmental and social risks when financing projects
Principles for Responsible Investment (PRI)	2006	Referred asset owners/institutional investors, investment managers, and service providers to incorporate ESG factors into their investment and ownership decision
International Integrated Reporting Council (IIRC)	2010	Framework for integrated reporting along the lines of six capitals (financial, manufactured, intellectual, human, social and relationship and natural)
International Finance Corporation Environmental and Social Performance Standards (IFC Performance Standards)	2012	Definition of IFC clients' responsibilities for managing environmental and social risks.
United Nations Sustainable Development Goals (SDGs)	2015	Collection of 17 interlinked global goals designed to be a blueprint to achieve a better and more sustainable future intended to be achieved by 2030
Global Sustainability Standards Board Global Reporting Initiative (GRI)	2016	Principles used by organizations to better understand, manage and communicate their impacts on sustainability-related issues
OECD Due Diligence Guidance for Responsible Business Conduct	2018	Guidelines covering non-binding principles and standards for responsible business conduct in a global context consistent with applicable laws and internationally recognized standards
Committee of Sponsoring Organizations of the Treadway Commission (COSO) and the World Business Council for Sustainable Development (WBCSD) Guidance for Applying Enterprise Risk Management to ESG-related risks	2018	Guidelines to overcome ESG-related risk challenges across the ERM process and provides methods for managing both upside and downside ESG-related risks.
United Nations Environment Programme Finance Initiative (UNEP FI)	2019	Principles aiming at aligning banks' business strategies with the objectives of the SDGs and the Paris Agreement
Sustainability Accounting Standards Board (SASB) Standards	2019	Standards that help companies disclose financially-material sustainability information to investors
World Economic Forum (WEF) report on 'Measuring Stakeholder Capitalism'	2020	Common metrics and disclosures on non-financial factors can be used by companies to align their mainstream reporting on performance against ESG indicators and track their contributions to the SDGs
Frameworks specifically addressing environmental factors		
Recommendations of the Financial Stability Board Taskforce on Climate-related Financial Disclosures (TCFD)	2017	Framework to disclose climate-related risks and opportunities through their existing reporting processes.
International Capital Market Association Green Bond Principles	2017 1ST ed. updated 2021	Principles for the qualification of green bonds

Framework	Year	Content
Natural Capital Protocol + Supplement (Finance)	2018	Framework for organizations to identify, measure, and value their impacts and dependencies on natural capital.
Climate Bond Initiative Climate Bonds Standard	2018	Sector-specific eligibility criteria for assets and projects that can be labeled as green investments
Climate Disclosure Project (CDP), UN Global Compact (UNGC), World Resources Institute (WRI), and World Wildlife Fund (WWF) Science-Based Targets initiative (SBTi)	2018	Targets and guidelines referred to the Paris Agreement
Partnership for Carbon Accounting Financials Global GHG Accounting and Reporting Standard for the Financial Industry	2019	Guidelines for the specific asset class

Elaboration from EBA 2021.

Table 1.
International frameworks and standards defining ESG factors.

2.1 ESG risks: relevance and assessment

ESG factors are characterizing the definition of new strategies for banks and financial institutions. This paragraph starts from EBA's definition of ESG risks and shows some considerations about their evaluation and management.

According to EBA [3] "*ESG factors are environmental, social or governance matters that may have a positive or negative impact on the financial performance or solvency of an entity, sovereign or individual.*"

These risks may have different and typical features, due to their main causes and effects. ESG risks influence banking activity both in lending and in asset class allocation. For this reason, banks must classify ESG risks. By doing they must consider separately the three factors, Environmental, Social, and Governance. As concerns environmental risks, which are caused by a number of factors, banks must face both their physical impact and the effects of transition, as it is specifically happening in the so-called "green transition." Social risks are caused by the diffusion of social inequality, health troubles, or the exploitation of human labor. The governance risks are important as well; and for example they are caused by corruption or similar in the board of directors of the company.

This complex articulation of such risks imposes banks to become more selective in their activity. Moreover, these risks are also more difficult to be measured as they are mainly focused on subjective elements and all quantitative indicators are still to be defined. For this reason, ESG risks are considered systemic and can impact the financial system as a whole. Institutions need to build their resilience to ESG risks across different time horizons, by taking a comprehensive and forward-looking view, as well as early and proactive actions, under supervisory control.

According to EBA, it is necessary to include ESG risks into the banking regulatory and supervisory framework, giving a particular emphasis on climate and environmental risks although social and governance risks are already important and necessitate attention. The main attention to these risks is due to the fact that they seem to be the most relevant because of climate change and the governments' requirements to move toward "green economy" by converting the "brown business."

To manage these risks, their transmission channels must be considered and incorporated into disclosures, risk management, and supervision. ESG disclosure is very relevant for stakeholders interested in assessing banks' risks and their sustainable finance strategy [3]. This is why the Basel Third Pillar must be integrated and the non-financial reporting is linked to this need.

The analysis of ESG risks is very important because it is considered by supervisors as the new frontier to reach a resilient business model and risk management system to ensure banks' preparedness for ESG-related challenges. ESG risks-related considerations must be fully taken into account in the definition of strategies and objectives, as the same must be done integrating ESG risks in governance structures, and managing these risks as drivers of financial risks. The actual regulatory framework is based on these actions expected by banks and the new supervisory and evaluation process (SREP) will be performed including these risks [2].

The materialization of ESG factors has consequences on banks' performance because it is linked to all financial risks, such as credit, market, operational, liquidity, and funding risks. In general, we can maintain that ESG risks can be defined as the negative materialization of ESG factors through their counterparties or invested assets [3]. For example, if a bank grants a loan to a company that is suffering under the transition risk and costs of a green economy, its difficulties will influence the bank's credit position and credit risk. This happens because this company will have problems in loan repayment and reimbursement due to the high expenses caused by the transition itself.

It is evident that ESG risks must be considered under a double perspective, proposed by EBA as an outside-in and inside-out perspective. According to the first dimension, banks can be impacted by ESG risks through their counterparties and invested assets, but at the same time, they may be impacted by or have an impact on (inside-out perspective) ESG factors. Even if both perspectives are important, the inside-out becomes much more relevant. The relationship between the inside-out and outside-in perspective is explained by the double materiality, which is divided into financial materiality and environmental and social materiality.

The double materiality implies that banks must measure and evaluate both the internal choices and the influence of the external behavior of companies and clients referring to ESG factors. The financial materiality can be explained by considering the effects on the company's economic and financial activities. The environmental and social materiality refers to the influence of the above-mentioned company's economic and financial activities on ESG factors themselves. With a circular process, this influence may cause, at the same time, financial materiality.

The assessment of ESG risks is done using three different methods—portfolio alignment method, risk framework method, and exposure method.

At the core of the portfolio alignment method, there is the meaning of alignment. According to this method banks, investors and supervisors will consider how far portfolios are aligned with globally agreed targets. This method could mainly be used for strategic purposes rather than risk management purposes because it does not explain the link between the global targets and the risk indicators of the bank.

The risk framework method includes the climate-stress test. This method is particularly relevant for climate risk, which is a forward-looking risk and stress testing over a future time horizon is, therefore, a useful tool for modeling climate risk impacts. On the contrary, the other ESG risks are in general more backward-looking.

The risk framework method focuses on the sensitivity of portfolios and the impact that climate change has on the real risk of the exposures. The actions to face the risk are derived from the level of measured sensitivity or direct risk of losses considering the current level of environmental factors (or climate factors, more specifically) and the possible developments under the selected scenario. The application of this method brings to a risk-based adjusted portfolio in the medium-long term and makes it possible to consider also internal components of banking and trading book.

An exposure method is a tool that banks can apply directly to the assessment of individual counterparties and individual exposures, even in isolation. This method is based on a direct evaluation of the performance of exposure in terms of its ESG attributes. This method can be used to complement the standard assessment of financial risk categories. Thanks to this approach, there is a calibration at the specific company level. It is possible to put in evidence the specific sensitivities to ESG factors of different segments and sub-segments of economic activity. This method suits well to all three aspects of ESG.

This method is considered the most suitable if compared with the others. Even if it is not based on complex scenario analysis, it considers backward-looking metrics and makes banks able to classify their ESG risks' exposures. This method gives banks the possibility to take adequate decisions to face ESG risks. The exposure method has developed some methodologies that can bring to ESG risks measurement. Regulators classify them in the following four methodologies—a. ESG ratings provided by specialized rating agencies; b. ESG evaluations provided by credit rating agencies; c. ESG evaluation models developed by banks in-house for their own assessment; and d. ESG scoring models developed by asset managers and data providers.

With the first methodology ESG ratings are provided by specialized rating agencies. They are stand-alone ratings on ESG factors, and consider the risk exposure to ESG factors. Rating agencies consider also the ability of the management to afford risks and to catch opportunities. These methodologies are generally built on a quantitative analysis of key issues identified for each company, but they also consider qualitative information collected by analysts from public information and engagement with companies.

In the case of ESG evaluations provided by credit rating agencies (e.g., S&P ESG), these evaluations integrate ESG factors into the standard credit analysis. They measure how ESG factors affect both certain scorecard components such as cash flows and leverage, and elements outside of the scorecard. They contribute to giving additional input to the existing financial risk assessment. Anyway, some difficulties in comparing ESG ratings by different providers are present as they include the different weights applied to the individual elements of ESG factors.

The internal methodologies have been developed by larger banks that were organizing their information systems on the basis of internal data deriving from wide data sets concerning their customers. These are internal and need the validation of regulatory authorities to be compliant with the existing rules. Finally, the ESG scoring models developed by asset managers and data providers, are publicly available.

Even if there are a number of methodologies, they are still improving both by banks and by regulators and they can be still considered at the early stages of development. These methods are very different both for the factors that are considered and for the results. They also differ for time horizons and for these reasons banks are experimenting with them all on different basis and portfolios. Anyway, the exposure origination is very important because it shows the future composition of a bank's portfolio and signals to counterparties, investors, and wider market participants that investments are no longer sustainable and supported by the financial sector. This is true and relevant because the EBA Guidelines on Loan Origination and Monitoring are oriented to consider ESG factors as taken into account in banks' credit risk appetite, policies and procedures.

The analysis of ESG risks requires a real ESG disclosure; this means that banks must map all business units and divisions on the basis of ESG risks' framework and above all on the basis of the inside-out and outside-in perspective.

This mapping is finalized to manage the risk of conflicting or inconsistent information being disclosed; to ensure consistency and/or alignment of the disclosure; and to identify the overlaps in the reporting pillars where common reporting metrics can be considered. This kind of risk disclosure is important as it is the expression of internal analysis and mapping of ESG risks, which must be constantly monitored in the next future. This mapping can be considered as an absolute improvement of Basel Third Pillar.

2.2 Climate-related risks

The environmental aspect is really important as it is considered as the core for climate risk. Climate risk has a double dimension; in fact, banks and financial institutions are both impacted by and contribute to climate risks. For this reason, regulators are prioritizing appropriate climate risk disclosures as part of ensuring the broader transition of the financial industry to more sustainable, and positively impactful business models. According to the Financial Stability Board [4], climate risk must be considered by banks as physical risk and transition risk.

Physical risk is *the possibility that the economic costs of the increasing severity and frequency of climate-change-related extreme weather events, as well as more gradual changes in climate, might erode the value of financial assets, and/or increase liabilities* [4]. It is evident from the definition that physical risk is based on the effects of extreme weather events that have physical consequences leading to damage to the value of financial assets or collateral held by banks. This may also imply an increase in credit risk because companies have their assets and properties destroyed becoming unable to pay or banks have investments in financial assets of the same companies.

Transition risk *relates to the process of adjustment toward a low-carbon economy. Whilst such an adjustment may be a necessary part of the global economy's response to climate change, shifts in policies designed to mitigate and adapt to climate change could affect the value of financial assets and liabilities* [4]. This risk puts in evidence the broader economic adjustment toward a low-carbon economy with the presence of a range of other factors, such as the emergence of disruptive technology.

Many stakeholders are interested in these two dimensions of climate risk and want to understand banks' strategies in financing the transition to a zero-carbon economy. Under EBA's requirement banks are required to disclose information on climate risks, mitigation action, and green asset ratio [5].

The disclosure about climate risks is due to the fact that according to EBA it is important to put in evidence how climate change may reinforce and worsen other risks in banks' balance sheets. Concerning mitigating actions banks must inform about what they have in place to address those risks including financing activities that reduce carbon emissions.

With the Green Asset Ratio, it is possible to understand how institutions are financing activities that will meet the publicly agreed Paris agreement objectives of climate change mitigation and adaptation based on the EU taxonomy of green activities. The Green Asset Ratio is based on the EU taxonomy. It is a measure of the financial support that banks are willing to give to sustainable activities. Through this ratio, it is possible to put in evidence the assets that can be considered environmentally sustainable as they are referred to grant finance to activities of climate change mitigation on climate change adaptation. It is important in setting strategies, and even a bank with a low Green Asset Ratio can identify how it wants to change its financing activities over time to meet the Paris agreement objectives and measures. It gives information about a strategy that must be monitored. It is expected by EBA to receive from counterparties subject to NFRD disclosure obligations reliable data for the Green Asset Ratio from December 2022, developing a framework that identifies the required disclosure standards and their materiality triggers. The most commonly referenced framework in the case of climate disclosures is the TCFD framework, which is recognized by regulators in the EU and is considered as guidance on climate-related disclosures.

Banks and financial institutions are exposed to climate-related risks through both their own operational impacts and the activities of their borrowers, customers, or counterparties. According to the outside-in and inside-out approaches, banks that provide loans or trade the securities of companies with direct exposure to climate-related risks suffer and accumulate climate-related risks via their credit and equity operations. In addition, as the markets for lower-carbon and energy-efficient alternatives grow, firms may assume material exposures in their lending and investment businesses.

The ECB Guide [5] represents a shared document that shows how relevant are a disclosed analysis of such risks to grant that banks are managed in a sound and safe way. The relevance of climate-related risks is really great and the ECB has declared that banks conducted a self-assessment in light of the supervisory expectations outlined in the guide and to draw up action plans on that basis. The self-assessment plans will be considered by ECB as the first step toward more accurate monitoring of climate risk among all typical financial risks. This importance is also evident in the declaration of the climate-related risks stress test that will be run by ECB during this year.

2.2.1 Physical risks

As it has been described above, physical risks are specifically referred to as natural catastrophes and the economic losses caused by them; and this situation has increased in the last decades. The number of some types of extreme weather events has globally increased. Such events have become more likely or more severe due to the effects of climate change, and it is known that further warming will intensify them and consequently the negative effects at the basis of the increase of climate risk.

Physical risks include losses stemming from changes in physical capital because natural disasters destroy infrastructure and divert resources toward reconstruction and replacement. These risks affect also human capital, through deterioration in health and living conditions. The hard conditions due to the physical risks may have consequences on future expectations with a reduction of investment, given the prevailing uncertainty about future demand and growth prospects.

If there is no action to reduce the effects of climate change, physical risks will continue to increase in the future. The frequency and severity of extreme weather events might increase non-linearly and become increasingly correlated with each other over time. The consequences of physical risks can affect mainly market and credit risks.

The climate risk consequences may influence the value of financial assets causing losses for banks, investors, and financial institutions. The losses are the expression of market risk, but they are not directly caused by negative movement of financial variables (i.e., interest rates or assets prices), instead, their origin is connected with the losses due to the material destruction due to physical risk. As concerns credit risk it is almost easier to be understood as it is the consequence of the impossibility to repay and/or to reimburse loans, because of the physical destruction of assets, things, or the death of human beings. It is evident that banks are in presence of a large and composite number of risks and aspects of the same risk [4].

The impact of physical risk is not easy to be estimated with the effect on a bank's assets. Estimates are based on a number of assumptions and subject to numerous sources of uncertainty concerning the global emissions with the potential increases in global temperatures and the severity of extreme weather events. So, the macroeconomic scenario and the variation in financial assets value are highly uncertain. Finally, there are the uncertainties associated with the future path of climate change and its impact on asset prices. Heating temperatures are increasing climate risk and physical risk in particular. They seem to be unavoidable, and this will cause an increase of negative effects on the financial system and assets prices [6, 7]. As physical risks are different in the sector and geographical areas, market and credit risks may be affected by these differences. This condition reinforces the situation in which other differences and in particular significant losses derive also from the disruption at the national level, and concentrated in certain countries with and exposure to operational risks that could disrupt firms' operations, and affect other firms (financial and non-financial) provided by banks' financial services amplifying risks for financial stability.

2.2.2 Transition risks

It is known the necessity of bringing the temperature to be below 2° C above pre-industrial level. Transition risks stem from the possible process of adjustment to a low carbon economy, and its possible effects are expected on the value of financial assets and liabilities. Such a transition to a low carbon economy would imply significant structural changes to the economy, including a major reallocation of investment. This could have a significant impact on firms involved in the production of fossil fuels, as well as other sectors whose business models rely on using such fossil fuels or that are energy intensive. The effect changes in asset prices with consequences on banks' portfolios. These prospective effects might have also the consequence of reallocating financial resources from highly risky sectors or businesses tied, for example, in fossil fuels to new and less pollutant activities, by doing so supporting a real transition to a green economy. We can affirm that there will be a transformation of banks' strategies and the support of market segments devoted to new and more sustainable sectors. We can say that the transition risks represent the lever to accelerate banks' contribution to a renewal of economy and financial flows besides the real beginning of sustainable finance. On the contrary, a disorderly transition to a low-carbon economy, unanticipated by market participants, could have a destabilizing effect on the financial system. The most relevant effect will be an increase in credit risk due to the instability of such companies operating in brown sectors and receiving loans from banks. A transition to a low-carbon economy might reduce some borrowers' capacity to generate sufficient income to service and repay their debts [8]. From this situation, banks are forced to face a higher credit risk, which is the result of a double scenario. The former is connected to the well-known difficulties in payments, and the latter is the increasing risks connected with the reduction of collateral value [7]. Transition scenarios are not able to catch all policy, technology and/or consumer preferences they change very rapidly. Moreover firms' vulnerability to transition risks isn't easy to be evaluated; in fact it is not only due to the firms' operations, but also to their suppliers and customers.

3. Banking regulation

Since time regulators are exploring this kind of risk and its widespread and are also analyzing possible ways to reduce them. However, the control of climate and ESG risks is at an early stage [9–11]. In the Appendices at the end of the chapter, there are the main initiatives that show the timeline and the complexity of the regulators' activity with regard to ESG disclosure, climate risk analysis, and reporting for banks.

In this context, financial regulators are defining the principles about which climate risks are managed by banks. This interest derives from the necessity to reduce their impact both for banks themselves and for the financial system as a whole. Supervisory expectations aim at covering some institutional risk management elements (i.e., governance, strategy, scenario analysis, and/or risk management) and some financial standard-setting bodies are also starting to work on supervisory guidance related to climate risk. In fact, till now climate risks are considered as the worst for financial stability.

For example, scenario analysis can be used to quantify the totality of exposures of banks to climate-related risks within their framework and this is also called "climate stress test" [5]. There is also a significant approach to consider macro-prudential policies to mitigate climate risks to save the stability of the financial system, by giving banks a major resilience.

A large number of guidelines, best practices, and notices are the evidence that banking regulation shows a kind of difficulties to make a unitary proposal. As it has been said climate risk has a "liquid" structure that makes it really complex for banks to define their ambits and strategies.

3.1 Banking supervision and ESG factors

The further evolution is the complete introduction of the ESG factors and ESG risks in the supervisory process and all control systems. These risks are not yet explicitly included in the CRD, the IFD, or in the SREP guidelines; at the same time, the consideration of these factors by supervisory authorities should be made with respect to the principle of proportionality, that links the conditions of each bank and its exposure to risks specifically referred to their dimension, context, and background [3].

Any way the integration of ESG risks into the supervisory review will be implemented gradually, considering the development of the related methodologies for the qualitative and quantitative assessment of ESG risks. The first step is the integration of these factors in the strategies and policies adopted by banks, with an improvement of the corporate and risk culture, and of the risk management frameworks. Only after the initial period when ESG risks will be completely introduced in banking management and there will be structured data, the supervisory assessment might cover all risks with the analysis of capital and liquidity.

The mechanism of the supervisory review is based on the consideration of the risk profile, but also the business model and the strategies adopted by the bank. Moreover, another check should be compliant with the IFD and IFR and with the financial risks afforded by the bank. The supervisory review is defined on the basis of the SREP elements; and so there is the business model analysis, the evaluation of the internal governance, of the internal controls, the analysis of the risks to capital and to liquidity and funding.

ESG factors are ESG matters that may have different impacts on banks' financial performance because they can turn into ESG risks as financial risks as they are in the analysis of the supervisory process and in particular of the assessment of the viability and sustainability of banks' business model. For this reason, supervisors are interested in the forward-looking analyses implemented by the banks themselves, in non-financial reporting that contains a number of information useful to discover the level of attention to a sustainable economy and in the bank's ESG ratings. The supervisory process is changing in line with these new risks; banks are compelled to show their capacity and ability to afford and manage adequately their impact. New business models and a new and more effective supervisory function should be a forward-looking assessment of the future business environment.

3.2 Analysis of the business model and the ESG risk perspective

In the previous paragraphs, the relevance of ESG factors and their possible characteristic of being a source of risks have been described. In addition, climate risk is considered one of the most important and actual risks in banks' regulation. These two assumptions are influencing also banks' business models.

Banks are organizing their activities to control their CO_2 impact. At the same time, it is entering new selective methods in granting funds to green projects, avoiding the greenwashing trap that could increase ESG risks.

The business model is analyzed both under a quantitative dimension and from a qualitative point of view. The new business model being influenced by new risks requires also different capital adequacy. This adequacy is measured with respect to the capacity of absorbing ESG risks, while the qualitative analysis aims at the evaluation of the bank's performance considering its risk appetite, but also the presence of other drivers.

According to EBA and Basel Committee [3, 6], to understand the impact of ESG factors on the current business model, the quantitative analysis should be based on the consideration of the portion of the bank's profitability that derives from assets that are more exposed to ESG risks. The differences in the profitability of conventional loans and loans that include ESG risk-related objectives must be compared as the concentration of assets, highly exposed to ESG risks. The geographical concentration of lending or deposit-taking from households in a region where the economy heavily depends on carbon-intensive industries or that is prone to disasters is an example of the possible effects of ESG risks. The consequence is the search of assets and liabilities with more complex variables. For this reason, regulators are presenting new guidelines and banks are looking for new schemes for the development of more effective strategies.

3.3 ESG risks and capital adequacy

From the previous discussion, it is evident that ESG risks impact the existing financial risks (e.g., credit risk, market risk, and operational risk). If it is so, it is evident that regulators and supervisors need to consider the impact on capital requirement [11]. According to the function of capital requirement, its entity is tied to the classification of risks to be faced. The risk-weighted assets are expressed on the basis of quantitative inputs classified by each bank starting from authorities' rules and regulations. The definition of capital requirement for ESG risks is influenced by their measurement and it is not yet well complied. In fact, as concerns climate-related risks and environmental risks a number of quantitative indicators are developing; on the contrary social and governance risks are mainly managed through qualitative methods. The supervisory position is focused on the way used to manage these risks, or better to analyze how banks are becoming aware of these risks. Right now the relationship under monitoring is the effects on credit risk profile.

As concerns ESG climate risk and environmental risks in determining capital adequacy is relevant the consideration that they are long term risk; in fact, the physical impact of environmental change and/or because previously insufficient political action forces a sudden and comprehensive transition.

Consequently, the supervisory process will be adapted to review whether and how the banks ensure that their banking book is sustainable in the medium to long term. To simulate the condition of risk, banks can adopt scenario analysis that gives a measure of the bank's resilience.

Supervisory activity tests capital adequacy by considering both qualitative and quantitative information. Anyway, the most important aspect is referred to the quantitative methodologies in which supervisory authorities assess bank's risk measurement tools. Starting from this approach to measure the relationship between credit risk and ESG risk, the standard credit risk assessment is used to take into account the impact of ESG risks. As credit risk is assessed in the short to medium term, the use of forward-looking metrics is relevant to measure the impact of ESG factor on bank's own exposure to credit risk. This evaluation is important to measure the sustainability of long-term loans in the bank's banking book. In determining the capital requirement, the maturity of the loan portfolio is more and more important to absorb the impact of ESG risks. The starting point is connected to the evaluation of the awareness of how ESG risks drive credit risk for each portfolio and the connection with the risk appetite framework of the bank. For this reason, supervisors might check that institutions have properly embedded the material ESG factors into their rating assignment and review process.

The above-mentioned geographical variable is relevant also for determining capital adequacy; in fact, as said, the location has an influence on physical risk, so the higher is the risk of natural disaster, the higher should be the capital requirement to cover unexpected risks.

Even if there is the incorporation of ESG risks into the review of the credit quality of the portfolio, this causes a number of questions, one of which is the availability of reliable data and information. Supervisors will consequently check that the credit strategy is fully aligned and properly reflects the underlying ESG risk appetite. Performing these assessments also implies controlling how the responsibilities for implementing and monitoring the ESG-related targets are set.

The control of credit and loans implies the analysis of loans originating. At the end of this step, it means that it is necessary to identify projects, activities, and criteria used to select environmentally sustainable lending. This analysis is a guide to avoid greenwashing activities that might require a higher capital level, with a higher risk level [10]. This check on loan activity to quantify the capital requirement is necessary to cover the bank from the reputational risk, it might incur in.

While the link between ESG risks and liquidity and funding is seen by institutions as more indirect, it is deemed important to not overlook these links when evaluating the risks to liquidity and funding; ESG factors could also result in funding issues for institutions or make some assets less liquid. The evaluation of liquidity needs in the short and medium term, in particular, whether ESG risks could cause net cash outflows that negatively impact the institution's liquidity position.

The analysis of ESG risks is still at an early stage, also because it is not yet simple in banking activity but it is relevant also for supervisory authority to assess the adequacy of internal capital to face these risks.

4. Conclusion

Environmental conditions and climate changes are influencing banking activity and regulators' duties. For a few years, ESG factors are impacting financial context and are inducing managers to adopt new approaches in running their business. Banks are changing their methods to consider the principles of sustainable finance both as concerns the banking book and consequently the loans activity, but also the new green investments. On the other side, climate changes and climate-related risks have demonstrated that the brown economy must leave the place to a green economy.

This new approach has induced banks to consider new risks deriving from the ESG factor and from climate change itself. Banking managers are reshaping their risk management scheme introducing also ESG and climate-related risks.

The framework is aggravated by the fast evolution of the social and governance models that must be structured in a new way.

Regulators and supervisors are running in giving guidelines and new frameworks to induce banks to pay more and more attention to these risks.

The whole supervisory process is reshaping by introducing the measurement of ESG risks and climate-related risks but the greatest problem is due to the huge relevance of these risks and the overlapping of rules, regulations, and guidelines that are still at an early stage but are renewing the banking activity whose main role to bring the economy to put in practice a real new green deal.

Appendices and nomenclature

CRD	Directive 2013/36/EU – Capital Requirement Directive
CRR	Regulation (EU) 2019/876 – Capital Requirement Regulation
FMP	Financial market participant
IFD	Directive (EU) 2019/2034 – The Investment Firms Directive
IFR	Regulation (EU) 2019/2033
LCBMR	Regulation (EU) 2019/2089 – The Low Carbon Benchmark Regulation
NFDR	Directive 2014/95/EU – The Non-Financial Reporting Directive
RTS	Regulatory Technical Standards
SFDR	Regulation (EU) 2019/2088 – The Sustainable Finance Disclosure Directive
SREP	Supervisory Review and Evaluation Process
Taxonomy	Regulation (EU) 2020/852
TCFD	Task Force on Climate-related Financial Disclosures

A. Appendix 1 – ESG risks timeline implementation

Year/Date	
2018	
	Banks must consider NFDR
2020	
February	EBA launches consultation about the revision of NFDR
April	LCBMR in force
September	EBA opens a survey on Pillar 3 disclosure on ESG risks
November	Opening of EBA's consultation on management and supervision of ESG risks for credit institutions and investment firms
December	LCMBR level II in force
	Closing of IFRS consultation on Sustainable Reporting
2021	
February	Closing of EBA's consultation on management and supervision of ESG risks for credit institutions and investment firms
	SFDR final draft RTS on indicators for the adverse impact of environment delivered to EC
March	Opening of EBA consultation on draft ITS on Pillar 3 disclosure
	SFDR principal website disclosure obligations apply to sustainability risk management; PAis; and remuneration policy
June	Proposal regarding the review of NFRD
	Closing of EBA consultation on draft ITS on Pillar 3 disclosure
	EBA report on management and supervision of ESG risks
November	EBA on sustainable securitization
December	SFDR final draft RTS on indicators for social and human matters
	EBA's submission of the final draft of ITS on Pillar 3 disclosure
2021–2022	
	EBA guidelines and Standards on ESG integration in risk management and supervision
2022–2024	
	Publication of EBA discussion paper with a consultation on the classification and prudential treatment of assets from a sustainability perspective
2025	
	EBA final report on the classification and prudential treatment of assets from a sustainability perspective

B. Appendix 2 – Climate regulation timeline implementation

Year/Date	
2017	
	TCFD Guidelines available
2020	

Year/Date	
June	EU publishes guidelines on reporting of climate-related information
July	EU Taxonomy Regulation enters in force
2021	
	EBA delivers advice to EC on KPIs and methodology for disclosure under NFRD
June	EC adoption of a delegated act on the additional transparency requirement for financial and non-financial undertakings under the EU Taxonomy Regulation
2022	
January	EU Taxonomy Regulation delegated acts on climate change mitigation and adaptation to apply
2023	
	Application of all EU Taxonomy Regulation delegated acts other than on climate change mitigation and adaptation

Author details

Rosaria Cerrone
Department of Management and Innovation Systems (DISA - MIS), University of Salerno, Fisciano, SA, Italy

*Address all correspondence to: rocerro@unisa.it

References

[1] Kern A. Environmental Sustainability. In: Kern a. Principles of Banking Regulation. 1st ed. Cambridge: Cambridge University Press; 2019. pp. 347-371. DOI: 10.1017/9781108551557

[2] ECB. The State of Climate and Environmental Risk Management in the Banking Sector. 2021. Available from: https://www.bankingsupervision.europa.eu/ecb/pub/pdf [Accessed: 2021-12-10]

[3] EBA. On Management and Supervision of ESG Risks for Credit Institutions and Investment Firms. EBA/REP/2021/18. 2021. Available from: https://www.ngfs.net/en/overview-environmental-risk-analysis-financial-institutions [Accessed: 2021-10-01]

[4] Financial Stability Board. The Implications of Climate Change for Financial Stability. 2020

[5] ECB. Guide on climate-related and environmental risks Supervisory expectations relating to risk management and disclosure. 2020. Available from: https://www.bankingsupervision.europa.eu/ecb/pub/pdf/ssm.202011finalguideonclimate-relatedandenvironmentalrisks~58213f6564.en.pdf [Accessed: 2021-03-10]

[6] Basel Committee on Banking Supervision. Climate-Related Financial Risks: A Survey on Current Initiatives April 2020. Available from: https://www.bis.org/bcbs/publ/d502.pdf [Accessed: 2021-10-10]. ISBN: 978-92-9259-375-9 (online)

[7] Battiston S, Dafermos Y, Monasterolo I. Climate risks and financial stability. Journal of Financial Stability. 2021;**54**:1-6. DOI: 10.1016/j.jfs.2021.100867

[8] Park H, Kim JD. Transition towards green banking: Role of financial regulators and financial institutions. Asian Journal of Sustainability and Social Responsibility. 2020;**5**(5):2-25. DOI: 10.1186/s411180-020-00034-3

[9] Bruno M, Lagasio V. An overview of the European policies on ESG in the banking sector. Sustainability. 2021;**13**(1264):1-10. DOI: 10.3390/su132212641

[10] NGFS. Overview of Environmental Risk Analysis by Financial Institutions 2020. Available from: https://www.ngfs.net/en/overview-environmental-risk-analysis-financial-institutions [Accessed: 2021-12-01]

[11] Feridun M, Güngör H. Climate-related Prudential risks in the banking sector: A review of the emerging regulatory and supervisory practices. Sustainability. 2020;**12**(13), 5325:1-20. DOI: 10.3390/su12135325

Section 4

Bank Profitability

Chapter 5

Determinants of Banking Profitability in Portugal and Spain: Evidence with Panel Data

Maria Elisabete Duarte Neves, Joana Monteiro and Carmem Leal

Abstract

This article aims to study the determinants of banking performance in the countries of the Iberian Peninsula, Portugal and Spain. To achieve the proposed objective, the methodology of panel data was used, specifically the estimation method Generalized Method of Moments (GMM-system). An unbalanced panel of 267 banks was used, of which 122 belong to the Portuguese banking sector and 145 to the Spanish banking sector. Two variables were used as performance measures, the average return on total assets (ROAA) and the average return on equity (ROAE). The results show that bank profitability is generally influenced by internal variables, and not so much by sector-specific or macroeconomic variables. Therefore, the results suggest that management decisions are the ones that most influence performance. We conclude that bordering countries, despite having different economies, have very similar influences on bank profitability.

Keywords: determinants of Bank profitability, Portugal, Spain, Iberian Peninsula, GMM system

1. Introduction

Financial institutions and in particular banks capture savings from economic agents that have higher levels of liquidity to lend to those that lack liquidity [1]. When these transactions are efficient, the economy and the financial sector of the countries tend to become more solid and stable [2].

According to the financial literature ([2, 3] among others), banking performance is affected both by internal determinants and by factors external to the bank. Thus, it is consensual that the internal factors result from policies applied by their managers. Meanwhile, the external determinants that, as they are exogenous to the institution, are not within the reach of the bank's direction and management. However, they can be predicted. And if the external factors are anticipated by the banks, they will be able, on time, to face the less favorable situations.

External factors can also, according to the literature ([2, 3], among others), be divided into two categories, industry-specific factors, and macroeconomic factors.

These variables are determined by characteristics inherent to the types of institutions, as well as the economic and legal environment of the country in question [4].

Thus, through the estimation technique used by Arellano and Bond [5], Arellano and Bover [6], and Blundell and Bond [7], the Generalized Method of Moments (GMM), models that will allow obtaining more efficient results will be estimated. to possible endogeneity problems.

Thus, this study aims to determine the profitability of banks operating in Portugal and Spain in the period between 2011 and 2016. The sample consists of 267 banks in the Iberian Peninsula, of which 122 are Portuguese and 145 are Spanish. Overall, the results show that internal factors are the ones that most affect bank profitability in the three samples. The variables capital, operational efficiency, and the annual growth of deposits are the factors that best explain the profitability of the banking sector, both when considering individual countries and in the joint sample. The rest of the work is organized as follows: The second section presents the most relevant studies on the subject and hypotheses accordingly. Next, the research design is presented, which includes the sample data, the variables, and the estimation method. In Section 4 the main results are discussed and finally, in Section 5 the conclusions, limitations, and lines of future research are presented.

2. Literature review

Several authors [4, 8–13] showed that the determinants of bank profitability can be internal and external, and it is also possible that external factors can be subdivided into specific industry factors and macroeconomic factors.

Internal factors are specific to banks and are normally controlled by management [8, 14]. While exogenous factors derive from the country's economic and legal environment, they do not depend on the manager [3, 4, 14]. According to these authors, internal determinants can include asset structure, asset quality, capital, operational efficiency, revenue diversification, annual deposit growth, and size.

Likewise, among the external factors we can highlight ownership, whether the banks are listed or not, the inflation, and economic growth. All these variables were used in the aforementioned studies.

2.1 Bank specific determinants

2.1.1 Asset structure

Banks tend to diversify their loan portfolio and increase liquidity to reduce risks, particularly in times of crisis [14]. Much of the literature [9, 10] agrees that this action, to other safer assets, should cause profitability to increase more quickly. These operations tend to increase operational maintenance costs, however, García-Herrero et al. [15] argue that profit should also increase.

It should be noted that the increase in the level of credit can cause a high liquidity risk, if the manager does not effectively reduce its liabilities or if it does not know how to properly finance the increase in assets [10, 11]. If these operations are carried out well, the increase in loans will increase the bank's revenues, therefore it will also increase profitability [16]. Therefore, Saona [12] and Trujillo-Ponce [10] found a positive relationship between the relative percentage of loans in a bank's assets and its profitability. Also, Tan et al. [16] confirmed that liquidity risk exerts a positive influence when considering

ROAA as a measure of bank profitability in Chinese banks, however, there is a negative relationship when considering ROAE. On the other hand, Trabelsi and Trad [17] empirically showed that asset structure negatively influences ROAA and positively influences ROAE. Guru et al. [8] and Rumler and Waschiczek [9] emphasize that the asset structure negatively influences bank profitability.

Thus, it can be seen that there is no consensus regarding the sign and significance of this variable with profitability. On the one hand, more loan amounts mean higher turnover and, in principle, more results. However, more loans also translate into more processing costs, higher chances of credit losses, and the cost of maintaining required capital reserves.

Thus, according to the literature, we expose hypothesis one, with no pre-defined sign.

Hypothesis 1—There is a significant relationship between the composition of banks' assets and their profitability (with no defined sign).

2.1.2 Asset quality

According to Trabelsi and Trad [17], this variable indicates the economic and financial situation of banks, as it warns us of financial vulnerability, assessing their resilience to financial shocks.

In fact, in unfavorable times, there may be an increase in bad debt assets, causing banks to distribute a portion of their gross margin for provisions, to cover any loan losses [10]. These operations are associated with a credit risk that affects bank profitability [3]. Thus, with an increase in impairment losses on loans and accounts receivable, the quality of the assets of banking institutions may be negatively affected [10]. Mester [13] also showed that the increase in loan quality is associated with an increase in bank operating costs, which may have an opposite effect to that expected.

Empirical analyzes by Alshatti [18], Athanasoglou et al. [2], Trabelsi and Trad [17], and Trujillo-Ponce [10] found a negative association between the quality of bank assets and their profit. Similarly, Dietrich and Wanzenried [3] showed a negative influence of asset quality on bank profitability during the time of crisis (2007–2009). Garcia and Guerreiro [19], on the other hand, were faced with a negative relationship when this variable was associated with ROAA, but when they use ROAE, this relationship is positive.

In contrast, Saona [12] showed a positive relationship between asset quality and profitability of Latin American banks. The author argues that this sign is observed because Latin American banks charge their customers with paying higher prices for services provided to combat the costs associated with credit risk. He also claims that these transactions are possible because the interest of investors is not protected in those countries. Following this literature, we propose the following hypothesis:

Hypothesis2—There is a significant relationship between the quality of assets and their profitability (with no defined sign).

2.1.3 Capital

Capital refers to the amount of own funds available to support banking activity, exerting a safety net in case of hostile developments [14]. Banks with a high net worth on assets are seen as safer and less risky banks compared to institutions with lower capital, that is, well-capitalized banks are able to cope with times of crisis [3, 8]. In fact, according to Iannotta, Nocera, and Sironi [20], a better capitalization of banks may reflect a higher quality of management. This association can help banks finance their assets with lower interest rates, as the risk of bankruptcy is reduced [3, 15], thus making increase your profitability.

However, Djalilov and Piesse [14] suggest that the increase in financing costs due to the high level of capital could negatively affect bank profitability. Thus, the authors found a positive relationship between capital and profitability in the countries that made the initial transaction, however, the countries of the former USSR did not show any relationship between capital and the profitability of their banks. Dietrich and Wanzenried [3] also showed that in the pre-crisis period, capital did not influence the profitability of the Swiss banking sector, but between 2007 and 2009 they had a significantly negative ROAA. On the other hand, Knezevic and Dobromirov [11] show that the profits of Serbian national banks are not influenced by capital, on the other hand, foreign banks are negatively influenced.

Trujillo-Ponce [10] showed that Spanish banks are positively influenced by capital when profitability is calculated using ROAA, however, when it is related to ROAE, they present a negative relationship. In contrast, the Portuguese banks analyzed by Garcia and Guerreiro [19] showed a negative association with ROAA, but insignificant with ROAE.

Other studies, such as Alshatti [18], Athanasoglou et al. [2], Rumler and Waschiczek [9], Saona [12] and Trabelsi and Trad [17] show a positive relationship between return and equity on assets. While the studies by Guru et al. [8] and Shehzad, De Haan and Scholtens [21] have a negative sign.

According to the exposed literature, the following hypothesis is proposed:

Hypothesis 3—There is a significant relationship between the capital ratio of banks and their profitability (with no defined sign).

2.1.4 Operational efficiency

Beccalli et al. [22] argue that efficiency represents the minimization of inputs (that is, consuming fewer inputs for the same level of results) or the maximization of outputs (producing more outputs for the same amount of inputs). To this, authors such as Beccalli et al. [22] and García-Herrero et al. [15], call it *X*-efficiency (best practice indicator). According to some studies [2, 4], operational efficiency is one of the indicators that most influence bank profitability. Thus, for profitability to be high, the degree of efficiency of the financial institution's management must also be high [2, 3], that is, the reduction of operating costs (administrative expenses, employees' salaries, property expenses, among others) and, simultaneously, the increase in income, lead to a high level of bank profitability [11].

Traditionally, the operational efficiency of the banking sector is calculated using the cost-to-income (CIR) ratio, that is, expenses to income, with a high value reflecting more inefficiency. Therefore, it is expected that expenses will be lower than revenues so that efficiency will positively influence banks' profitability.

Thus, some showed a negative association between bank efficiency and profit [3, 8, 10, 11, 19, 21].

For example, Ding et al. [4] concluded that the Chinese banking sector is more efficient than US banking institutions in times of crisis, however, after the crisis, the US overlaps China. Tan et al. [16] found that efficiency in Chinese banks negatively influences ROAA and positively ROAE.

According to the literature cited, the fourth hypothesis is presented:

Hypothesis 4—There is a positive relationship between operational efficiency and your bank profitability.

2.1.5 Revenue diversification

Banking activities can be divided into traditional activities and non-traditional activities, both of which are important for bank profitability. According to Trujillo-Ponce [10], non-traditional activities arise for diversification, trying, in this way, to generate new sources of income complementing traditional activities. In this sense, Stiroh and Rumble [23] follow in stating that financial institutions have to make more profitable sources that are generated by non-traditional activities so that they increase profitability levels and manage to survive the competition.

However, DeYoung and Rice [24] argue that one cannot put all the emphasis on non-traditional activities, due to the consequent increase in profitability, since, if they are not associated with traditional activities, they become an unsound strategy, thus putting, concerned the possible profit.

Even so, studies have concluded that revenue diversification has a positive impact on profitability above the spread [25]. While Saona [12] presented a negative sign for this relationship. Tan et al. [16] showed a positive relationship between non-traditional activities and ROAA, but a negative one with ROAE. However, Elsas, Hackethal and Holzhäuser [26], Stiroh and Rumble [23], and Trujillo-Ponce [10] did not find significant differences to be able to state that diversity affects profitability.

As per the provisions, it appears that there is a relationship between the diversity of revenues and the profitability of the banking sector. Accordingly, the following hypothesis arises:

Hypothesis 5—There is a significant relationship between revenue diversity and bank profitability (with no defined sign).

2.1.6 Deposit growth

In general, deposits represent stable and cheaper resources than other types of financing, and, to this extent, they contribute to increasing bank profitability [15]. But the global financial crisis led banks to adopt aggressive policies, mortgaging their margins at the expense of paying higher rates, which contributed to the decrease in profitability [10].

Dietrich and Wanzenried [3] state that an increase in deposits also implies attending to numerous factors, such as operational efficiency, as banks must be able to convert deposit liabilities into revenue-generating assets, taking into account good credit quality. However, high deposit growth rates also attract additional competitors, affecting the profitability of banking institutions.

Thus, Trujillo-Ponce [10] did not find any relationship between the growth rate of bank deposits and Spanish bank profitability. However, Garcia and Guerreiro [19] found that the growth of deposits intervenes positively in ROAA, but that it has no statistical significance in ROAE. In contrast, Dietrich and Wanzenried [3] are faced with a negative influence on ROAA and a positive influence on ROAE.

In harmony with the exposed literature, the following hypothesis is put forward:

Hypothesis 6—There is a significant relationship between the growth rate of deposits and bank profitability (no defined sign).

2.1.7 Bank size

The size of banks is one of the characteristics that have traditionally been used to determine their levels of profitability because, in principle, the bigger the bank, the greater the use of synergies and economies of scale, leading to a reduction in expenses and, consequently, an increase in results and profitability [14, 20]. Saona [12] claims that a large bank will incur in large operations, therefore, it will be associated with a higher risk, which, consequently, will cause the institution to charge higher margins, positively influencing profit.

However, a bank that is too large may incur diseconomies of scale as it will have an increase in variable costs, such as operating, bureaucratic and marketing expenses, negatively affecting bank profitability [2, 3]. According to García-Herrero et al. [15], the increase in size can make bank management difficult due to the occurrence of aggressive competitive strategies.

Therefore, empirical investigations [12, 16, 17] have found a positive and significant relationship between profitability and size.

Dietrich and Wanzenried [3] showed that in Switzerland the largest banks are the least profitable, following Berger and Mester [27] who had concluded the same.

In another sense, Ding et al. [4] showed that the large US banks after the crisis were the ones that were able to restructure the fastest and obtain higher levels of profitability. Once the authors had obtained a negative relationship during the crisis. Also, Elsas et al. [26] and Knezevic & Dobromirov [11] found a negative and significant relationship between size and profitability. Other empirical research does not find any significant relationship between profitability and bank size [2, 9, 10, 18, 28].

Following the exposed literature, we proposed hypothesis 7:

Hypothesis 7—There is a significant relationship between the bank's size and its profitability (with no defined sign).

2.2 Industry-specific determinants

2.2.1 Ownership

Banks can be private or public institutions, the private ones belong, essentially, to private entities (more than 50% of these institutions) and the public ones, mainly, to the State. Berger and Mester [27] argue that the more external investors there are, the greater the control, the greater the efficiency, consequently the greater the profitability.

However, there is much empirical evidence that this variable does not influence the institution's profit [2, 18, 28].

DeYoung and Rice [24] and Knezevic and Dobromirov [11] found a negative relationship between ROAE and ROAA, respectively. Dietrich and Wanzenried [3] also concluded that ROAA is negatively influenced by the type of property, however, this is not statistically significant when the performance index is the ROAE.

In contrast, Rumler and Waschiczek [9] show that banks with public capital positively influence ROAE. Under these points of view the following hypothesis is placed:

Hypothesis 8—There is a significant relationship between the nature of bank ownership and its profitability (with no defined sign).

2.2.2 Stock exchange quotation

According to Beccalli et al. [22], information on the earnings of institutions can be incorporated into stock prices, however, changes in stock prices do not properly reflect the extent of changes in earnings. Dietrich and Wanzenried [3] argue that the fact that listed banks negatively affect institutions' profits makes them subject to greater requirements, such as additional reporting and greater market scrutiny. This fact may affect the profitability of banks with the additional costs that they entail. However, financial institutions listed on the stock exchange that has a positive influence on performance will suffer greater pressure from the financial market (shareholders, financial analysts, etc. ...).

Iannotta et al. [20] showed that the stock market positively affects bank profitability.

On the other hand, Dietrich and Wanzenried [3] faced a negative influence when using ROAA. García-Herrero et al. [15] showed that banks present on the stock exchange are not more profitable than those that are not.

By the way, the hypothesis to be tested will be:

Hypothesis 9—Banks listed on the stock exchange have greater profitability than unlisted ones.

2.3 Macroeconomic determinants

2.3.1 Inflation

Inflation can influence profitability depending on how it interferes with operating income and costs. Thus, if management manages to forecast the inflation rate, it can regulate interest rates appropriately, to increase revenues faster than costs [11]. Otherwise, banking costs will be higher than revenues and will negatively affect the profitability of banking institutions.

Athanasoglou et al. [2], García-Herrero et al. [15], Guru et al. [8], Rumler and Waschiczek [9], Saona [12], and Tan et al. [16] confirmed that the relationship between inflation and bank profitability is positive. However, Djalilov and Piesse [14] and Shehzad et al. [21] did not find a significant relationship between profitability and this variable. Trabelsi and Trad [17] and Trujillo-Ponce [10], in turn, showed that ROAA is positively influenced by the inflation rate while ROAE is negatively affected.

Following the literature, we propose the following hypothesis:

Hypothesis 10—There is a direct relationship between inflation and bank profitability (with no defined sign).

2.3.2 Economic growth

Economic growth varies over the years as the economy goes through several economic cycles. On the one hand, if the country's economic conditions are unfavorable, this could mean an increase in banks' provisions due to the loss of credit and the poor quality of assets mortgaged to profitability. On the other hand, if the country's economic conditions are favorable, the demand for credit from households and companies will increase and, consequently, so will profitability [10, 14].

However, Saona [12] concluded that in periods of strong economic growth, banks may tend to adjust their margins, leading to lower results and profitability. That said, Athanasoglou et al. [2], Dietrich and Wanzenried [3], Lee and Kim [28], Rumler and Waschiczek [9], Trabelsi and Trad [17], and Trujillo-Ponce [10] show a positive relationship between economic growth and economic profitability. While other investigations [11, 14, 15] have not found any relationship between economic growth and bank profitability. However, Saona [12] and Shehzad et al. [21] showed a negative association between Gross Domestic Product (GDP) and bank profitability. Finally, Garcia and Guerreiro [19] concluded that GDP negatively affects the banking sector if it is analyzed with the ROAE profit indicator, however, if it is related to ROAA, the sign becomes insignificant.

In line with the provisions, we propose the following hypothesis to be tested: Hypothesis 11—The country's GDP influences bank profitability.

3. Research design

3.1 Sample data

The sample, for the period between 2011 and 2016, is composed of 267 Iberian banks, of which 122 are Portuguese and 145 are Spanish. All databases without complete data for at least four consecutive years were excluded, a necessary condition for second-order correlation estimation [5]. As the second-order correlation is a GMM assumption, and this will be the estimation method used, this correlation must be tested [29]. Data to calculate bank- and industry-specific variables are sourced from Orbis Bank Focus, Bureau van Dijk database. While the macroeconomic variables come from The World Bank[1].

3.2 Sample variables

3.2.1 Dependent

ROAA and ROAE have traditionally been used as measures of banking performance and to that extent are also the variables that we will use as dependent variables.

The average return on total assets (ROAA) is the ratio between Ebit and total assets [2, 30]. Garcia and Guerreiro [19] state that ROAA portrays management efficiency and is, therefore, an imminently economic indicator. Return on average equity (ROAE) is the ratio of net income to equity [2]. Rumler and Waschiczek [9] suggest that ROAE is a more popular performance measure among financial analysts.

This indicator translates into shareholder returns and, as such, there may be pressure from shareholders to distribute results, threatening the capitalization of banks. we know that the asset may be valued at acquisition cost, which can lead to the undervaluation or overvaluation of the elements that comprise it, thus influencing the ROAA ratio.

3.2.2 Independent variables

Table 1 presents the explanatory variables to be used in the regression models, highlighting their internal origin, intrinsic to management, or external, without direct influence from the manager.

3.3 Methodology

Considering ROAE and ROAA as the dependent variables and the independent variables as defined previously, we obtain the following models:

$$\begin{aligned} \mathrm{ROAE}_{it} = {} & \beta_0 + \beta_1 \mathrm{AS}_{it} + \beta_2 \mathrm{AQ}_{it} + \beta_3 \mathrm{EQ}_{it} + \beta_4 \mathrm{CIR}_{it} + \beta_5 \mathrm{RD}_{it} + \beta_6 \mathrm{ADG}_{it} \\ & + \beta_7 \mathrm{SIZE}_{it} + \beta_8 \mathrm{Owner} + \beta_9 \mathrm{Quoted} + \beta_{10} \mathrm{INF}_{it} + \beta_{11} \mathrm{GDP}_{it} + + \mu_{it} \end{aligned} \tag{1}$$

[1] https://data.worldbank.org/.

Variables	Designation	Proxy	Theoretical foundation
Asset Structure	AS	Total Loans /Total Assets	Alshatti [18], García-Herrero et al. [15], Sharma et al. [1] and Trujillo-Ponce [10]
Asset Quality	AQ	Provisions for Loan Losses/ Total Loans	Athanasoglou et al. [2], Dietrich e Wanzenried [8], Saona [12]
Equity	EQ	Equity/Total Assets	Alshatti [18], Garcia and Guerreiro [19], Knezevic and Dobromirov [11] and Trabelsi and Trad [17]
Cost to Income ratio	CIR	Total Expense/Total Revenue	Dietrich and Wanzenried [3], Knezevic and Dobromirov [11] and Saona [12]
Revenue Diversification	RD	Non-interest income/gross income	Tan et al. [16]
Annual Deposit Growth	ADG	(Total Deposits$_t$—Total Deposits$_{t-1)}$/Total Deposits$_{t-1}$)	Dietrich and Wanzenried [3], Garcia and Guerreiro [19] and Trujillo-Ponce [10]
Size	Size	Ln (total Assets)	Alshatti [18], Djalilov and Piesse [14], Knezevic and Dobromirov [11], Tan et al. [16]; Trujillo-Ponce [10]; Neves, Proença and Dias [31]
Owner	Owner	Dummy variable—takes value 1 if it has Public ownership and 0 if Private	
Quoted	Quoted	Dummy variable—1 if quoted 0 otherwise	
Inflation	INF	Annual Inflation Rate at Constant Prices	Knezevic and Dobromirov [11]; Trujillo-Ponce [10]
GDP	GDP	Real Gross Domestic Product Growth	Athanasoglou et al. [2], Dietrich e Wanzenried [3], Garcia e Guerreiro [19] Rumler e Waschiczek [9]

Table 1.
Specific characteristics of banks, industry-specific characteristics, and macroeconomic factors.

$$\begin{aligned}\mathrm{ROAA_{it}} &= \beta_0 + \beta_1\mathrm{AS_{it}} + \beta_2\mathrm{AQ_{it}} + \beta_3\mathrm{EQ_{it}} + \beta_4\mathrm{CIR_{it}} + \beta_5\mathrm{RD_{it}} + \beta_6\mathrm{ADG_{it}} \\ &\quad + \beta_7\mathrm{SIZE_{it}} + \beta_8\mathrm{Owner} + \beta_9\mathrm{Quoted} + \beta_{10}\mathrm{INF_{it}} + \beta_{11}\mathrm{GDP_{it}} + +\mu_{it}\end{aligned} \tag{2}$$

To estimate these models, the GMM dynamic model was used, initially proposed by Arellano and Bond [5] and improved by Arrellano and Bover [6] and Blundell and Bond [7]. By using the GMM method, we solve two fundamental problems such as endogeneity and unobserved heterogeneity [14, 15, 29].

4. Results

4.1 Descriptive statistics

This chapter describes descriptive statistics (mean, minimum, maximum, and standard deviation) for the variables used in the sample. From what can be seen in **Table 2**, the study shows a positive mean of the dependent variables for all the years under observation. It is also observed, in the three samples, that the means of the independent variables are mostly positive, except GDP in the samples from the Iberian Peninsula and Portugal. Regarding the standard deviation, it can be seen that the annual growth of deposits is the variable that presents the highest value for the samples from the Iberian Peninsula and Spain. While Portugal presents the asset quality variable with the greatest discrepancy to the average.

4.2 Discussion results

Table 3 presents the results for the banks of Portugal and Spain as the Iberian Peninsula, and **Table 4** an individual analysis of the determinants that affect the profitability of these two border countries. Thus, economic growth exhibits a statistically significant and positive sign for the joint analysis (**Table 3**). Such evidence may be due to the increase in credit on the part of families and companies after the financial crisis. As well as, a decrease in bad debt assets, during some favorable economic growth of the countries. Since in favorable growth situations, borrowers can meet their debts. By the provisions, hypothesis 11 is corroborated, following the results found by Lee and Kim [28], Rumler and Waschiczek [9], and Trabelsi and Trad [17]. Regarding inflation, this influences positively and significantly both the Iberian banking sector and the Portuguese banking sector (**Table 4**). However, banking in Portugal is only influenced by the operating performance index, which is the ROAA. In this way, hypothesis 10 is supported by the studies by Rumler and Waschiczek [9], Tan et al. [16], and Trujillo-Ponce [10]. This reveals that the managers of the banks under analysis can predict the rate of inflation, properly regulating interest rates so that revenues increase faster than expenses. On the other hand, an increase in inflation can also translate into an increase in the purchasing power of the population in general, so this increase can mean more deposits, more credit compliance, safer, therefore more profitability. The asset structure presents a negative and statistically significant result concerning the ROAE of the sample of Iberian and Portuguese banks. In fact, the asset structure of Spanish banks (**Table 4**) also shows the same sign for both dependent variables. By the provisions, it is clear that it is possible to corroborate hypothesis 1. This evidence is supported by the results of Rumler and Waschiczek [9] and Tan et al. [16]. This means that the banking sector is not able to efficiently manage and increase the loan portfolio in the period under review. A period that is characterized by strong competition and banking competitiveness, as banks were under great pressure to attract customers. However, an increase in the loan portfolio implies increases in operating costs, so if interest rates are not well adjusted, they will become incapable of supporting operating expenses, harming banks' profitability. As well, the increase in the loan portfolio can also lead to a high risk of credit defaults. It appears that the sign of the variable capital is positive in both Tables. That said, hypothesis 3 is corroborated. This evidence shows that Portuguese and Spanish banks are well-capitalized.

Regarding **Table 3**, Banks that present better levels of capital denote a lower risk of bankruptcy, they are considered.

with lower financing costs, therefore they can obtain higher gross margins, which leads to higher levels of profitability. These results are in line with the investigations of Garcia and Guerreiro [19], Trujillo-Ponce [10], and Saona [12]. Consistent with hypothesis 2, the results in **Table 4** show that asset quality negatively and significantly affects the ROAA of Portuguese banks and both performance indicators relative to Spain. This is due to the increase in impairment losses on loans, which negatively

			Iberian Peninsula		Portugal					Spain		
Variables	**Mean**	**Minimum**	**Maximum**	**Standard Deviation**	**Mean**	**Minimum**	**Maximum**	**Standard Deviation**	**Mean**	**Minimum**	**Maximum**	**Standard Deviation**
ROAE	2.815	−596.314	516.159	37.512	2.196	−131.397	516.159	36.318	3.173	−596.314	348.454	34.985
ROAA	0.415	−17.502	19.236	2.394	0.136	−17.502	17.239	2.519	0.576	−14.037	19.236	2.299
AS	51.070	0.000	99.967	23.947	47.727	0.143	98.125	22.333	53.066	0	99.967	25.958
AQ	14.442	0.000	1884.362	137.350	33.507	0.002	1884.362	220.676	2.650	0	140.937	19.738
EQ	13.987	−7.831	99.987	18.277	13.827	−5.607	93.253	13.128	14.078	−7.831	99.987	20.56033
CIR	67.954	0.200	872.730	49.619	10.582	1.22	620.690	43.900	66.363	0.200	872.730	51.072
RD	44.500	0.000	550.000	34.369	44.428	0	179.604	24.204	44.570	0	550.000	42.111
ADG	393.336	−98.914	184025.500	8323.199	6.649	−77.243	172.352	22.625	577.918	−98.914	184025.5	8970.098
SIZE	6.119	4.113	9.127	1.146	5.807	4.360	8.139	0.991	6.299	4.113	9.127	1.159
OWNER	0.023	0.000	1	0.151	0.030	0	1	0.171	0.018	0	1	0.142
Quoted	0.038	0.000	1	0.191	0.030	0	1	0.171	0.044	0	1	0.199
INF	1.289	−0.500	3.653	1.478	1.426	−0.278	3.653	1.524	1.182	−0.500	3.196	1.342
GDP	−0.319	−4.028	3.432	2.304	−0.877	−4.023	1.822	2.054	0.117	−2.928	3.432	2.26

Table 2.
Descriptives statistics.

	ROAE					ROAA				
	Coefficient	St. Deviation	*Z*	*P*-value		Coefficient	St. Deviation	*Z*	*P*-value	
Constant	−16.763	(77.231)	−0.22	0.828		−7.288	(7.646)	−0.95	0.341	
AS	−0.222	(0.103)	−2.15	0.032	**	−0.011	(0.008)	−1.36	0.174	
AQ	−0.176	(0.149)	−1.18	0.239		−0.001	(0.019)	−0.06	0.995	
EQ	1.173	(0.570)	2.06	0.040	**	0.191	(0.059)	3.24	0.001	***
CIR	−0.352	(0.042)	−8.38	0.000	***	−0.021	(0.004)	−5.11	0.000	***
RD	−0.019	(0.025)	−0.78	0.434		0.001	(0.003)	0.19	0.847	
ADG	0.018	(0.007)	2.48	0.013	**	0.003	(0.001)	4.10	0.000	***
SIZE	6.515	(10.884)	0.60	0.549		1.255	(1.129)	1.11	0.266	
OWNER	99.912	(95.047)	1.05	0.293		1.815	(4.439)	0.41	0.683	
Quoted	−35.332	(30.531)	−1.16	0.247		−6.798	(5.114)	−1.33	0.184	
INF	2.452	(1.002)	2.45	0.014	**	0.255	(0.091)	2.79	0.005	***
GDP	1.218	(0.290)	4.20	0.000	***	0.064	(0.029)	2.16	0.031	**
Sargan			16.01318 (11)	0.1406				10.57061 (11)	0.4799	
Wald			215.79 (12)	0.0000				69.20 (12)	0.0000	
AR (1)			0.43101	0.6665				−1.9816	0.0475	
AR (2)			−1.5599	0.1188				−0.13714	0.8905	

*In the table above, all the variables are those included in the literature review. In order to understand the reading of the results, we still need to know that: (i) the values in parentheses represent the asymptotic standard errors compatible with heteroscedasticity problems; (ii) **,*** represent the statistically significant coefficients at the level of 10%, 5% and 1%, respectively; (iii) The Sargan test has a p value greater than 5%, which means that the instruments are valid and the values between relatives represent degrees of freedom; (iv) The Wald test has a p-value less than 5% indicating that the set of coefficients is asymptotically distributed as $\chi 2$ under the null hypothesis without significance, the degrees of freedom are represented in parentheses; (v) The Arellano-Bond test is asymptotically distributed as N (0,1) under the null hypothesis of no serial correlation. The AR(2) test indicates that there is no second-order serial correlation.*

Table 3.
Estimation results of models 1 and 2 for the Iberian Peninsula.

	Portugal								Spain							
	ROAE				ROAA				ROAE				ROAA			
	Coefficient	St. Deviation	Z	P-value	Coefficient	St. Deviation	Z	P-value	Coefficient	St. Deviation	Z	P-value	Coeficiente	Erro padrão	Z	P-value
Constant	173.441	(166.815)	1.04	0.298	1.824	(7.023)	0.26	0.795	87.620	(24.922)	3.52	0.000 ***	10.126	(4.790)	2.11	0.035 **
AS	−0.512	(0.214)	−2.39	0.017 **	−0.009	(0.008)	−1.11	0.266	−0.454	(0.084)	−5.42	0.000 ***	−0.034	(0.009)	−3.83	0.000 ***
AQ	−0.366	(0.479)	−0.76	0.455	−0.081	(0.036)	−2.23	0.026 **	−4.471	(0.387)	−11.55	0.000 ***	−0.448	(0.049)	−9.19	0.000 ***
EQ	1.934	(0.405)	4.78	0.000 ***	0.133	(0.033)	3.98	0.000 ***	0.775	(0.251)	3.09	0.002 ***	0.092	(0.043)	2.14	0.032 **
CIR	−0.543	(0.103)	−5.24	0.000 ***	−0.032	(0.003)	−10.07	0.000 ***	−0.370	(0.027)	−13.62	0.000 ***	−0.031	(0.003)	−11.89	0.000 ***
RD	−0.051	(0.026)	−1.91	0.056 *	−0.004	(0.001)	−2.51	0.012 **	−0.031	(0.025)	−1.23	0.217	−0.004	(0.003)	−1.16	0.247
ADG	0.248	(0.064)	3.90	0.000 ***	0.018	(0.003)	5.85	0.000 ***	0.044	(0.025)	1.73	0.084 *	0.003	(0.001)	2.25	0.025 **
SIZE	−22.012	(24.628)	−0.89	0.371	−0.050	(0.934)	−0.05	0.957	−5.009	(3.175)	−1.58	0.115	−0.796	0.586	−1.36	0.174
OWNER	−27.070	(73.281)	−0.37	0.712	0.772	(6.379)	0.12	0.904	−700.091	(920.457)	−0.76	0.447	−119.784	(211.781)	−0.57	0.572
Quoted	−80.435	(67.069)	−1.20	0.230	12.742	(13.500)	0.94	0.345	3.412	(3.327)	1.03	0.305	−0.279	(0.296)	−0.94	0.347
INF	2.128	(1.514)	1.41	0.160	0.214	(0.052)	4.12	0.000 ***	−1.592	(1.143)	−1.13	0.260	0.005	(0.099)	0.05	0.960
GDP	0.571	(0.575)	0.99	0.321	−0.013	(0.042)	−0.30	0.762	0.106	(0.477)	0.22	0.824	0.044	(0.044)	0.99	0.323
Sargan			7.240062 (11)	0.7793			7.007189 (11)	0.7985			7.754619 (9)	0.5591			12.96967 (9)	0.1640
Wald			1720.97 (12)	0.0000			12162.61 (12)	0.0000			5941.12 (13)	0.0000			784.38 (13)	0.0000
AR (1)			0.5725	0.5670			−2.1586	0.0309			−1.1767	0.2393			−1.6326	0.1025
AR (2)			−0.80537	0.4206			−0.4231	0.6722			−0.78984	0.4296			0.00352	0.9972

*In the table above, all the variables are those included in the literature review. To understand the reading of the results, we still need to know that: (i) the values in parentheses represent the asymptotic standard errors compatible with heteroscedasticity problems; (ii) *,**,*** represent the statistically significant coefficients at the level of 10%, 5% and 1%, respectively; (iii) The Sargan test has a* p-value *greater than 5%, which means that the instruments are valid and the values between relatives represent degrees of freedom; (iv) The Wald test has a* p-value *less than 5% indicating that the set of coefficients is asymptotically distributed as* $\chi 2$ *under the null hypothesis without significance, the degrees of freedom are represented in parentheses; (v) The Arellano-Bond test is asymptotically distributed as* N (0,1) *under the null hypothesis of no serial correlation. The AR(2) test indicates that there is no second-order serial correlation.*

Table 4.
Estimation results for Portugal and Spain.

affects the performance of banking institutions. Naturally, in dire economic cycles, which is the case in the sample period, households tend to default on credit. Therefore, the period from 2011 to 2016 is marked by losses of millions of euros in loans to customers, which was noted in the financial statements of institutions. And once banks have a significant increase in bad debt assets, they tend to distribute their gross margin to cover expected losses [10]. This result is in line with the results obtained by Alshatti [18], Athanasoglou et al. [2], Trabelsi and Trad [17] and Trujillo-Ponce [10].

Regarding the operational efficiency variable, it manifests itself with a negative and significant sign in both Tables. The negative and significant coefficient of the cost-to-income ratio shows that poor expenditure management is one of the main contributors to poor profitability performance. In other words, to obtain a higher performance it is necessary to have a decrease in expenses and/or an increase in income [11]. The result obtained is under the empirical analysis by Dietrich and Wanzenried [3] and Shehzad et al. [21], that is, the higher the CIR, the lower the efficiency and therefore the profitability.

The annual growth rate of deposits is showing a statistically significant and positive sign. Indeed, hypothesis 6 is corroborated, following the result obtained in the investigation by Dietrich and Wanzenried [3] and Garcia and Guerreiro [19]. The increased demand for deposits increases bank profitability both in the Iberian Peninsula and in Portugal and Spain. Banks may be benefiting from the increased purchasing power of depositors following the effects of the financial crisis. To that extent, there will be no need to incur aggressive policies (which can negatively affect performance through lower margins) to attract a greater number of depositors. Finally, as happened with the authors Saona [12] and Tan et al. [16], and corroborating hypothesis 5, the results of Portuguese banking show a negative and significant sign for the variable revenue diversification, for both profitability indicators. This result suggests that non-traditional activities, by themselves, do not boost Portuguese banking profitability.

Also, DeYoung and Rice [24], had already warned that if banks did not associate these activities with traditional activities, they could incur losses. Despite this, this result may be due to charges, for example, with securities. As a means of recapitalization, to comply with the rules established by the Basel III agreement, banks were subject to CoCos (Contingent Convertible Bonds) bonds, however, the financial charges with the high-interest rates of these bonds may have harmed the banks' performance. Portuguese.

It should be noted that the significant variables in the three samples always show the same sign, which somehow gives credibility to the results found. In the sample of Spanish banks, it is possible to verify that the explanatory variables are exactly the same using the ROAA or the ROAE as dependent variables, which similarly suggests that the explanatory variables were well selected. In general, when operating profitability is used as a performance measure, the variables that remain significant in all samples are bank capitalization, operating efficiency measured by the CIR and the growth of deposits.

Likewise, when using ROAE as a performance measure, the signs and significance of these variables remain unchanged and the composition of assets is added as a determinant of return on equity. These results suggest that the role of managers is fundamental in defining and monitoring capital and deposit growth ratios to improve performance. Furthermore, it is necessary to improve operational efficiency as well as maximize the asset structure, which in a highly competitive environment has not been able to increase bank profitability levels.

5. Conclusion

The economic and financial stability of banking institutions is important for the economic stability of the country where the sector is located. Therefore, satisfactory levels of profitability can translate into the stable financial health of countries.

This study aimed to analyze the factors that influence the profitability of Portuguese and Spanish banks, during a period between 2011 and 2016.

The empirical study was carried out considering three sub-samples to observe the Iberian Peninsula as a whole, and each country individually in order to understand the differences in the determinants of profitability in these two border countries. However, our results show that the profitability of Portuguese and Spanish banks is mostly influenced by the same internal variables, which shows that, probably, the fact that they are neighboring countries can lead to similar behavior of managers. These management decisions are those that exert the greatest influence on bank profitability.

In particular, it can be seen that the performance of banks, both in the Iberian Peninsula as a whole and in Portugal or Spain, is positively influenced by demand from depositors. Likewise, it is possible to verify that the more capital the financial institutions of both countries hold, the better their capacity to face adverse situations.

Finally, it is concluded that if Iberian banks do not efficiently manage their expenses and costs, they incur a poorly applied operational policy, negatively influencing the profitability of these institutions.

Therefore, despite different economic systems, Portugal and Spain have similar internal banking policies. This may be due to the strong presence of Spain in the Portuguese financial sector, establishing management methods that are very similar to each other.

Since in this work, only Iberian banks were used and to that extent, the sample is small, which may constitute a limitation in the extrapolation of these results, we propose to analyze in future work a broader set of countries with different legal and institutional environments, using an example to an additional efficiency model such as the DEA.

Acknowledgements

This work is supported by national funds, through the FCT—Portuguese Foundation for Science and Technology under the project UIDB/04011/2020.

Author details

Maria Elisabete Duarte Neves[1,2*], Joana Monteiro[2] and Carmem Leal[2]

1 Polytechnic of Coimbra, Coimbra Business School Research Centre|ISCAC, Quinta Agrícola-Bencanta, Coimbra, Portugal

2 Centre for Transdisciplinary Development Studies, University of Trás-os-Montes and Alto Douro, Vila Real, Portugal

*Address all correspondence to: mduarteneves@gmail.com

References

[1] Sharma D, Sharma AK, Barua MK. Efficiency and productivity of banking sector: A critical analysis of literature and design of conceptual model. Qualitative Research in Financial Markets. 2013;**5**(2):195-224

[2] Athanasoglou PP, Brissimis SN, Delis MD. Bank-specific, industry-specific and macroeconomic determinants of bank profitability. Journal of International Financial Markets, Institutions and Money. 2008;**18**(2):121-136

[3] Dietrich A, Wanzenried G. Determinants of bank profitability before and during the crisis: Evidence from Switzerland. Journal of International Financial Markets, Institutions and Money. 2011;**21**(3):307-327

[4] Ding N, Fung H-G, Jia J. Comparison of Bank profitability in China and the USA. China & World Economy. 2017; **25**(1):90-108. DOI: 10.1111/cwe.12188

[5] Arellano M, Bond S. Some tests of specification for panel data: Monte Carlo evidence and an application to employment equations. The Review of Economic Studies. 1991;**58**(2):277. DOI: 10.2307/2297968

[6] Arellano M, Bover O. Another look at the instrumental variable estimation of Erro-components model. Journal of Econometrics. 1995;**68**(1):29-51. DOI: 10.1016/0304-4076(94)01642-D

[7] Blundell R, Bond S. Initial conditions and moment restrictions in dynamic panel data models. Journal of Econometrics. 1998;**87**(1):115-143. DOI: 10.1016/S0304-4076(98)00009-8

[8] Guru BK, Staunton J, Balashanmugam B. Determinants of commercial bank profitability in Malaysia. Journal of Money, Credit, and Banking. 2002;**17**:69-82

[9] Rumler F, Waschiczek W. Have changes in the financial structure affected bank profitability? Evidence for Austria. European Journal of Finance. 2014;**22**(10):803-824. DOI: 10.1080/1351847X.2014.984815

[10] Trujillo-Ponce A. What determines the profitability of banks? Evidence from Spain. Accounting and Finance. 2013; **53**(2):561-586. DOI: 10.1111/j.1467-629X.2011.00466.x

[11] Knezevic A, Dobromirov D. The determinants of Serbian banking industry profitability. Economic Research-Ekonomska Istrazivanja. 2016; **29**(1):459-474. DOI: 10.1080/1331677X.2016.1174390

[12] Saona P. Intra- and extra-bank determinants of Latin American banks' profitability. International Review of Economics and Finance. 2016;**45**: 197-214. DOI: 10.1016/j.iref.2016.06.004

[13] Mester LJ. A study of bank efficiency taking into account risk-preferences. Journal of Banking & Finance. 1996; **20**(6):1025-1045

[14] Djalilov K, Piesse J. Determinants of bank profitability in transition countries: What matters most? Research in International Business and Finance. 2016;**38**:69-82

[15] García-Herrero A, Gavilá S, Santabárbara D. What explains the low profitability of Chinese banks? Journal of Banking & Finance. 2009;**33**(11): 2080-2092

[16] Tan Y, Floros C, Anchor J. The profitability of Chinese banks: Impacts

of risk, competition and efficiency. Review of Accounting and Finance. 2017;**16**(1)

[17] Trabelsi MA, Trad N. Profitability and risk in interest-free banking industries: A dynamic panel data analysis. International Journal of Islamic and Middle Eastern Finance and Management. 2017;**10**(4):454-469. DOI: 10.1108/IMEFM-05-2016-0070

[18] Alshatti AS. Determinants of banks' profitability—the case of Jordan. Investment Management and Financial Innovations. 2016;**13**(1):84-91. DOI: 10.21511/imfi.13(1).2016.08

[19] Garcia MTM, Guerreiro JPSM. Internal and external determinants of banks' profitability. Journal of Economic Studies. 2016;**43**(1):90-107. DOI: 10.1108/JES-09-2014-0166

[20] Iannotta G, Nocera G, Sironi A. Ownership structure, risk and performance in the European banking industry. Journal of Banking & Finance. 2007;**31**(7):2127-2149

[21] Shehzad CT, De Haan J, Scholtens B. The relationship between size, growth and profitability of commercial banks. Applied Economics. 2013;**45**(13): 1751-1765. DOI: 10.1080/00036846.2011.637896

[22] Beccalli E, Casu B, Girardone C. Efficiency and stock performance in European banking. Journal of Business Finance & Accounting. 2006;**33**(1–2): 245-262

[23] Stiroh KJ, Rumble A. The dark side of diversification: The case of US financial holding companies. Journal of Banking & Finance. 2006;**30**(8):2131-2161

[24] DeYoung R, Rice T. Noninterest income and financial performance at US commercial banks. Financial Review. 2004;**39**(1):101-127

[25] Narwal KP, Pathneja S. Effect of bank-specific and governance-specific variables on the productivity and profitability of banks. International Journal of Productivity and Performance Management. 2016;**65**(8):1057-1074. DOI: 10.1108/IJPPM-09-2015-0130

[26] Elsas R, Hackethal A, Holzhäuser M. The anatomy of bank diversification. Journal of Banking & Finance. 2010; **34**(6):1274-1287

[27] Berger AN, Mester LJ. Inside the black box: What explains differences in the efficiencies of financial institutions? Journal of Banking & Finance. 1997; **21**(7):895-947

[28] Lee JY, Kim D. Bank performance and its determinants in Korea. Japan and the World Economy. 2013;**27**:83-94. DOI: 10.1016/j.japwor.2013.05.001

[29] Neves MED. Payout and firm's catering. International Journal of Managerial Finance. 2018;**4**(7):734

[30] Neves ME, Proença C. Intellectual capital and financial performance: Evidence from Portuguese banks. International Journal of Learning and Intellectual Capital. 2021;**18**(1):93-108. DOI: 10.1504/IJLIC.2020.10031817

[31] Neves ME, Proença C, Dias A. Bank profitability and efficiency in Portugal and Spain: A non-linearity approach. Journal of Risk and Financial Management. 2020;**13**(11):284. DOI: 10.3390/jrfm13110284

Section 5

Financial Assets and Pandemics

Chapter 6

Pandemics and Financial Assets

Pattarake Sarajoti, Pattanaporn Chatjuthamard and Suwongrat Papangkorn

Abstract

There have been several pandemics in the history of mankind. One of the major pandemics was the Spanish flu that took place in 1918, in which millions of lives were lost globally. Despite significant advances in science and medicine since then, the COVID-19 pandemic has still caused major impacts around the world. As evidenced, pandemics not only cause social and public health implications, but also cause effects on the economy as well. This chapter addresses the ill effects of pandemics on the economy and presents how the financial markets and financial institutions were influenced and how they responded to the pandemics. More specifically, this chapter identifies the effects of the pandemics on various assets (e.g., crude oil, gold, currencies, equity, bonds, and cryptocurrencies) around the world. In addition, the chapter also presents evidence of corporates' characteristics relative to their responses to the ill effects of the pandemics.

Keywords: pandemics, COVID19, capital markets, financial markets, financial assets, corporate governance

1. Introduction

It is now almost evident that our world seems to have entered into an infinite loop of new outbreaks of variants of the coronavirus that led to the COVID 19 pandemic. Beginning in early 2020, the coronavirus spread throughout the world and caused concern, as reflected in the world stock indexes. Even in the third year of this ongoing pandemic, it is clear that, despite vaccination and awareness, the new variant Omicron is causing investors to panic [1, 2]. Due to the extreme impacts of these epidemics, it is critical to investigate pandemics and their pessimistically veiled aspects to develop effective strategies. In this chapter, we will explore how this health outbreak impacted the economy and financial markets and how market participants responded to the pandemic.

The rest of the chapter is organized as follows. In the following sections, we review the literature on how the pandemic impacts the equity market and provide a brief discussion on how COVID-19 differs from other crises. Section 3 presents a discussion of how the pandemics impact other financial assets, including communities, foreign exchange, and cryptocurrencies. The fourth section analyzes corporate characteristics relative to their responses to the ill effects of the pandemic. Lastly, we end with the concluding remarks.

2. Pandemic and financial market

2.1 Prior pandemic

Throughout human history, there have been numerous health outbreaks, such as foot and mouth disease, severe acute respiratory syndrome (SARS), bird flu (H5N1), and swine flu (H1N1). During the SARS outbreak in 2003, a total of 8098 people worldwide became sick, and 774 people died. Even though SARS is contagious and spread by close person-to-person contact, it is short-lived, with only 8 months separating the first reported case and the end of the crisis. While Ebola was first seen in West Africa, unlike other outbreaks, Ebola killed 86 people on the first day of the disease. It has shown fatality rates ranging from 25–90% in past outbreaks. These outbreaks have significant social and economic impacts, such as increasing social tension and people's health as well as the economy.

Barro et al. [3] calculated that the death rate of the 1918–1920 Spanish influenza pandemic would imply a 6- to 8-percentage-point drop in GDP and consumption in a typical country. Other researchers, on the other hand, have shown that a health outbreak can have a significant impact on the stock market and real economic activity. During the SARS outbreak, for example, the growth rate of household income fell by more than 3% [4], while the average price of Hong Kong real estate fell by 1.6% [5]. In the same way, Ichev & Marinč [6] found that the 2014–2016 Ebola outbreak events were followed by bad financial market returns.

The epidemic had the most serious impact on the tourism industry: hotels, restaurants, theme parks, and airlines. Chen et al. [7] found that within a month of the SARS outbreak, Taiwanese hotel stocks experienced steep declines in earnings and stock prices (approximately 29%), while the manufacturing, retail trade, and banking industries were less affected. Meanwhile, some industries benefited from concerns about health outbreaks. During the SARS outbreak, the biotechnology sector emerged stronger [7]. Similarly, the study by Donadelli et al. [8] documented that disease-related news has a positive impact on pharmaceutical stocks. As a result, investors shifted their assets from the financial market to the relatively low-risk real sector [9].

The impact of the health outbreak does not only affect the economy and investors' behavior; it also influences corporations' operations and strategies. Health outbreaks have led to great uncertainty about future cash flow, and investors may reduce investment due to uncertain demand and limited budgets. Besides the uncertainty of the epidemic, which increases default rates on credit cards and mortgages [10], the cost of bank loans, restrains the volume of bank lending [11]. While the approval of vaccines significantly mitigates the adverse impact of the outbreak [11].

Media coverage of major disasters, such as the Ebola outbreak, can heighten anxiety, depression, and terror, leading to risk aversion and pessimism among investors. Del Giudice and Paltrinieri [12] investigated observed monthly flows of geographically specialized equity mutual funds in African countries during the Ebola outbreak. They discovered that the disease outbreak had a statistically significant negative impact on monthly net flows. The effect was especially strong when linked to the event's media coverage. In a similar vein, Ichev and Marinč [6] proposed that outbreak events are more relevant for companies that are geographically closer to both the outbreak's birthplace and the financial markets.

In short, the external and unexpected shocks from health outbreaks can affect economic trends and suddenly change investors' sentiment. The magnitude of the adverse impact also depends on the industry, media coverage, and geographic area.

2.2 Why is the COVID-19 crisis different from other crises?

In 2008, the global financial crisis triggered a massive liquidity crisis as authorities hurried to implement emergency assistance packages to save financial institutions and enterprises. It saw the demise of well-known financial institutions such as Lehman Brothers, Freddie Mac, and Fannie Mae, as well as Northern Rock. It's important to recognize that the pandemic issue is very different from the global financial crisis of 2008. The COVID-19 pandemic is a health-related disaster that has far-reaching consequences not just for global economies but also for our everyday lives.

While no two epidemics are comparable, the current pandemic is fundamentally different from previous outbreaks. COVID-19 is much more dangerous than previous outbreaks [13–15]. Compared to other health outbreaks, the number of deaths COVID-19 has caused (more than 5.64 million people as of January 28, 2021) is actually more comparable with previous flu pandemics. More stringent public health measures that disrupt economic activity were implemented in response to the pandemic. As a result, the COVID-19 pandemic disaster has paralyzed the world more than any other crisis. Empirical evidence also suggests that the impact of European and US markets during the era of COVID-19 is high as compared to the GFC time [16]. Additionally, the implied volatility index (VIX), also known as the "fear gauge," has moved and has risen to its highest level since the GFC, while the US 10-year treasury yield index has fallen to a new low [17]. In addition, unlike other disease outbreaks, only WHO's public health risk announcements related to COVID-19 had a significant negative effect on stock markets, at least for 30 days [18].

Overall, no pandemic is likely to have had such a devastating economic impact as COVID-19, which caused a near-total shutdown of social and economic activity.

2.3 Equity market and COVID-19

In December 2019, the COVID-19 outbreak was triggered in the city of Wuhan, which is in the Hubei province of China. More than 2 years have passed, and the virus is still spreading over the planet. Although China was initially the epicenter of the outbreak, instances are now being reported in a variety of other nations. The impact of the outbreak was not only the slowing down of the Chinese economy with interruptions to production, the functioning of global supply chains has also been disrupted. The outbreak triggered fears and uncertainty in the financial markets, resulting in lower market returns and increased stock market volatility [18–22]. As a result, investors suffered significant losses in a short period of time due to a very high level of risks [23]. This, in turn, has led to more financial market turmoil and made the economic shock even worse. Compared to previous pandemics, there was more borrowing and more debt among businesses and households during this time. This makes the short-term shocks more powerful than in the past.

During periods of high economic policy uncertainty, especially during COVID-19, economic policy uncertainty has a significant impact on the financial stock market and affects investment returns. Various studies have examined the impact of investor sentiment on the stock market during the pandemic. Some researchers use the VIX as a proxy for investors' general attitude or tone toward future cash flows and investment risk of a particular security or financial market (e.g., [15, 24, 25]). An increase in VIX indicates a greater need for risk protection and higher market volatility. In particular, the VIX is used to quantify investors' fear. One of the early studies by Baker et al. [14] examined the US stock market volatility based on the daily news headlines and found that the pandemic had an unprecedented effect on VIX, especially after February 24, 2020. In addition, they argued that no prior infectious disease outbreak has resulted in daily stock market swings as dramatic as the response to COVID-19 developments in 2020. One of the possible explanations for this result would be the government's limits on commercial activity and deliberate social separation, which have powerful consequences in a service-oriented economy.

Other researchers focused on the implied volatility derived from stochastic volatility models (e.g., [26–28]). For instance, Mirza et al. [28] evaluated the price reaction, performance, and volatility timing of European investment funds during the outbreak. They found that social entrepreneurship funds outperformed their counterparts during the epidemic. These results reflect the reality that as the world becomes increasingly uncertain, investors are putting more emphasis on social aspects. Stock volatility, however, is not directly observed in practice, but rather inherently latent. Thus, some researchers recommend using so-called realized volatilities, which are calculated by adding the squared intraday interval return, as a proxy for volatility. Chatjuthamard et al. [29] separated the realized volatility into continuous and discontinuous jump components to investigate the impact of COVID-19 on the global stock market. They found that an increasing the growth rate of COVID-19 confirmed cases would lead to increased volatility and jumps while reducing the return. Besides, they also found that the risk from COVID-19 overshadows economic, financial, and political risks. Overall, these studies highlight the fact that COVID-19 caused pronounced market movements, extreme volatility, and unprecedented disruption to the economy.

Though the pandemic has been found to disrupt the financial market, some industries have been more affected than others. In the wake of the pandemic, some industries (such as transportation, hotels, and restaurants) have ceased operations, while others continue to operate to provide basic requirements (e.g., communication, healthcare, and pharmaceuticals). As a result, investment and consumption patterns have shifted dramatically. Some of the losses are attributable to investors' realistic estimate that profits may drop as a result of the pandemic's effects. For instance, Mazur et al. [30] found that during March 2020, natural gas, food, healthcare, and software sectors performed abnormally well, generating high returns, whereas petroleum, real estate, entertainment, and hospitality stocks plummeted considerably, losing more than 70% of their market capitalizations.

In light of the growing disruptions caused by the COVID-19 pandemic, the information flow related to the pandemic is critical. The higher media coverage in the pandemic period led to negative sentiments which caused markets to decline and volatility to rise. This view is supported by Haroon and Rizvi [31], who found panic by news outlets has been linked to increased stock volatility and the association is stronger for industries severely affected by the pandemic's occurrences. Researchers show the number of confirmed COVID-19 cases and deaths could be predictive factors of financial assets, such as stock volatility [19, 32], oil prices [33], and cryptocurrencies [34]. Similarly, Baker et al. [14] documented that news related to COVID-19, both positive and negative, is the dominant driver of large daily U.S. stock market moves. With technological advancement, a growing body of literature seems to agree that investors' attention and trends measured by internet activities, such as Google Trends, Twitter tweets, and other social media trends, could possess predictive power for trading volume and volatility of financial assets. This view is supported by Chatterjee and French [35], who documented that equity market volatility and liquidity are more sensitive to the uncertainty contained in tweets, as measured by the Twitter market uncertainty index (TMU), during the outbreak. Interestingly, previous research has established that fake news and media coverage during the outbreak has had an adverse effect on some countries' stock market returns [36].

The timeframe could be considered another determinant of the impact of the coronavirus on the global market. The global market's uncertainty increased when the coronavirus moved from epidemic to pandemic stage (11th March 2020 onwards) [37]. The equity market dramatically fell during the pandemic stage, evident from the higher negative return.

Another factor that could impact the relationship between the COVID-19 situation and the stock market is government interventions. The government has played a critical role in addressing the crisis caused by this disease outbreak. During the recent pandemic, governments implemented a variety of policies to mitigate the pandemic's impact. Globally, travel bans (i.e., closing international borders), lockdowns (i.e., restricting people's movement), and fiscal stimulus and relief packages (e.g., monetary policy, interest rates, quantitative easing, and corporate bond liquidity stabilization fund) were implemented. Stock markets responded positively to these policies because they could slow the spread of the disease and potentially calm panic. This view is supported by Narayan et al. [38], who investigated the effects of the G7 countries' government responses to the pandemic. They discovered that stock markets reacted favorably to government policies, particularly lockdowns. Baker et al. [14] agreed, finding that lockdowns and voluntary social distancing were the primary reasons why the US stock market reacted much more negatively to COVID-19 than to previous pandemics.

Government interventions signal changes in future economic conditions, which may affect company cash-flow expectations and, as a result, stock prices. As a result, investors may revise their portfolios, resulting in increased volatility within and across asset classes. In line with this notion, Zaremba et al. [39] investigate the relationship between COVID-19 pandemic policy responses and stock market volatility in 67 countries. Surprisingly, their findings suggested that stringent policy responses increase return volatility and that the effect is unrelated to the increase in confirmed COVID-19 cases and deaths. One implication of these findings is that, while government interventions may slow the spread of the pandemic, they may also increase volatility in financial markets, resulting in widespread sales of risky assets.

Though in previous health crises, the geographical location of the outbreak determined the relationship between the event and the financial market, globalization has brought economies closer together and strengthened the interdependence of financial markets around the world. The number of COVID-19 deaths in one country influences not only the performance of the local stock market but also the stock markets of other countries and commodities. Akhtaruzzaman et al. [40], for instance, found that listed firms across China and G7 countries experience a significant increase in conditional correlations between their stock returns as the pandemic's trajectory develops. China and Japan appeared to be net spillover transmitters, implying that financial contagion follows a pattern similar to virus infection. He et al. [41] suggested that the impact of COVID-19 on the European and US stock markets has a spillover effect on the Asian stock markets, particularly China. In addition, they also reported no evidence to suggest that the outbreak has had a negative impact on these countries' stock markets greater than the global average, as measured by the S&P Global 1200 index.

Conversely, some authors claim that the pandemic has accelerated the trend of de-globalization and de-dollarization [42]. Okorie and Lin [43] observe that the fractal contagion effect occurs only in the short run and that it disappears in the middle and long run for both stock market return and volatility. Similarly, Ali et al. [37] split the timeframe into three phases, beginning with casualties in China (which shows China as the epicenter of the epidemic), moving to the start of casualties in Europe (which shows Europe as the epicenter of the epidemic), and finally, when casualties began in the United States (the new epicenter). Unlike in previous pandemics, the levels of volatility in the Chinese market did not change significantly during all three phrases, indicating a lower level of global integration and early efforts by the authorities to stop the virus's spread.

When faced with the unknown upheaval of the coronavirus crisis, investors fear and avoid taking any risks, leading them to engage in irrational behavior. After the GFC, investors are more sensitive to asset losses. As a result, they are more likely to imitate the behavior and actions of other investors based on private information or public knowledge about their behavior. This irrational behavior can lead to significant mispricing and might create additional risks in financial markets. In finance, this kind of action is also known as herding behavior. Prior literature suggested that, under extreme market conditions induced by COVID-19, herding behavior is more pronounced for upside market movement, lower market trading volume, and lower market volatility [44]. Similar results are also found in the cryptocurrency market [45] and crude oil market [46].

Everyone has an incomplete view of the world. But we form a complete narrative and fill in the gaps. Our past experiences shape who we are today, as well as our decision-making process. Likewise, it has been suggested that prior exposure to similar events can influence risk aversion and investment decisions [47]. This notion is also true during the recent pandemic. Researchers found supporting evidence for the imprint theory in the behavioral bias of investors. Investors who have previously experienced such crises are more likely to react promptly than those without such experience or imprints. In addition, the timely attention and proactive responses to coronavirus situations of both individuals and governments are more prominent in nations with previous health outbreak experiences [48]. It was found that during the COVID-19, countries that had SARS 2003 saw less return and volatility spillover between stock markets [49]. This could imply that companies with past pandemic experience were found to make better decisions in the coronavirus outbreak. However, researchers also found that the experience of the current pandemic also impacted investors' decisions. Brands with names resembling aspects of the "coronavirus" began to experience abnormal losses and sustained periods of trading volatility [50]. Likewise, Yue et al. [51]'s findings showed that households that know someone infected with COVID-19 lose confidence in the economy and are more likely to change their risk behavior and become risk-averse.

In view of all that has been mentioned so far, it seems that the recent pandemic COVID-19 has exacerbated financial market volatility and the economic shock. Nevertheless, the impacts of COVID-19 are heterogenous across industries, time frames, governments, and the flow of information.

3. Alternative investment and COVID-19

As investors worry about the pandemic's economic consequences, the volatility has spiked, in some cases to levels last seen during the global financial crisis. Market liquidity has deteriorated significantly and investors embraced alternative investments in their portfolio for higher returns and shifting away from low-yield debt securities. As part of this trend, precious metals [52–55], bitcoin [52, 53], commodities [56, 57], and foreign exchange currencies [54, 58, 59] are all considered safe-haven assets in periods of financial crisis.

Precious metals, such as gold, silver, platinum, and palladium, are considered effective diversifiers against stock market returns in several developed and emerging economies. They can help investors build a portfolio that mitigates the downside market risk. Ji et al. [56] evaluated the safe-haven role of assets from December 2019 to March 2020. By observing the downside risk (i.e., the left-tail of the return distribution), they argued that gold has an irreplaceable role in preserving the value of investment during the recent crisis. Besides, many countries have adopted unconventional macroeconomic measures in response to the COVID-19's impact on the exchange rate and to prevent disruption in the long-term downward trend in exchange rate volatility. And gold serves as a safe-haven asset to protect against the risk of exchange rate depreciation [60].

Yet, with the unique characteristics of COVID-19, gold could not always act as a safe haven. This view is supported by Akhtaruzzaman et al. [52], who found that gold served as a safe-haven asset for stock markets only from December 31, 2019 to March 2020. However, from March 17 to April 24, 2020, gold failed to protect investor wealth and became a hedge instead. This interesting result confirms the findings reported by Cepoi [36], who observed the gold return has a nonlinear positive correlation with the stock markets, which intensifies during extreme bearish and bullish periods, indicating that gold does not behave as a safe-haven asset. Likewise, Cheema et al. [54] suggested that during the pandemic, investors might have lost trust in gold and preferred liquid and stable assets rather than gold. Taken together, it is unclear whether gold acts as a safe haven during the COVID-19 turmoil.

Some claim that cryptocurrency or digital currency is distinct from financial assets and that it might be viewed as a new form of virtual gold. It is frequently portrayed as a panacea capable of replacing financial institutions and protecting the global financial system from sovereign risk and vulnerability [61]. Furthermore, the cryptocurrency appears to be unrelated to stock market returns [61, 62] and exchange rate [63]. Therefore, they are an ideal asset to reduce financial risks during periods of crisis. During the COVID-19, some researchers suggested that cryptocurrencies, such as Bitcoin, could play an important role as a safe haven (for example see [64–66]). Goodell and Goutte [65] applied wavelet methods to daily data of COVID-19 deaths and Bitcoin prices from December 31, 2019 to April 29, 2020, demonstrating that the intensity of the COVID-19 crisis caused a rise in Bitcoin prices. Similarly, Caferra and Vidal-Tomás [66] suggested that, unlike traditional stock markets, cryptocurrencies only experienced a brief moment of financial panic during COVID-19 because of the lack of a link between digital currency and the actual economy. Bouri et al. [53] also found that bitcoin is the least reliant and has a competitive advantage over gold and other commodities.

Nonetheless, some researchers argue that cryptocurrencies, such as bitcoin and ethereum, only exhibit short-term safe-haven properties as well as high volatility [67]. Cryptocurrencies appeared as speculative assets and presented more systematic risk than investments in the stock markets during COVID-19 [50, 54]. Conlon and McGee's [68] finding suggested that, rather than acting as a safe haven, Bitcoin may instead increase portfolio downside risk relative to holding the S&P 500 alone. Yet, not all cryptocurrencies behave in the same manner. Goodell and Goutte [69] examine the role of COVID-19 in the paired co-movements of four cryptocurrencies and seven equity indices. They found that the co-movements between cryptocurrencies and equity indices gradually increased as the pandemic escalated. However, they also found that tether behaved differently from other cryptocurrencies. It moved negatively with equity markets both before and during the COVID-19 outbreak. One explanation for this result would be that the stablecoin tether has particular utility as a vehicle for liquidity, and one tether is supposed to be backed by one dollar. Hence, the properties of the tether are similar to those of fiat currency rather than digital currency. This finding is also consistent with Hasan et al. [70], who found Tether has emerged as a strong new safe haven during the pandemic.

In addition to gold and cryptocurrency, currencies and commodities can also potentially offer a safe-haven role in financial markets. Alali [58], or example, says that the Swiss franc is a good investment during a time when there is a lot of diseases. Similarly, Cheema et al. [54] also found the Swiss franc served as a strong safe haven during both the Global Financial Crisis of 2008 and the COVID-19 pandemic. Nevertheless, some studies suggest that cross-currency hedge strategies are likely to fail during this period. Umar and Gubareva [59] detected a positive relationship between the panic level, as measured by the Pavenpack Coronavirus Panic Index, and the dynamics of leading fiat currencies, such as the Euro, British pound, and Renminbi currencies.

The coronavirus has been labeled a pandemic; thus, its effects are expected to be seen throughout multiple countries, regions, and continents. To put it another way, it is likely to have an impact on worldwide demand and supply of products and services, particularly commodity prices. Ji et al. [56] show that soybean commodity futures remain robust as safe-haven assets during the current pandemic. There is also evidence of a positive relationship between commodity price returns and the global fear index (GFI), confirming that commodity returns increase as COVID-19 related fear rises [57]. In addition, Salisu et al. [57] also suggested that the commodity market offers better safe-haven properties than the stock market. Just like other financial assets, the properties of commodities are heterogeneous. Oil prices seem to have dropped a lot since the pandemic started, but food commodity futures like soybeans made money on average during the COVID-19 pandemic [56].

Considering all of this evidence, it seems that which asset is considered as a safe-haven asset during the COVID-19 turmoil. These inconsistent results are common findings in financial literature, suggesting that the relationship between financial assets is dynamic. Safe-haven assets can change over time [52, 70]. For example, gold may have been perceived as a safe haven during the early stages of the COVID-19, but as the pandemic progressed, gold has become a hedging asset instead.

4. Corporate in the midst of the pandemic

While some researchers have focused on how the financial markets react to the pandemic situation, other researchers have focused on firm actions and characteristics during the outbreak. As mentioned earlier, the pandemic would impact the corporate operation. Governments are shutting down huge sectors of their economies, ostensibly to stop the spread of infectious diseases but potentially putting the vast majority of businesses in danger of running out of cash. While the effect is temporary for some firms, many firms will experience it in the long term, leading to financial distress. Under these circumstances, corporate funding is becoming increasingly important to prevent liquidity issues from becoming solvency issues (e.g., [71–73]). There is evidence suggesting that during the early phase of the pandemic, firms were able to raise substantial amounts of external financing by drawing down lines of credit from banks and by accessing the public market [74]. Besides, the rating risk induced by the COVID-19 shock could impact the firms' decisions on the source of funding. Firms on the cusp of being downgraded to non-investment status (i.e., firms with a BBB rating) are likely to behave most aggressively to increase their cash-holding through their credit lines with banks, while AAA- to A-rated firms manage to maintain access to liquidity through the public capital market, that is, by issuing bonds and equity. In contrast to existing evidence on bond maturities in previous crises, firms chose to issue bonds with maturities that exceeded those of bonds issued before by the same firms, as well as the average maturities during normal times [75]. Considering all of this evidence, it seems that during the early part of the crisis, firms were able to raise funds quickly when the lockdowns began and cash flow shortfalls emerged. This suggests that lessons from previous crises have helped inform the policy response to the current pandemic.

A large number of published studies suggest that corporate governance could mitigate the negative effects of the health crisis (e.g., [76, 77]). Corporate governance practices are being tested and questioned in the aftermath of the COVID-19 outbreak. When it comes to meeting stakeholder expectations, businesses must make difficult decisions. In this situation, stakeholders would expect management to be quick to adapt and change the firm's policies and processes. The pandemic, with its heavy toll on both social and financial aspects, has highlighted the importance of societal responsibility. According to Albuquerque et al. [76], firms with high environmental and social (ES) scores experienced lower stock price declines than other firms. This finding highlights how ES policies can help build resilience in the face of the COVID-19 pandemic. Similarly, Broadstock et al. [77] discovered that firms with high ESG (environmental, social, and governance) performance have lower downside risk and are more resilient during turbulent times, particularly during the COVID-19-caused financial crisis. According to the evidence reviewed here, corporate governance may strengthen corporate immunity to the COVID-19 pandemic.

Despite the fact that the COVID-19 shock was global, not all firms were impacted in the same way, and they did not respond in the same way. Firms with a high level of financial flexibility can more easily fund a cash flow shortfall caused by the COVID-19 shock. Furthermore, the uncertainty caused by the COVID-19 pandemic increases stakeholders' demand for societal responsibility.

5. Conclusion

Pandemics are large-scale infectious disease outbreaks that can significantly increase morbidity and mortality over a wide geographic area. Furthermore, the recent COVID-19 virus outbreak demonstrates how infectious diseases spread quickly in open economies and can jeopardize a country's economic stability. The impact of the COVID-19 pandemic will be devastating to the global economy, as it has been in previous crises. In comparison to previous crises, COVID-19 differs from other economic shocks in many ways, including the causes and the public policy response. As the pandemic spread, governments around the world halted economic activity, and panic caused by the economic consequences and uncertainty resulted in a stock market crash. Because of technological advancements, news travels faster than ever before, causing more panic and fear of more bad news. The volatility caused by the crisis influenced many investors' perceptions and behaviors. For higher returns and portfolio diversification, investors turned to alternative investments such as commodities, cryptocurrencies, and foreign exchange. Nonetheless, as the pandemic spread, those alternative investments did not always result in lower downside risk and higher yield.

The pandemic has had an impact on businesses all over the world, but the damage has not been distributed evenly. Certain industries have suffered more than others, and many face an uncertain future. Firms would need to increase liquidity in their businesses as well as maintain good corporate governance in response to the crisis in order to create resilience during the pandemic outbreak.

Author details

Pattarake Sarajoti[1], Pattanaporn Chatjuthamard[2] and Suwongrat Papangkorn[3*]

1 Research Unit in Finance and Sustainability in Disruption Era, SASIN School of Management, Chulalongkorn University, Bangkok, Thailand

2 Center of Excellence in Management Research for Corporate Governance and Behavioral Finance, SASIN School of Management, Chulalongkorn University, Bangkok, Thailand

3 SASIN School of Management, Chulalongkorn University, Bangkok, Thailand

*Address all correspondence to: suwongrat.papangkorn@sasin.edu

References

[1] Baldwin R, Tomiura E. Thinking ahead about the trade impact of COVID-19. In: Baldwin R, di Mauro BW, editors. Economics in the Time of COVID-19. London: CEPR Press; 2020

[2] Goodell JW. COVID-19 and finance: Agendas for future research. Finance Research Letters. 2020;**35**:101512. DOI: 10.1016/j.frl.2020.101512

[3] Barro RJ, Ursúa JF, Weng J, Ursúa Dodge JF, Weng Ever Life J. The Coronavirus and the Great Influenza Pandemic: Lessons from the "Spanish Flu" for the Coronavirus's Potential Effects on Mortality and Economic Activity. Working Paper No.: 26866. Massachusetts: National Bureau of Economic Research; 2020. DOI: 10.3386/W26866

[4] MacKellar L. Pandemic influenza: A review. Population and Development Review. 2007;**33**(3):429-451. DOI: 10.1111/j.1728-4457.2007.00179.x

[5] Wong G. Has SARS infected the property market? Evidence from Hong Kong. Journal of Urban Economics. 2008;**63**(1):74-95. DOI: 10.1016/j.jue.2006.12.007

[6] Ichev R, Marinč M. Stock prices and geographic proximity of information: Evidence from the Ebola outbreak. International Review of Financial Analysis. 2018;**56**:153-166. DOI: 10.1016/J.IRFA.2017.12.004

[7] Chen MH, Jang SC, (Shawn), Kim WG. The impact of the SARS outbreak on Taiwanese hotel stock performance: An event-study approach. International Journal of Hospitality Management. 2007;**26**(1):200-212. DOI: 10.1016/J.IJHM.2005.11.004

[8] Donadelli M, Kizys R, Riedel M. Dangerous infectious diseases: Bad news for Main street, good news for wall street? Journal of Financial Markets. 2017;**35**:84-103. DOI: 10.1016/J.FINMAR.2016.12.003

[9] Zhang Z, Ma C, Hu H, Li H. Will infectious disease outbreaks cause a decline in investment of real sector firms? Evidence form 2003 SARS outbreak in China. Applied Economics. 2021;**53**(59):6820-6838. DOI: 10.1080/00036846.2021.1949431

[10] Houle JN, Collins JM, Schmeiser MD. Flu and finances: Influenza outbreaks and loan defaults in US cities, 2004-2012. American Journal of Public Health. 2015;**105**(9):e75-e80. DOI: 10.2105/AJPH.2015.302671

[11] Gong D, Jiang T, Lu L. Pandemic and bank lending: Evidence from the 2009 H1N1 pandemic. Finance Research Letters. 2021;**39**:101627. DOI: 10.1016/J.FRL.2020.101627

[12] del Giudice A, Paltrinieri A. The impact of the Arab spring and the Ebola outbreak on African equity mutual fund investor decisions. Research in International Business and Finance. 2017;**41**:600-612. DOI: 10.1016/J.RIBAF.2017.05.004

[13] Alfaro L, Chari A, Greenland AN, Schott PK. Aggregate and firm-level stock returns during pandemics, in real time. National Bureau of Economic Research. 2020:w26950

[14] Baker SR, Bloom N, Davis SJ, Kost K, Sammon M, Viratyosin T. The unprecedented stock market reaction to COVID-19. The Review of Asset Pricing Studies. 2020;**10**(4):742-758. DOI: 10.1093/rapstu/raaa008

[15] Jackwerth J. What Do index options teach us about COVID-19? The Review of Asset Pricing Studies. 2020;**10**(4):618-634. DOI: 10.1093/rapstu/raaa012

[16] Shehzad K, Xiaoxing L, Kazouz H. COVID-19's disasters are perilous than global financial crisis: A rumor or fact? Finance Research Letters. 2020;**36**:101669. DOI: 10.1016/J.FRL.2020.101669

[17] Leduc S, Liu Z. The Uncertainty Channel of the Coronavirus. Economic Letters, Federal Reserve Bank of San Francisco. 07 March 2020. pp. 1-5

[18] Schell D, Wang M, Huynh TLD. This time is indeed different: A study on global market reactions to public health crisis. Journal of Behavioral and Experimental Finance. 2020;**27**:100349. DOI: 10.1016/J.JBEF.2020.100349

[19] Al-Awadhi AM, Alsaifi K, Al-Awadhi A, Alhammadi S. Death and contagious infectious diseases: Impact of the COVID-19 virus on stock market returns. Journal of Behavioral and Experimental Finance. 2020;**27**:100326. DOI: 10.1016/j.jbef.2020.100326

[20] Ashraf BN. Stock markets' reaction to COVID-19: Cases or fatalities? Research in International Business and Finance. 2020;**54**:101249. DOI: 10.1016/j.ribaf.2020.101249

[21] Erdem O. Freedom and stock market performance during Covid-19 outbreak. Finance Research Letters. 2020;**36**:101671. DOI: 10.1016/j.frl.2020.101671

[22] Ramelli S, Wagner AF. Feverish stock Price reactions to COVID-19. The Review of Corporate Finance Studies. 2020;**9**(3):622-655. DOI: 10.1093/rcfs/cfaa012

[23] Zhang D, Hu M, Ji Q. Financial markets under the global pandemic of COVID-19. Finance Research Letters. 2020;**101528**:101528. DOI: 10.1016/j.frl.2020.101528

[24] Altig D, Baker S, Barrero JM, Bloom N, Bunn P, Chen S, et al. Economic uncertainty before and during the COVID-19 pandemic. Journal of Public Economics. 2020;**191**:104274. DOI: 10.1016/j.jpubeco.2020.104274

[25] Cheng I-H. Volatility markets underreacted to the early stages of the COVID-19 pandemic. The Review of Asset Pricing Studies. 2020;**10**:635-668. DOI: 10.1093/rapstu/raaa010

[26] Alan NS, Engle RF, Karagozoglu AK. Multi-regime Forecasting Model for the Impact of COVID-19 Pandemic on Volatility in Global Equity Markets. NYU Stern School of Business. 15 June 2020. DOI: 10.2139/ssrn.3646520

[27] Basuony MAK, Bouaddi M, Ali H, EmadEldeen R. The effect of COVID-19 pandemic on global stock markets: Return, volatility, and bad state probability dynamics. Journal of Public Affairs. 2021:e2761. DOI: 10.1002/pa.2761

[28] Mirza N, Naqvi B, Rahat B, Rizvi SKA. Price reaction, volatility timing and funds' performance during Covid-19. Finance Research Letters. 2020;**36**:101657. DOI: 10.1016/j.frl.2020.101657

[29] Chatjuthamard P, Jindahra P, Sarajoti P, Treepongkaruna S. The effect of COVID-19 on the global stock market. Accounting & Finance. 2021;**61**(3):4923-4953. DOI: 10.1111/acfi.12838

[30] Mazur M, Dang M, Vega M. COVID-19 and the march 2020 stock market crash. Evidence from S&P1500. Finance Research Letters. 2020;**38**:101690. DOI: 10.1016/j.frl.2020.101690

[31] Haroon O, Rizvi SAR. COVID-19: Media coverage and financial markets behavior—A sectoral inquiry. Journal of Behavioral and Experimental Finance. 2020;**27**:100343. DOI: 10.1016/J.JBEF.2020.100343

[32] Baig AS, Butt HA, Haroon O, Rizvi SAR. Deaths, panic, lockdowns and US equity markets: The case of COVID-19 pandemic. Finance Research Letters. 2021;**38**:101701. DOI: 10.1016/J.FRL.2020.101701

[33] Narayan PK. Oil price news and COVID-19—Is there any connection? Energy Research Letters. 2020;**1**(1):13176

[34] Sahoo PK. COVID-19 pandemic and cryptocurrency markets: An empirical analysis from a linear and nonlinear causal relationship. Studies in Economics and Finance. 2021;**38**(2):454-468. DOI: 10.1108/SEF-09-2020-0385

[35] Chatterjee U, French JJ. A note on tweeting and equity markets before and during the Covid-19 pandemic. Finance Research Letters. 2021;**102224**:17. DOI: 10.1016/J.FRL.2021.102224

[36] Cepoi C-O. Asymmetric dependence between stock market returns and news during COVID-19 financial turmoil. Finance research letters. 2020;**36**:101658. DOI: 10.1016/j.frl.2020.101658

[37] Ali M, Alam N, Rizvi SAR. Coronavirus (COVID-19) — An epidemic or pandemic for financial markets. Journal of Behavioral and Experimental Finance. 2020;**27**:100341. DOI: 10.1016/J.JBEF.2020.100341

[38] Narayan PK, Phan DHB, Liu G. COVID-19 lockdowns, stimulus packages, travel bans, and stock returns. Finance Research Letters. 2021;**38**:101732. DOI: 10.1016/J.FRL.2020.101732

[39] Zaremba A, Kizys R, Aharon DY, Demir E. Infected markets: Novel coronavirus, government interventions, and stock return volatility around the globe. Finance Research Letters. 2020;**35**:101597. DOI: 10.1016/j.frl.2020.101597

[40] Akhtaruzzaman M, Boubaker S, Sensoy A. Financial contagion during COVID–19 crisis. Finance Research Letters. 2020;**101604**:101604. DOI: 10.1016/j.frl.2020.101604

[41] He Q, Liu J, Wang S, Yu J. The impact of COVID-19 on stock markets. Economic and Political Studies. 2020;**8**(3):275-288. DOI: 10.1080/20954816.2020.1757570

[42] Tokic D. Long-term consequences of the 2020 coronavirus pandemics: Historical global-macro context. Journal of Corporate Accounting & Finance. 2020;**31**(3):9-14. DOI: 10.1002/jcaf.22448

[43] Okorie DI, Lin B. Stock markets and the COVID-19 fractal contagion effects. Finance Research Letters. 2020;**101640**:101640. DOI: 10.1016/j.frl.2020.101640

[44] Wu G, Yang B, Zhao N. Herding behavior in Chinese stock markets during COVID-19. Emerging Markets Finance and Trade. 2020;**56**(15):3578-3587. DOI: 10.1080/1540496X.2020.1855138

[45] Mandaci PE, Cagli EC. Herding intensity and volatility in cryptocurrency markets during the COVID-19. Finance Research Letters. 2021:102382. DOI: 10.1016/J.FRL.2021.102382

[46] Chang CL, McAleer M, Wang YA. Herding behaviour in energy stock markets during the global financial crisis, SARS, and ongoing COVID-19*. Renewable and Sustainable Energy

Reviews. 2020;**134**:110349. DOI: 10.1016/J.RSER.2020.110349

[47] Wang M, Keller C, Siegrist M. The less you know, the more you are afraid of—A survey on risk perceptions of investment products. Journal of Behavioral Finance. 2011;**12**(1):9-19. DOI: 10.1080/15427560.2011.548760

[48] Ru H, Yang E, Zou K. Combating the COVID-19 pandemic: The role of the SARS. Imprint. 2021;**67**(9):5606-5615. DOI: 10.1287/MNSC.2021.4015

[49] Bissoondoyal-Bheenick E, Do H, Hu X, Zhong A. Learning from SARS: Return and volatility connectedness in COVID-19. Finance Research Letters. 2021;**41**:101796. DOI: 10.1016/J. FRL.2020.101796

[50] Corbet S, Hou Y, Hu Y, Lucey B, Oxley L. Aye Corona! The contagion effects of being named Corona during the COVID-19 pandemic. Finance Research Letters. 2021;**38**:101591. DOI: 10.1016/J.FRL.2020.101591

[51] Yue P, Gizem Korkmaz A, Zhou H. Household financial decision making amidst the COVID-19 pandemic. Emerging Markets Finance and Trade. 2020;**56**(10):2363-2377. DOI: 10.1080/ 1540496X.2020.1784717

[52] Akhtaruzzaman M, Boubaker S, Lucey BM, Sensoy A. Is gold a hedge or a safe-haven asset in the COVID–19 crisis? Economic Modelling. 2021;**102**:105588. DOI: 10.1016/J.ECONMOD.2021.105588

[53] Bouri E, Shahzad SJH, Roubaud D, Kristoufek L, Lucey B. Bitcoin, gold, and commodities as safe havens for stocks: New insight through wavelet analysis. The Quarterly Review of Economics and Finance. 2020;**77**:156-164. DOI: 10.1016/J. QREF.2020.03.004

[54] Cheema MA, Faff RW, Szulczyk K. The 2008 global financial crisis and COVID-19 pandemic: How safe are the safe haven assets? [homepage on the internet]. SSRN Electronic Journal. Elsevier BV. 2021:42. DOI: 10.2139/ SSRN.3590015

[55] Gürgün G, Ünalmiş I. Is gold a safe haven against equity market investment in emerging and developing countries? Finance Research Letters. 2014;**11**(4):341-348. DOI: 10.1016/J. FRL.2014.07.003

[56] Ji Q, Zhang D, Zhao Y. Searching for safe-haven assets during the COVID-19 pandemic. International Review of Financial Analysis. 2020;**71**:101526. DOI: 10.1016/J.IRFA.2020.101526

[57] Salisu AA, Akanni L, Raheem I. The COVID-19 global fear index and the predictability of commodity price returns. Journal of Behavioral and Experimental Finance. 2020;**27**:100383. DOI: 10.1016/J.JBEF.2020.100383

[58] AlAli MS. Safe haven assets: Are they still safe during Covid-19 pandemic period? European Journal of Economic and Financial Research. 2020;**4**(1):91-98. DOI: 10.5281/zenodo.3777255

[59] Umar Z, Gubareva M. A time–frequency analysis of the impact of the Covid-19 induced panic on the volatility of currency and cryptocurrency markets. Journal of Behavioral and Experimental Finance. 2020;**28**:100404. DOI: 10.1016/J. JBEF.2020.100404

[60] Tanin TI, Sarker A, Brooks R. Do currency exchange rates impact gold prices? New evidence from the ongoing COVID-19 period. International Review of Financial Analysis. 2021;**77**:101868. DOI: 10.1016/J.IRFA.2021.101868

[61] Bouri E, Molnár P, Azzi G, Roubaud D, Hagfors LI. On the hedge

and safe haven properties of bitcoin: Is it really more than a diversifier? Finance Research Letters. 2017;**20**:192-198. DOI: 10.1016/J.FRL.2016.09.025

[62] Baur DG, Hong KH, Lee AD. Bitcoin: Medium of exchange or speculative assets? Journal of International Financial Markets, Institutions and Money. 2018;**54**:177-189. DOI: 10.1016/J.INTFIN.2017.12.004

[63] Baur DG, Dimpfl T, Kuck K. Bitcoin, gold and the US dollar – A replication and extension. Finance Research Letters. 2018;**25**:103-110. DOI: 10.1016/J.FRL.2017.10.012

[64] Corbet S, Hou Y, (Greg), Hu Y, Larkin C, Oxley L. Any port in a storm: Cryptocurrency safe-havens during the COVID-19 pandemic. Economics Letters. 2020;**194**:109377. DOI: 10.1016/J.ECONLET.2020.109377

[65] Goodell JW, Goutte S. Co-movement of COVID-19 and bitcoin: Evidence from wavelet coherence analysis. Finance Research Letters. 2021;**38**:101625. DOI: 10.1016/J.FRL.2020.101625

[66] Caferra R, Vidal-Tomás D. Who raised from the abyss? A comparison between cryptocurrency and stock market dynamics during the COVID-19 pandemic. Finance Research Letters. 2021;**43**:101954. DOI: 10.1016/J.FRL.2021.101954

[67] Mariana CD, Ekaputra IA, Husodo ZA. Are bitcoin and Ethereum safe-havens for stocks during the COVID-19 pandemic? Finance Research Letters. 2021;**38**:101798. DOI: 10.1016/J.FRL.2020.101798

[68] Conlon T, McGee R. Safe haven or risky hazard? Bitcoin during the Covid-19 bear market. Finance Research Letters. 2020;**35**:101607. DOI: 10.1016/J.FRL.2020.101607

[69] Goodell JW, Goutte S. Diversifying equity with cryptocurrencies during COVID-19. International Review of Financial Analysis. 2021;**76**:101781. DOI: 10.1016/J.IRFA.2021.101781

[70] Hasan MB, Hassan MK, Rashid MM, Alhenawi Y. Are safe haven assets really safe during the 2008 global financial crisis and COVID-19 pandemic? Global Finance Journal. 2021;**50**:100668. DOI: 10.1016/J.GFJ.2021.100668

[71] Liu Y, Qiu B, Wang T. Debt rollover risk, credit default swap spread and stock returns: Evidence from the COVID-19 crisis. Journal of Financial Stability. 2021;**53**:100855. DOI: 10.1016/J.JFS.2021.100855

[72] Ding W, Levine R, Lin C, Xie W. Corporate immunity to the COVID-19 pandemic. National Bureau of Economic Research. 2020;**141**:802-830

[73] Fahlenbrach R, Rageth K, Stulz RM. How Valuable Is Financial Flexibility when Revenue Stops? Evidence from the COVID-19 Crisis. The Review of Financial Studies. 2021;**34**(11):5474-5521. DOI: 10.1093/rfs/hhaa134

[74] Acharya V, v., Steffen S. The risk of being a fallen angel and the corporate dash for cash in the midst of COVID. The Review of Corporate Finance Studies. 2020;**9**(3):430-471. DOI: 10.1093/RCFS/CFAA013

[75] Halling M, Yu J, Zechner J. How did COVID-19 affect firms' access to public capital markets? The Review of Corporate Finance Studies. 2020;**9**(3):501-533. DOI: 10.1093/RCFS/CFAA008

[76] Albuquerque R, Koskinen Y, Yang S, Zhang C. Resiliency of environmental

and social stocks: An analysis of the exogenous COVID-19 market crash. The Review of Corporate Finance Studies. 2020;**9**(3):593-621. DOI: 10.1093/rcfs/cfaa011

[77] Broadstock DC, Chan K, Cheng LTW, Wang X. The role of ESG performance during times of financial crisis: Evidence from COVID-19 in China. Finance Research Letters. 2021;**38**:101716. DOI: 10.1016/J.FRL.2020.101716

Section 6

Financial Performance Measures

Chapter 7

Looking beyond the Numbers: Determinants of Financial Performance of Portuguese Wine Firms

Carmem Leal, Bernando Cardoso, Rogério Bessa, José Vale, Rúben Nunes and Rui Silva

Abstract

This chapter focuses on the analysis of the determinants of financial performance (FP) of Portuguese wine firms. Unbalanced panel data were analyzed using fixed-effects regression. The sample consisted of 386 Portuguese wine firms, for the period 2014–2017. FP is the dependent variable of this study, having been measured through return on assets (ROA) using as explanatory variables debt-to-equity, net working capital, current ratio, days payable out-standing (DPO), and days receivables outstanding (DRO). The results show: (1) DRO, debt-to-equity and net working capital are the variables that best explain the FP measured by ROA; (2) Debt-to-equity and DRO have a negative relationship with ROA, whereas current ratio, working capital, and DPO have a positive relationship with profitability measured by ROA. The findings suggest that there are other qualitative elements in the wine sector, beyond numbers, that support the explanation of its performance. The way this industry is heavily controlled affects its success. Furthermore, factors such as the style of corporate governance and the lengthy production cycle can have a significant impact on its FP. it is strongly advised that qualitative approaches be employed in conjunction with quantitative research in future studies to obtain the most comprehensive and accurate results.

Keywords: financial performance, wine firms, liquidity, profitability, panel data, R software

1. Introduction

Winemaking is one of the most representative economic activities in a number of countries, owing to the wide range of fine products available and the convergence of producers' know-how, craftsmanship, and traditions.

The wine industry has been studied from a variety of perspectives. In recent years, the culture of quality wine has been bolstered by significant investments made by both large corporations and medium-and-small-sized businesses. This study focuses on the factors that influence winemakers' economic and financial performance.

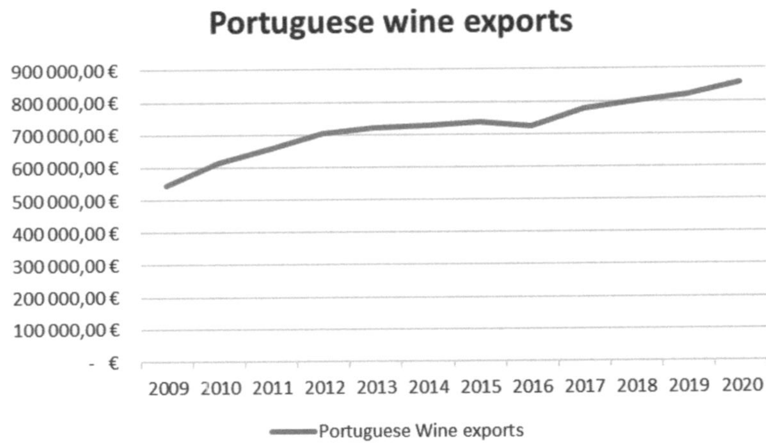

Figure 1.
Evolution of Portuguese wine exports from 2009 to 2020. Source: Instituto do Vinho e da Vinha, in *https://www.ivv.gov.pt/np4/9865.html.*

The evolution of the wine firm's level of exports in Portugal can be used to assess its importance. As shown in **Figure 1**, the value of exports in thousands of euros nearly doubled from 2009 to 2020.

In 2019, the overall value of exported food commodities will be around 7.4 million euros, with wine exports accounting for roughly 15% of the total [1]. These figures alone can indicate the importance of this industry for Portugal, in addition to the quality of the products and their international renown. As a result, it appeared appropriate to investigate this sector's financial performance.

Over the last four decades, little attention has been paid to the area of short-term finance, specifically working capital management (WCM). This can happen for a number of reasons, the first of which is that decisions about working capital are made on a daily basis. As a result, their individual impact is negligible. Second, unlike capital investment decisions, these routine decisions are reversible over time. However, many research studies, such as see Refs. [1, 2], have shown that WCM has a significant impact on a firm's profitability. Talha et al. [3] observed that aggressive liquidity management improves operating performance and is typically associated with higher corporate values.

The economic recovery has increased managers' awareness of short-term financial management and associated flows. Firms were forced to manage their short-term financing policies more efficiently during a recession and with a decrease in investment strength on the part of the banking sector.

As a result, issues concerning working capital management have become as important as capital structure, financial autonomy, and liabilities. This paradigm shift was accelerated by the economic downturn, during which efficient working capital management contributes exponentially to increased business performance [1].

Not only in the context of crisis but also on a daily basis, the possibility of acquiring a level of debt that might compromise shareholders' wealth is a very real problem. Thus, it is up to managers to align the financial structure with the organization's resources to ensure corporate sustainability, always safeguarding the obligations of the commitments assumed.

Financial management and short-term decision-making must, therefore, be understood as important tools for medium and long-term business objectives that can guarantee them a successive improvement of processes and, consequently, an efficient business.

The efficient allocation of resources allows the increase of business gains, but only when there is continuous fulfillment of obligations toward the others. Thus, to ensure this financial balance, the proper management of short-term resources using the analysis of ratios is one of the main factors for maintaining the organization's health [2].

One of the main objectives of short-term management is to ensure the existence of liquidity in firms since this is one of the most important assumptions for organizational success. Without efficient liquidity management, the guarantee of compliance with business obligations can be compromised due to a lack of cash, which can enhance decision-making that entails an increased risk for the company's sustainability.

Short-term management is critical for the wine sector and allows the guarantee of business continuity in a sector where the competition is fierce.

The wine sector is vulnerable to the costs of raw materials and external supplies and services that predominate in frequency during a production cycle, given the activities that will attract income. In this way, it is necessary to understand how short-term management can contribute to the maintenance of good yields, such as those related to a firm's assets.

The main objective of this investigation is to understand the impact of liquidity measures on the financial performance of wine firms. Thus, the relationship between ROA, days payable outstanding (DPO), days receivables outstanding (DRO), net working capital (NWC), debt-to-equity ratio, and current ratio (CR) will be analyzed. The goals of this research are to determine whether the DRO and debt-to-equity ratio have a negative relationship with the ROA and whether this has a significant relationship with the indicators of DPO, working capital, and current ratio. The current study will be conducted for a sample of 303 wine firms over a four-year period. The remainder of this study is organized as follows. Section 2 reviews the related literature and develops our hypotheses. Section 3 explains how we measure our key variables and specifies the empirical model used for hypothesis testing. Section 4 describes our data and summary statistics. Section 5 discusses our main empirical findings and reports the results of our robustness checks, Section 6 concludes and sets out some final reflections.

2. Literature review and hypothesis development

2.1 Liquidity and working capital

Liquidity represents the ability of an asset to convert to cash, and it is regarded as a precondition to ensure that firms are able to meet their short-term obligations [3, 4].

The current ratio is used as a liquidity criterion and measures the capacity of firms to meet their current obligations, typically due in 1 year. Excessive liquidity indicates accumulated idle funds, and inadequate liquidity not only adversely affects the creditworthiness of the firm but also interrupts the production process and hampers its earning capacity to a great extent. Keeping this indicator at an optimum level implies ensuring an adequate level of current assets, which must be above that of short-term liabilities [5].

Following this reasoning, we can anticipate that an increase in the current liquidity will lead to an increase in profitability as some literature has proved [6–9]. However, a high level of this indicator can be a sign of over liquidity, with possible adverse effects on the profitability as is indicated by research findings of [10–13].

In a study conducted in the Republic of Serbia, the authors analyzed the impact of traditional liquidity indicators on the profitability in the meat processing industry using data from official financial reports of the firms for the period from 2016 to 2019 and concluded that liquidity has no effects on profitability of those firms [14]. Similar results were obtained by Pervan and Višić in the Croatian manufacturing industry for the period from 2002 to 2010 [15].

As evidence, there is no consensus on the existence and quality of the relationship between liquidity and profitability. Thus, the first hypothesis of this study can be stated as follows:

Hypothesis 1: There is a possible impact of liquidity on the profitability of Portuguese wine firms.

Working capital (WC) is an approach to improving a company's liquidity, profitability, and value [4, 16]. Working capital management provides enough cash to meet the short-term obligations and operating costs of a firm [17, 18], and its main purpose is to free up capital that has been locked up in day-to-day operations to boost liquidity. Even for companies with promising long-term prospects, working capital integrates short-term financial management with strategic decisions, impacting profitability, risk, and so value [19]. Academicians, managers, and policymakers have recognized the importance of effective WCM in a firm's survival in the aftermath of the global financial crisis [20].

"WC can be viewed as a statically, as a 'stock' value, or dynamically as a 'flow' value" [4]. In the first case, WC is defined as a company's current assets minus its current liabilities and is referred to as net working capital in this scenario. In the latter case, working capital requirements are inextricably linked to the process of earning and spending money, and they are a part of the cycle of activities that this process entails.

The most common measure of working capital management is the cash conversion cycle (CCC) [21, 22]. CCC is defined as the time lag between the collection of revenue from the sales of finished goods or services and the payment to the suppliers for the purchase of raw materials. The cash conversion cycle comprises of days receivables outstanding (DRO), days inventory outstanding (DIO), and days payable outstanding (DPO). A shorter CCC could be driven by a shorter DRO, a shorter DIO, or a longer DPO [23, 24]. The aim is to reduce the length of the CCC to a reasonable minimum, the shorter the CCC, the lower the capital requirements, improving the firm's profitability [16, 25].

The relationship between firm profitability and WCM has become exceedingly popular among academics [26, 27].

Despite major variances in working capital practices throughout businesses and even within industries over time, there is widespread agreement on the negative association between shorter DRO and DIO, and hence shorter CCC, and greater profitability [7, 13, 25, 28, 29]. The role of DPO in WCM is unclear and unexplored. In empirical studies, DPO is often negatively correlated to profitability [10]. Since the negative effect was also sometimes found to be insignificant, this relation remains unclear. In this regard, we formally state our second and third hypotheses as follows:

Hypothesis 2.1: The DRO is negatively related to the profitability of Portuguese wine firms.

Hypothesis 2.2: The DPO is related to the profitability of Portuguese wine firms.

Net working capital (NWC) is a measure of a firm's liquidity that is intended to be positive since it is defined as the difference between a firm's current assets and current liabilities [10, 30]. NWC is predicted to have a favorable impact on a company's profitability; nevertheless, the importance of NWC in a specific company is decided by macroeconomic conditions, which have a substantial impact on the company's investments and financing. Managing NWC effectively means maximizing shareholder profit while minimizing the risk of a firm's failure [13]. There is an enormous amount of studies about the possible relationship between NWC and profitability, but there is no consensus. A significant number of studies suggest the existence of a negative impact of working capital management on a company's profitability [7, 8, 10, 13, 25, 28, 31], supporting the premise that an aggressive strategy of WCM positively influences a company's profitability. Nonetheless, the results of some studies show otherwise [11, 32–34]. These authors point out the positive impact of WCM on companies' profitability and success, thus supporting a conservative strategy (e.g., positive impact of NWC). These discrepancies could be attributed to the inconsistency and volatility of economic (and other) conditions in the various countries and environments where the studies were conducted, the analysis of various industries, differences in the distribution of company types within samples, different methods and approaches used in the analysis, and so on [11]. This leads to the following hypothesis:

Hypothesis 3: There is a possible impact of NWC on the profitability of Portuguese wine firms.

2.2 Leverage and profitability

Many empirical researches have been conducted on the relationship between leverage and profitability; nevertheless, the results of these investigations are inconclusive. This indicates that the impact of leverage on performance is greatly dependent on the circumstances, and theories such as pecking order, capital structure, and agency theory can help explain the discrepancies [35].

Various studies in developed countries such as the United States, France, Belgium, the United Kingdom, Italy, and Germany demonstrate a positive association between debt and profitability [36–38]. Others, on the other hand, show that a company's leverage is inversely associated with its profitability, suggesting that a larger debt ratio leads to lower profitability [39–41]. There are also authors who argue that there is no connection between the two concepts [42].

In general, more evidence in developing countries supports the concept that leverage and profitability are negatively linked than the other way around [43–45]. Other research shows mixed or nonlinear outcomes when it comes to the impact of financial leverage on performance [46, 47]. Following existing literature, we present the fourth hypothesis:

Hypothesis 4: There is a possible impact of leverage on the profitability of Portuguese wine firms.

3. Research methodology

3.1 Data and sample selection

The sample of the study is composed of 412 wine firms operating in Portugal from 2014 to 2017. After eliminating the firms with missing values, insufficient and extreme data, an unbalanced panel 9,264 firms firm-year observations on 386 firms is finally obtained.

Because of its benefits, the panel data approach is used. First, the panel data technique may account for unobservable heterogeneity. Second, it removes or minimizes estimation bias and data multicollinearity concerns [48].

R software was used to collect and analyze panel data. The ideal starting point for the analysis was to generate summary descriptive statistics to provide an overview of the panel data set under investigation. The sample minimum, sample maximum, mean, and standard deviation were thus the basic summary statistics. The intensity and direction of the relationship between the study variables were determined using correlation analysis. Univariate plotting was done before estimating panel data models. Because panel or time series stochastic features might be trending, random walk (drift), or both trend and drift, this aided in displaying data and summarizing its distribution [49]. Finally, diagnostic tests were performed, and the hypotheses were tested using a panel regression analysis approach.

3.2 Study variables

In this study accounting metrics were given primacy over market measures, following previous literature, while evaluating the wine business, which has extremely distinctive characteristics [50, 51]. Inspired from these arguments, as dependent variables in this study, return on assets (ROA) was used as a proxy for firm profitability in line with some of the prior studies [14, 39, 50, 51]. Please see **Table 1** for the variable definition.

3.3 Data analyses

The main justification for using a fixed-effects panel model is to eliminate the influence of serially correlated errors [52]. The main difference between the fixed-effects and the random-effects models is that the variation between entities is believed to be random and uncorrelated with the independent variables [53]. The advantage of fixed- and random-effects models over the OLS method is that they allow researchers to adjust for all stable characteristics of each company included in the sample over the study period.

After obtaining the results of the OLS, fixed-effects, and random-effects, the F-test is used to select between the fixed-effects and the OLS. Furthermore, the Lagrange Multiplier (LM) test of Breusch and Pagan [54] is used in the selection of the random-effects and the OLS. Because the F test is significant in all of the models, it reveals that the Fixed-effects method outperforms the OLS method. The Hausman (1978) test is

	Formula
DSO (days)	$\frac{Accounts\ Receivable}{Total\ Credit\ Sales} x365$
DPO (days)	$\frac{Accounts\ payable}{Cost\ of\ Goods\ sold} x365$
Current ratio	$\frac{Current\ Assets}{Current\ Liabilities}$
Debt to equity ratio (%)	$\frac{Total\ Liabilities}{Total\ Shareholders'\ Equity}$
Net working capital (€)	Total Current Assets – Total Current Liabilities
Return on assets (€)	$\frac{Net\ income}{Total\ Assets}$

Table 1.
Variables definition.

then used to determine whether the fixed-effects or random-effects method is superior. Because the Hausman test is significant, the results favor the fixed-effects method [55].

The model tested was:

$$ROA_{t,i} = \alpha_t + \beta_1 DRO_{i,t} + \beta_2 DPO_{i,t} + \beta_3 DTE_{i,t} + \beta_4 CR_{i,t} + \beta_5 NWC_{i,t} + \eta_i \quad (1)$$

4. Empirical results

Table 2 reports summary statistics (mean) for the main variables used in this study. The mean for ROA is 3% in 2014 and 4.75% in 2017. The mean days receivable outstanding is 163 in 2014 going down to 158 days in 2017. The mean days payable outstanding is 231 in 2014 going up to 246 days in 2017. The mean of debt-to-equity and current ratio are approximately 0.98 and 7, respectively, going down in 2017 to 0.81 and 5,39, respectively. Finally, the net working capital presents in 2014 the mean value of 1,448,068 €, going up to 1,802,862 € in 2017.

	N	2014	2015	2016	2017
ROA %	386	3.07	3.84	3.83	4.75
DRO (days)	386	163	156	166	158
DPO (days)	386	231	393	293	246
Debt-to-equity	386	0.98	0.92	0.90	0.81
Current ratio	386	7.05	4.72	5.90	5.39
Net working capital	386	1,448,068 €	1,641,146 €	1,759,999 €	1,802,862 €
Return on Assets (€)	386	0,04 €	0,05 €	0,04 €	0,05 €

Table 2.
Wine firms – descriptive statistics (mean).

ROAt,i = αt + β1DSOi,t + β2DPOi,t + β3DTEi,t + β4CRi,t + β5NWCi,t + ηi			
Independent variables	**β**	***Std. Error***	***p-value***
DRO	−7.7958e−05***	1.8959e−05	˂0.01
DPO	3.9019e−06	8.6471e−06	0.65
Debt to equity (DTE)	−1.1657e−04***	4.6579e−05	0.01
Current ratio (CR)	1.9768e−04	1.9845e−04	0.32
Net working capital (NWC)	2.4266e−09**	1.3339e−09	0.04
F test for individual effects			
F = 5,2814	**df1 = 301**	**df2 = 878**	**p-value ˂ 2.2e-16**
alternative hypothesis: significant effects			

R^2 = 0.0935.
***Represents significance at 5% level.*
****Represents significance at 1% level.*

Table 3.
Model estimation – (fixed effects-dependent variable – ROA).

All these values evolve in a positive direction, as well as expected according to theory.

Table 3 presents the results obtained. The regression coefficients show that DRO (−7.7958e-05) and DTE (−1.1657e-04) have a negative influence on ROA and are significant at the 1% level. As can be seen in **Table 2**, both DPO (3.9019e-06) and CR (1.9768e-04) have a positive influence on ROA. However, the positive influence of DPO and CR on ROA is not statistically significant. Finally, NWC (2.4266e-09) has a statistically significant positive influence on ROA and is significant at the 5% level. Apart from these results, the F value in fixed-effects is highly significant, meaning that the model has appropriate fit measures (**Table 2**).

The computed R^2 was approximately 10% showing that there are some other variables that can explain the profitability of Portuguese wine firms. The liquidity measures can explain 10% of their ROA during the period of 2014 to 2017.

5. Discussion

The higher the ROA, the more efficient the firm's performance in relation to its assets. The amount of efficiency in a firm's performance might be an alternative in encouraging stockholders to invest in a firm. According to the results presented the Portuguese wine firms show an upward in terms of ROA for the period analyzed.

When it comes to the independent variables, it is clear that DRO has a negative and considerable impact on ROA. This suggests that the firms with the longest wait time for payment from their customers are the least profitable. To properly manage their CCC, they should work to close this gap. The outcome is comparable to the findings of [7, 13, 25] which, consequently, leads to the acceptance of hypothesis 2.1. Following the findings reported by [39, 56], the coefficient for accounts payable management, measured with DPO, is positive but not significant, giving evidence to reject hypothesis 2.2. The work of Yazdanfar and Öhman [38] that looked at the evolution of working capital management and its impact on profitability and shareholder value of 115 German companies, discovered that DPO has a positive but not significant association with ROA and they have discussed the importance of DPO has a positive sign [56], on the purpose of CCC theory, and not negative as some others authors defend [7, 13, 25, 28, 31]. Moodley et al. [56] proposed another dependent variable in place of ROA to capture the true effects of CCC and follow the theory.

The results also show that the Portuguese wine firms have high levels of debt (but in a downward trend) and the relationship of debt-to-equity on ROA is significantly negative, implying that a higher debt ratio results in lower profitability, as previously found by Čavlin et al.; Dawar; and Balakrishnan and Fox [14, 43, 45], leading to the acceptance of hypothesis 4. The result obtained contradicts the works of Wald; Margaritis and Psillaki; Yazdanfar and Öhman [36–38] that stated that developed countries tend to find a positive relationship between debt and profitability. Despite its status as a developed country, Portugal's industry is more comparable to that of developing countries, where managers use debt to pay the previous debt (even having idle funds) relying heavily on short-term debt, demonstrating no strategy for correct debt use, financing, for example, long-term investments recurring to short-term debt.

The liquidity, measured by the current ratio, was found positively linked to profitability, but the influence was not significant. The estimated sign is consistent with past research, but the model revealed that liquidity had no impact on the profitability of Portuguese wine firms, as Čavlin et al. [14] presented in their study about meat processing activity in the Republic of Serbia. In this sense, it is not possible to accept the first hypothesis of this study.

In terms of NTW's potential impact on ROA, the calculated model revealed a positive and significant effect, verifying our third hypothesis. This result follows [11, 31–33] showing a conservative approach to working capital management by Portuguese wine firms. They appear to prefer longer CCC cycles to pursue an aggressive strategy.

6. Conclusion, implications, and limitations

Winemaking is one of the most representative economic activities in several countries as a result of the variety of fine products and the convergence of know-how, craftsmanship, and traditions of producers and Portugal is a respected country of producers with excellent and well-known products.

The wine sector has been studied from various aspects. In recent years, the culture of quality wine has been enhanced also through sizeable investments by both large corporations and medium- and small-sized companies.

However, the most relevant research databases (Web of Science, Scopus, Google Scholars, and EBSCO) indicate a scarcity of research on the economic and financial performance of these types of businesses.

Taking this into account, it is feasible to conclude that this study contributes to the literature on financial analysis of the wine business by addressing a gap in the literature on financial indicators of liquidity and performance.

In this sense, the purpose of this research is to demonstrate the importance of short-term financial indicators on the profitability of Portuguese wine firms.

The profit position of a firm is influenced by numerous factors and in this study, the authors wanted to additionally explore the impact of some liquidity indicators in the Portuguese wine firms in the period 2014–2017.

It was found that an increase in the level of net working capital increases profitability of the company and leverage was negatively related to ROA. Firms policies promoting the decrease of DRO result in increased profitability. In this sense, the guarantee of low levels of general indebtedness helps wine firms increase their profitability.

The above speaks in favor of a conservative strategy of working capital management of Portuguese wine firms and this position is in line with the type of firms. Mostly of Portuguese wine firms are family firms and their management strategy tends to be more conservative than non-family firms [51].

The estimation model emphasized that the profitability of Portuguese wine firms, measured by ROA, is less explained by liquidity variables than by other qualitative variables, such as management style (whereas the family is on the Board, or not) and financing policies.

The poor adjustment might be also associated with the specificities of the wine sector, the fact that it is a regulated market, which is largely geared toward exports (variable not included in the estimation model), usually with more traditional or less professional management and which have a specific production cycle (with long periods of the operating cycle).

In terms of practical implications, we were able to show that, on average, the Portuguese wine sector manages its cash cycle conservatively, likely because it is a family-run business with few naturally aggressive managers or risk-takers, and that, based on the findings, they are not properly concerned with liquidity measures in their daily management. It is critical to enlarge and update this sample to more firmly establish these conclusions.

To better explain the performance of these organizations, and overcome some limitations, future developments must include:

- An updated sample, divided into family firms and non-family firms, with internationalization level included;
- Inclusion of other dependent variables, such as EBITDA or ROE, as well as independent variables, such as firm size;
- A comparative analysis of firms from other wine-producing countries and.
- Inclusion of qualitative variables such as governance and/or reward systems.

Acknowledgements

This work is supported by national funds, through the FCT – Portuguese Foundation for Science and Technology under the project UIDB/04011/2020.

Author details

Carmem Leal[1]*, Bernando Cardoso[2], Rogério Bessa[2], José Vale[3], Rúben Nunes[2] and Rui Silva[1]

1 CETRAD—University of Trás-os-Montes e Alto Douro, Vila Real, Portugal

2 University of Trás-os-Montes e Alto Douro, Vila Real, Portugal

3 CEOS.PP, Polytechnic Institute of Porto, Porto, Portugal

*Address all correspondence to: cleal@utad.pt

References

[1] FMMS. Exportações de bens e serviços: total e por produto [Internet]. Paris; 2021. Available from: https://www.pordata.pt/Portugal/Exportações+de+bens+e+serviços+total+e+por+produto+(base+2016)-2291-184657

[2] Liesiö J, Andelmin J, Salo A. Efficient allocation of resources to a portfolio of decision making units. European Journal of Operational Research. 2020;**286**(2): 619-636

[3] Talha M, Christopher SB, Kamalavalli AL. Sensitivity of profitability to working capital management: A study of Indian corporate hospitals. International Journal of Managerial and Financial Accounting. 2010;**2**(3):213-227

[4] Pass LC, Pike HR. An overview of working capital management and corporate financing. Managerial Finance. 1984;**10**(3):1-11

[5] Kestens K, Van Cauwenberge P, Vander BH. Trade credit and company performance during the 2008 financial crisis. Account &Finance. 2012;**52**(4): 1125-1151

[6] Baghiyan F. Working capital management, investment and financing constraints in companies listed on the Tehran, Iran stock exchange. Journal of Business and Economics Research. 2013; **2**(6):130-133

[7] Banos-Caballero S, Garcia-Teruel PJ, Martinez-Solano P. How does working capital management affect the profitability of Spanish SMEs? Small Business Economics. 2012;**39**(2):517-529

[8] Uyar A. The relationship of cash conversion cycle with firm size and profitability: An empirical investigation in Turkey. International Research Journal of Finance and Economics. 2009; **24**(2):186-193

[9] Al-Jafari MK, Samman H Al. Determinants of profitability: Evidence from industrial companies listed on Muscat Securities Market. Review of European Studies 2015;7:303.

[10] Eljelly AMA. Liquidity-profitability tradeoff: An empirical investigation in an emerging market. International Journal of Commerce and Management. 2004; **14**(2):48-61

[11] Gill A, Biger N, Mathur N. The relationship between working capital management and profitability: Evidence from the United States. Business and Economics Journal. 2010; **10**(1):1-9

[12] Raykov E. The liquidity-profitability trade-off in Bulgaria in terms of the changed financial management functions during crisis. Management Journal of Contemporary Management issues. 2017;**22**(1):135-156

[13] Deloof M. Does working capital management affect profitability of Belgian firms ? Journal of Business Finance Account. 2003;**30**(2001): 573-588

[14] Čavlin M, Tankosić JV, Miletić V, Ivaniš M. Analysis of the impact of liquidity on the profitability in the medium and large meat processing enterprises in the republic of Serbia. Економика пољопривреде. 2021;**68**(3): 789-803

[15] Pervan M, Višić J. Influence of firm size on its business success. Croatian Operational Research Review. 2012;**3**(1): 213-223

[16] Gitman LJ, Juchau R, Flanagan J. Principles of managerial finance. Pearson Higher Education AU. 2015

[17] Raheman A, Afza T, Qayyum A, Bodla MA. Working capital management and corporate performance of manufacturing sector in Pakistan. International Research Journal of Finance and Economics. 2010;**47**(1): 156-169

[18] Sah NB, Banerjee A, Malm J, Rahman A. A good name is better than riches: Family firms and working capital management. Journal of Behavioral and Experimental Finance. 2022 Mar;**1**(33): 100599

[19] Richards VD, Laughlin EJ. A cash conversion cycle approach to liquidity analysis. Financial Management. 1980;**9** (1):32-38

[20] Prasad P, Narayanasamy S, Paul S, Chattopadhyay S, Saravanan P. Review of literature on working capital management and future research agenda. Journal of Economic Surveys. 2019;**33**(3):827-861

[21] Adhikari HP, Krolikowski MW, Malm J, Sah NB. Working capital (mis) management—Impact of executive age. Account & Finance. 2021; **61**(1):727-761

[22] Malm J, Sah N. Litigation risk and working capital. Managerial Finance. 2019;**45**(1):88-102

[23] Mathuva DM. The influence of working capital management components on corporate profitability: A survey on Kenyan listed firms. Research Journal of Business Management. 2010; **4**:1-11

[24] Ashraf CK. The relationship between working capital efficiency and profitability. Journal of Account Management. 2012;**2**(3): 21-45

[25] Juan Garcia-Teruel P, Martinez-Solano P. Effects of working capital management on SME profitability. International Journal of Management Finance. 2007;**3**(2):164-177

[26] Seth H, Chadha S, Sharma SK, Ruparel N. Exploring predictors of working capital management efficiency and their influence on firm performance: An integrated DEA-SEM approach. Benchmarking An International Journal. 2020

[27] Ghosh DSK, Maji SG. Working capital management efficiency: A study on the Indian cement industry. Manag Accountant-Calcutta. 2004;**39**:363-372

[28] Pais MA, Gama PM. Working capital management and SMEs profitability: Portuguese evidence. International Journal of Management Finance. 2015; **11**(3):341-358

[29] Pratap Singh H, Kumar S. Working capital management: A literature review and research agenda. Qualitative Research in Financial Markets. 2014; **6**(2):173-197

[30] Korent D, Orsag S. The impact of working capital management on profitability of Croatian software companies. Zagreb International Review of Economics \& Business. 2018;**21**(1): 47-65

[31] Enqvist J, Graham M, Nikkinen J. The impact of working capital management on firm profitability in different business cycles: Evidence from Finland. Research in International Business and Finance. 2014;**32**:36-49

[32] Tahir M, Anuar MBA. The determinants of working capital

management and firms performance of textile sector in Pakistan. Qual & Quant. 2016;**50**(2):605-618

[33] Nazir MS, Afza T. Impact of aggressive working capital management policy on firms' profitability. IUP Journal of Applied Finance. 2009;**15**(8):19-30

[34] Angahar PA, Alematu A. Impact of working capital on the profitability of the Nigerian cement industry. European Journal of Account Auditing and Financ Research. 2014;**2**(7):17-30

[35] Baker HK, Saadi S, Dutta S, Gandhi D. The perception of dividends by Canadian managers: New survey evidence. International Journal of Management Finance. 2007

[36] Wald JK. How firm characteristics affect capital structure: An international comparison. Journal of Financial Research. 1999;**22**(2):161-187

[37] Margaritis D, Psillaki M. Capital structure, equity ownership and firm performance. J Bank & Finance. 2010;34 (3):621–632.

[38] Yazdanfar D, Öhman P. Debt financing and firm performance: An empirical study based on Swedish data. The Journal of Risk Finance. 2015

[39] Högerle B, Charifzadeh M, Ferencz M, Kostin KB. The development of working capital management and its impact on profitability and shareholder value: Evidence from Germany. Strategic Management. 2020;**25**(2):27-39

[40] Goddard J, Tavakoli M, Wilson JOS. Determinants of profitability in European manufacturing and services: Evidence from a dynamic panel model. Applied Financial Economics. 2005; **15**(18):1269-1282

[41] Baker M, Wurgler J. Market timing and capital structure. Journal of Finance. 2002;**57**(1):1-32

[42] Bae J, Kim S-J, Oh H. Taming polysemous signals: The role of marketing intensity on the relationship between financial leverage and firm performance. Review of Financial Economics. 2017;**33**:29-40

[43] Dawar V. Agency theory, capital structure and firm performance: Some Indian evidence. Managerial Finance. 2014

[44] Foong S-Y, Idris R. Leverage, product diversity and performance of general insurers in Malaysia. The Journal of Risk Finance. 2012

[45] Balakrishnan S, Fox I. Asset specificity, firm heterogeneity and financial leverage. Strategic Management Journal. 1993;**14**(1):3-16

[46] Jaisinghani D, Kanjilal K. Non-linear dynamics of size, capital structure and profitability: Empirical evidence from Indian manufacturing sector. Asia Pacific Management Review. 2017;**22**(3):159-165

[47] Lin F-L, Chang T. Does debt affect firm value in Taiwan? A panel threshold regression analysis. Applied Economics. 2011;**43**(1):117-128

[48] Hsiao C. Analysis of Panel Data. Cambridge: Cambridge University Press; 1986

[49] Kuhnert P, Venables B, Zocchi SS. An introduction to R: Software for statistical modelling & computing. Citeseer. 2005

[50] Dalci I. Impact of financial leverage on profitability of listed manufacturing firms in China. Pacific Account Review. 2018;**30**(4)

[51] Bresciani S, Giacosa E, Broccardo L, Culasso F. The family variable in the French and Italian wine sector. Euromed Journal of Business. 2016

[52] Singhania M, Mehta P. Working capital management and firms' profitability: Evidence from emerging Asian countries. South Asian Journal of Business Studies. 2017

[53] Dalci I, Ozyapici H. Working capital management policy in health care: The effect of leverage. Health Policy (New York). 2018;**122**(11):1266-1272

[54] Breusch TS, Pagan AR. The Lagrange multiplier test and its applications to model specification in econometrics. The Review of Economic Studies. 1980;**47**(1): 239-253

[55] Baltagi B. Econometric Analysis of Panel Data. 3rd edition. New York: John Wiley & Sons; 2001

[56] Moodley T, Ward M, Muller C. The relationship between the management of payables and the return to investors. South African Journal of Account Research. 2017;**31**(1):35-43

Chapter 8

Impact of Short-Term Management on Portuguese and Spanish Firms' Performance

Carmem Leal, Diogo Rocha and Elisabete Neves

Abstract

An effective and efficient working capital management ensures companies a greater ability to survive in an increasingly competitive and challenging business world and therefore plays a key role in the manager's operational and financial decisions. Thus, the main objective of this chapter is to show empirically the extent to which working capital management influences the measures of business performance evaluation. To achieve the proposed objective, the ROA, ROE, and Tobin's Q were used as measures of performance. For this study, data from Portuguese and Spanish companies were used, which are listed on Euronext Lisbon and the Madrid Stock Exchange, respectively, resulting in a final sample of 106 companies. The methodology used to test the hypotheses formulated was dynamic panel data methodology (with GMM system) for a period between 2010 and 2016. The results obtained in this research show, in a general way, that there are significant differences in the determinants of performance depending on the samples used, whether they are the Spanish Sample or the Portuguese Sample.

Keywords: working capital management, business performance measures, financial analysis, dynamic panel data, Iberian companies

1. Introduction

The literature on the corporate finance area has been directed toward long-term management, more specifically to investment issues [1], capital structure [2], dividends [3], and business evaluation [4].

Although medium- and long-term management (LTM) is extremely important for the creation of a company's value, it is necessary that short-term management is carefully treated, since individual LTM decisions cannot create value for the company alone.

More recently, companies have been placing greater emphasis on the impact that short-term management has on corporate performance because a large part of the account balances presented in the accounts relates to short-term investments and resources [5].

It should be noted that managers must perceive a balance between each component of short-term management to maximize the company's value and ensure a higher organizational performance as well as a better competitive advantage [6].

In the last years, and as a result of the increase in competitiveness among companies, the management of current assets as an aid in the search for greater profitability has been the target of the Academy's interest [5, 7, 8].

A wide range of authors [8–10] considers that the Cash Conversion Cycle (CCC) is one of the most important short-term management measures and, therefore, the most used to study this subject, since in these author's studies they measure the impact that this variable has on corporate performance.

Thus, the Cash Conversion Cycle assumes a relevant role in the present study, since it is considered that this variable encompasses a set of preponderant factors for the short-term management and the firms' survival. These factors can be translated into three concepts: Average Collection Period (ACP), Average Stocking Period (ASP), and Average Payments Period (APP). This being said, in this chapter, six models will be investigated and each of the dependent variables (ROA, ROE, and Tobin's Q) will have two models. The existence of two models for each of the dependent variables is due to the fact that in the first instance each of the components of the CCC (ACP, ASP, and APP) is tested individually, and only then the CCC is tested in a single variable. Each of the six previously referenced models will be tested on two samples, namely the Spain Sample and the Portugal Sample.

In this sense, the present work aims to analyze the impact of short-term management on the performance of Iberian companies. For this, some hypotheses will be raised according to the existing literature, that is intended to be corroborated, to understand which are the determining variables in the explanation of corporate performance. Specifically, there will be used as explanatory variables, the Cash Conversion Cycle, ACP, ASP and APP, and current ratio. On the other hand, leverage, firm size, and tangible fixed assets will be used as control variables.

Additionally, it is intended to increase the literature related to the topic addressed throughout this chapter, since this subject is still little debated and discussed. After the crisis of 2008, short-term management assumed a greater preponderance, and consequently, the number of published studies on short-term management [11] increased.

This study will be directed to large companies in Portugal and Spain, listed on the corresponding stock exchanges, for the period between 2010 and 2016. The final sample resulted in 106 companies, which resulted in a total of 660 observations.

In short, this article is organized as follows—in Section 2 the literature review and respective hypotheses will be presented. Section 3 presents the methodology for the study. Sections 4 and 5 will present the main results and the conclusion, respectively.

2. Literature review and hypothesis definition

In the financial literature, there are several measures of corporate performance evaluation. Some of these measures have been more consensual and are the so-called traditional measures [12].

Therefore, the fact that there is no specific performance measure that guarantees greater efficiency and effectiveness than the other measures lead to the use of three measures of performance evaluation, more specifically Return on Assets (ROA), Return on Equity (ROE), and Tobin's Q.

2.1 Average collection period (ACP)

The Average Collection Period is one of the components of the Cash Conversion Cycle and is characterized as the time (calculated in days or months) that, on average, companies take time to charge their customers what they sell to them.

According to García-Teruel, Deloof, Pais and Mathuva et al. [5, 9, 10, 13], when it comes to the relationship between ACP and performance, we find that the larger the firm's ACP, the smaller the business performance will be. In the specific case of García-Teruel et al. [5], a negative relationship between ACP and ROA arises because the companies increase the average time of receipt of their clients so that they can increase purchases. However, although with these companies increase sales, the consequent increase in the ACP implies a decrease in ROA. Thus, according to the authors, a more restrictive credit policy by reducing the payment time of the clients, contributes to better performance.

The negative relationship between accounts receivable and profitability found by the authors mentioned above suggests that less profitable companies will try to reduce the ACP promptly to close and reduce the differences in the Cash Conversion Cycle.

Regarding Tobin's Q as a performance measure, a positive relationship was observed between ACP and Tobin's Q in Ref. [14].

Regarding these studies, it is possible to define the following hypothesis:

H1: there is a significant relationship between the Average Collection Period and the corporate performance measures (with no predicted sign).

2.2 Average stocking period (ASP)

The Average Stocking Period shows how long a product on average is in stock, so, it is expected that the lower the ASP, the greater the turnover of the product.

García-Teruel, Deloof and Pais et al. [5, 9, 10] in their studies concluded that the ASP and performance are negatively related. In contrast, Mathuva et al. [13] determined a positive relationship between ASP and performance. For this author, the higher the company's level of stocks, the lower the likelihood of stock-outs of the company. However, Kim et al. [15] suggest that there are counterparts to the fact that there are large volumes of stocks of raw materials and commodities, and they argue that a large volume of stocks may increase the likelihood of goods not being sold or exceeding the validity date, thus contributing to the increase of losses, which implies the minimization of corporate profits.

According to the literature, and there being no consensus among the several studies, the hypothesis to be formulated will be the following:

H2: there is a significant relationship between the Average Stocking Period and the corporate performance measures (with no predicted sign).

2.3 Average payments period (APP)

The last component of the Cash Conversion Cycle to be presented will be the Average Payment Period. This ratio indicates the time (calculated in days or months) that, on average, companies take to pay their suppliers.

García-Teruel and Deloof et al. [5, 9] concluded that there is a negative relationship between APP and profitability. According to Deloof et al. [9], this happens because companies that have a bigger difficulty in settling their accounts with suppliers have lower profitability levels. In the same line of thinking, a study by Pais et al. [10] for

Portuguese SMEs, concluded that there is a negative relationship between APP and ROA.

However Mathuva et al. [13] argued that the larger the APP, the longer the period that the suppliers finance the company's activities. In this sense, the author identified a positive and significant relationship between APP and profitability.

Nurein et al. [14] using Tobin's Q as a performance measure, came to the conclusion that the APP is positively related to Tobin's Q, thus sharing Mathuva et al. [13] conclusion.

Considering the previous conclusions, it is possible to formulate the following hypothesis:

H3: there is a significant relationship between the Average Payments Period and the corporate performance measures (with no predicted sign).

2.4 Cash conversion cycle

The Cash Conversion Cycle was developed by Richards et al. [16] and characterizes as being the time interval since the company has expenses in the acquisition of raw materials from its suppliers until the moment it sells its products to its clients [17].

Uyar et al. [18] argues that companies with shorter CCC are more profitable because they are less dependent on external financing and therefore, they will have to bear lower costs than a company with a longer CCC, which consequently will make them more cost-effective.

Regarding Tobin's Q as an evaluation measure of performance, it is found that for Vural et al. [19] there is a positive and significant relationship between the Cash Conversion Cycle and Tobin's Q, so an increase in CCC will lead to an increase in Tobin's Q.

Despite this, Mohamad et al. [20] and Nurein et al. [14], when conducting two studies in Malaysia, concluded that CCC negatively affects Tobin's Q, arguing that a lower CCC means higher performance when measured according to Tobin's Q.

Although there is no unanimity in the empirical literature, the vast majority defends the existence of a negative relationship between CCC and corporate performance. Thus, the following hypothesis will be defined:

H4: there is a significant relationship between the CCC and the corporate performance measures (with no predicted sign).

2.5 Current ratio

Following Husna et al. [21] current ratio consists of the ease with which assets held by companies can be converted into means of payment, that is, the ability of companies to meet their obligations as they mature. According to Uyar et al. [18], the way companies manage their liquidity is fundamental regardless of their size.

Raheman and Eljelly et al. [22, 23] found a negative relationship between the current ratio and corporate performance. According to Eljelly et al. [23], the negative relationship results from the companies' need to constantly present high levels of liquidity, and this causes companies to arise unnecessary costs that will lead to loss of profitability.

Jose et al. [7] point out that there is a negative relationship between current ratio and performance, which results from the lack of efficient liquidity management, obliging companies to use external financing to meet the short-term obligations, which will entail costs for organizations, and therefore, the company's profitability will decrease.

However, Goddard, Fagiolo and Safdar et al. [24–26] show the existence of a positive relationship between the variables in question. According to Goddard et al. [24], the companies with the highest levels of liquidity, besides being the companies with the best profitability, are also the ones with the greatest ability and flexibility to adapt more quickly to the changes to which they are subject.

Following this reasoning Fagiolo et al. [25] argue that firms with higher levels of liquidity are able to overcome certain obstacles that may arise when companies resort to external financing.

Du et al. [27] conducting a study in Chinese companies, have concluded that there is a positive relationship between current ratio and Tobin's Q, which they justify with Holmström et al. [28] arguments since for these authors, companies that manage to maintain adequate levels of liquidity are able to avoid potential risks to the company, contributing to increase the company's value.

Considering the divergence in the previous results, the hypothesis to be formulated will be the following:

H5: there is a significant relationship between the current ratio and corporate performance measures (with no predicted sign).

2.6 Leverage

Leverage is a very important variable for companies because, in addition to the explicit costs that arise with leverage, a bad decision can increase the company's financial risk and, consequently, affect its profitability. The use of external financing would only leverage the ROE due to the effect of the fiscal economy of interest and on the assumption that ROA exceeds the average cost of borrowing.

Pais, Vural, Goddard and Muritala et al. [10, 19, 24, 29] argue that between debt and corporate performance (when measured through ROA, ROE, and Tobin's Q) there is a negative relationship.

Goddard et al. [24] argues that the negative relationship between variables arises because, during the period when companies are paying off the debt, they are losing investment opportunities in projects that could generate returns for the company.

Although many studies advocate the existence of a negative relationship between leverage and corporate performance, some authors stand up for the existence of a positive relationship between these variables.

Olokoyo et al. [30] conducting a study on 101 listed companies in Nigeria, concluded that debt positively influences Tobin's Q. However, when using ROA as an evaluation measure of performance, the author observes that leverage negatively influences ROA.

Also Berger and Adams et al. [31, 32] have concluded that there is not always a negative relationship between leverage and performance, that is, the fact that a company uses external financing does not mean less performance. Even more debt can imply more and better investments and this can leverage the company's profitability.

Regarding the divergence of opinions presented by the various studies, the hypothesis will be the following:

H6: there is a significant relationship between the leverage and the corporate performance measures (with no predicted sign).

2.7 Firm size

The firm size is a preponderant factor in investment decisions, in access to external financing, in access to capital markets, among others [33].

According to Jose, Banos-Caballero, Serrasqueiro and Lee et al. [7, 8, 34, 35], what makes large-scale enterprises more profitable is their ability to increase production while at the same time reducing the average cost of production and thus taking advantage of economies of scale.

Although the existing literature finds a positive relationship between firm size and performance, there are studies that prove the existence of a negative relationship between these variables. In this sense, Goddard et al. [24] show a negative relationship between firm size and profitability (ROA). For these authors, the reason behind this relationship is the less interference and control of the owners in the manager's activities, due to the increase of the size of the companies. In this way, the manager's investment options can increase their personal benefits, however, it contributes to the decrease of the company's performance.

In addition, Yoon et al. [36] shares the idea that increasing the size of the company beyond the ideal level can reduce the firm's performance.

So, in this sense, the following hypothesis is presented:

H7: there is a significant relationship between the firm size and the corporate performance measures (with no predicted sign).

2.8 Tangible fixed assets

Several studies [34, 37–39] show that tangible fixed assets can be a variable that has an impact on the performance of the firms, and as such will be used in this study as a control variable.

Asset tangibility refers to the composition of the asset of an organization. A company that has sufficient assets can use them as collateral in the event of liquidation, allowing the company easier access to external sources of financing, as Singh et al. [11] refer.

Serrasqueiro et al. [34] concluded that tangible fixed assets negatively influence corporate performance. The Portuguese authors followed the arguments of Serrasqueiro and Nucci et al. [34, 39] to support the result obtained in their study. The argument used by them advocates that companies that are more inclined to innovate and invest in R & D activities are those that present greater opportunities for long-term investment and, consequently, higher performance. In this way, companies that invest more in intangible assets will be more profitable than those that make their investments in tangible assets.

Maina et al. [38] concluded that there is a negative and significant relationship between tangible fixed assets and ROE. The authors add that companies that invest heavily in tangible assets will experience a decrease in ROE. This result goes against the one found by Muritala et al. [29]. This author found a negative and significant relationship between the two variables. As for the relationship found between tangible fixed assets and Tobin's Q, the results reveal a negative and significant relationship.

Considering all the studies presented for the tangible fixed assets the hypothesis to be formulated is the following:

H8: There is a significant relationship between tangible fixed assets and corporate performance measures (with no predicted sign).

3. Data, variables, and methodology

3.1 Sample

To carry out this research, a quantitative approach was used, based on the Amadeus database. Therefore, the sample of this article covers the period from 2010 to 2016, thus giving rise to an unbalanced panel with 106 non-financial companies, corresponding to a total of 660 observations.

This study's sample was limited to non-financial firms, since the companies from the financial sector have distinct characteristics from non-financial companies, and as such, they must be studied in an independent way [40, 41]. In addition to the financial companies, the companies of the sports sector were also eliminated from the sample, since they use a different accounting system in the preparation of their financial statements. Considering the sample's definition, companies that had little information for the desired indicators (e.g., did not have information for 4 consecutive years) were excluded [42].

3.2 Selection and description of variables

Considering the literature review, **Table 1** shows the form of calculation of each of the variables used in this article.

3.2.1 Estimation method

To test the proposed hypotheses, the dynamic panel data methodology was used. This methodology allows the only one-time model to aggregate time-series and cross-section data.

Dependent variables	**Method of calculation**
Return on assets (ROA)	$ROA = \frac{EBIT}{total\ assets}$
Return on equity (ROE)	$ROE = \frac{net\ profit}{equity}$
Tobin's Q	$Tobin's\ Q = \frac{market\ value}{total\ assets}$
Independent variables	**Method of calculation**
Average collection period (ACP)	$ACP = \frac{receivables}{turnover} \times 365$
Average stocking period (ASP)	$ASP = \frac{stocks}{cost\ of\ goods\ sold} \times 365$
Average payments period (APP)	$APP = \frac{payables}{cost\ of\ goods\ sold} \times 365$
Cash conversion cycle (CCC)	CCC = ACP + ASP – APP
Current ratio (CR)	$CR = \frac{current\ assets}{current\ liabilities}$
Leverage (Lev)	$Lev = \frac{debt}{total\ assets}$
Firm size (Size)	$\text{Size} = \log(total\ assets)$
Tangible fixed assets (Tang)	$Tang = \frac{tangible\ fixed\ assets}{total\ assets}$

Table 1.
Selection and description of variables.

According to Neves et al. [43], some of the advantages associated with the use of this methodology are—the control of individual heterogeneity, correction of endogeneity, the existence of less collinearity between variables, the possibility of handling high amounts of information, and greater efficiency in estimation.

Thus, unlike the cross-section analysis, panel data allows the control of individual heterogeneity. This point is fundamental for the accomplishment of the present work, since the performance of each company is directly related to the individual specificities of each one of the companies, and without the control of heterogeneity, the obtained results could be biased. Moreover, this methodology allows solving another fundamental point, namely endogeneity (which arises from the causal relationship that the various dependent variables (ROE, ROA, and Tobin's Q) may have with the explanatory variables of the study).

Consequently, endogeneity can be a problem in the model of the present work, and therefore, it is necessary to keep it controlled.

Specifically, we use all the variables on the right side of the model with t-1 mismatches for the level equations, as Blundell et al. [44] suggested, by deriving the system estimator used in this article.

The models to be tested throughout this article are presented below:

Model 1: $ROA_{it} = \beta_0 + \beta_1(ACP)_{it} + \beta_2(ASP)_{it} + \beta_3(APP)_{it} + \beta_4(CR)_{it} + \beta_5(Lev)_{it} + \beta_6(Size)_{it} + \beta_7(Tang)_{it} + \mu_{it}$

Model 2: $ROA_{it} = \beta_0 + \beta_1(CCC)_{it} + \beta_2(CR)_{it} + \beta_3(Lev)_{it} + \beta_4(Size)_{it} + \beta_5(Tang)_{it} + \mu_{it}$

Model 3: $ROE_{it} = \beta_0 + \beta_1(ACP)_{it} + \beta_2(ASP)_{it} + \beta_3(APP)_{it} + \beta_4(CR)_{it} + \beta_5(Lev)_{it} + \beta_6(Size)_{it} + \beta_7(Tang)_{it} + \mu_{it}$

Model 4: $ROE_{it} = \beta_0 + \beta_1(CCC)_{it} + \beta_2(CR)_{it} + \beta_3(Lev)_{it} + \beta_4(Size)_{it} + \beta_5(Tang)_{it} + \mu_{it}$

Model 5: $Tobin'sQ_{it} = \beta_0 + \beta_1(ACP)_{it} + \beta_2(ASP)_{it} + \beta_3(APP)_{it} + \beta_4(CR)_{it} + \beta_5(Lev)_{it} + \beta_6(Size)_{it} + \beta_7(Tang)_{it} + \mu_{it}$

Model 6: $Tobin'sQ_{it} = \beta_0 + \beta_1(CCC)_{it} + \beta_2(CR)_{it} + \beta_3(Lev)_{it} + \beta_4(Size)_{it} + \beta_5(Tang)_{it} + \mu_{it}$

4. Results and discussion

In this chapter, the main results of this article will be presented and discussed. Firstly, the Descriptive Statistics of each of the three samples will be presented and then the main results.

4.1 Descriptive statistics

Table 2 provides summary statistics (mean, standard deviation, minimum and maximum) of the variables used in the construction of the dependent and explanatory variables.

Table 3 presents summary statistics (mean, standard deviation, minimum and maximum) of the variables used in the construction of the dependent and explanatory variables.

4.2 Model 1: estimation

Based on **Table 4**, the fact that ACP negatively influences ROA means that Spanish companies will have to reduce their client's ACP so that they can increase the

Variables	Mean	Standard deviation	Minimum	Maximum
ROA	3.767568	9.055842	−34.73	53.01
ROE	2.907545	33.57112	−182.3	144.93
Tobin's Q	0.8021636	1.13628	0	7.42
ACP	92.63409	60.09211	0	279
ASP	21.59545	40.98847	0	298
APP	65.34773	45.43186	0	267
CCC	48.88182	71.83697	−190	387
CR	1.420523	0.8410572	0.09	9.67
Lev	0.6380227	0.2234283	0.1	2.52
Size	13.86105	2.264694	6.39	18.68
Tang	0.2906364	0.2153083	0	0.92

Table 2.
Descriptive statistics of Spain.

Variables	Mean	Standard deviation	Minimum	Maximum
ROA	2.483682	5.35625	−14.99	22.47
ROE	2.517182	24.36511	−164.57	66.28
Tobin's Q	0.3380296	0.3407419	0.01	1.82
ACP	94.32727	61.42473	0	294
ASP	32.35909	50.10339	1	279
APP	70.86364	41.08649	0	187
CCC	55.82273	76.83732	−131	399
CR	1.200591	0.8291296	0.13	7.54
Lev	0.6591364	0.1738621	0.07	1.09
Size	13.01314	1.990146	8.06	17.6
Tang	0.3101818	0.1919498	0	0.69

Table 3.
Descriptive statistics of Portugal.

	Coefficient	STD error	Z	P value
Const	−4.786997	5.971701	−0.80	0.423
ACP	−0.0448544	0.0134737	−3.33	0.001***
ASP	0.0024074	0.0154443	0.16	0.876
APP	0.0215348	0.0134551	1.60	0.109
CR	1.217,916	0.6472035	1.88	0.060**
Lev	−19.4286	2.739318	−7.09	0.000***
Size	1.371543	0.4403209	3.11	0.002***
Tang	7.386,296	5.573,588	1.33	0.185

	Coefficient	STD error	Z	P value
Sargan			23.91367(19)	0.1995
Wald			242.88(8)	0.0000
AR (1)			−36.218	0.0003
AR (2)			−0.09622	0.9233

*Note: the regression is performed using an unbalanced data panel consisting of 68 companies and 440 observations. The variables are duly defined in the data, variables, and methodology section. It should also be noted that: (i) *, **, and *** indicates significance levels at 10%, 5%, and 1% respectively; (ii) the Sargan test with a p value greater than 5% shows that the instruments are valid, and the values in parentheses of the test represent degrees of freedom; (iii) he Wald test has a p value less than 5% which means that the joint significance and the coefficients are significant distributed asymptotically as χ^2 under a null hypothesis without significance, with degrees of freedom in parentheses.*

Table 4.
Results of the model (1) for Spain.

performance of their companies. Thus, if companies manage to reduce their ACP, they will be able to reduce the CCC as well. Therefore, the results follow the reasoning of García-Teruel et al. [5] carried out in Spain as well the studies published by. The results are still in harmony with the studies of Pais and Yazdanfar et al. [10, 45], allowing to corroborate hypothesis 1 previously proposed.

The positive relationship between the current ratio and ROA validates hypothesis 5, as well as the studies carried out by Goddard and Safdar et al. [24, 26]. Goddard et al. [24] argues that the greater the level of liquidity of a company, the greater the company's ability to face changes of a competitive nature in the markets in which they operate.

Hypothesis 7 contemplates the possibility that the firm size is positively related to performance evaluation measures, and this hypothesis is corroborated by the results found in **Table 4**. According to Jose and Banos-Caballero et al. [7, 8] what makes the larger companies more profitable is the capacity to increase their production, reducing the average cost of production and taking advantage of economies of scale.

Finally, **Table 4** demonstrates a negative relation between leverage and ROA. This relationship supports hypothesis 6 and confirms the studies [10, 30]. According to Goddard et al. [24], the more leveraged firms are, less profitable will be, because while they are paying the debt they are, simultaneously, losing investment opportunities in projects that could generate a return to the company.

Table 5 shows a considerable number of significant variables when the evaluation measure of performance used is ROA, considering the estimated model for Portuguese companies.

The negative relation between APP and ROA found in this study follows the conclusions obtained by Pais et al. [10] for a study of large Portuguese firms. Banos-Caballero and Deloof et al. [8, 9] also reached this relationship, arguing that an increase in APP will lead to a decrease in profitability. The evidence found thus corroborates hypothesis 3.

As can be seen in **Table 5**, the more leveraged the company's capital structure, the greater ROA will be, so the results obtained validate hypothesis 6 and the results of Berger and Adams et al. [31, 32] who show that when a company uses external financing does not mean that there will be a decrease in corporate performance. For these authors, managers only need to be able to efficiently manage their resources,

	Coefficient	STD error	Z	P value
Const	−12.2367	2.629679	−4.65	0.000
ACP	0.006264	0.0079111	0.79	0.428
ASP	−0.0052733	0.0081643	−0.65	0.518
APP	−0.0319109	0.0072112	−4.43	0.000***
CR	0.2455387	0.3797602	0.65	0.518
Lev	5.954678	3.010078	1.98	0.048**
Size	0.9599293	0.1504516	6.38	0.000***
Tang	−4.681794	1.395103	−3.36	0.001***
Sargan			24.80384(19)	0.1671
Wald			3078.66(8)	0.0000
AR (1)			−1.5355	0.1246
AR (2)			1.0026	0.3160

*The regression is performed using an unbalanced data panel consisting of 37 companies and 220 observations. The variables are duly defined in the data, variables, and methodology section. It should also be noted that: (i) *, **, and *** indicates significance levels at 10%, 5%, and 1% respectively; (ii) the Sargan test with a p value greater than 5% shows that the instruments are valid, and the values in parentheses of the test represent degrees of freedom; (iii) the Wald test has a p value less than 5% which means that the joint significance and the coefficients are significant distributed asymptotically as χ^2 under a null hypothesis without significance, with degrees of freedom in parentheses.*

Table 5.
Results of the model (1) for Portugal.

since there is a reduction in cash flows, derived from the regular payment of the debt. In addition, companies sometimes take advantage of the financial leverage effect of increasing debt to increase their profitability levels.

One of the common relationships between Portugal's sample and Spain's sample is the existing positive relationship between firm size and ROA, thus confirming hypothesis 7, as well as the studies of [34, 45].

In the Spanish case, we observed a positive relationship between the current ratio and ROA. However, when estimating model 1 for Portuguese companies we verified that the current ratio is not significantly related to ROA.

Another difference between the two samples is due to the existence of a negative relationship between tangible fixed assets and ROA for Portuguese companies, thus being in conformity with hypothesis 8 previously placed.

4.3 Model 2: estimation

The estimation of model 2 for the large Spanish companies, in **Table 6**, makes it possible to verify that although the CCC is used to the detriment of the ACP, ASP, and APP, the significant relationships are the same in both models.

Also, based on **Table 6**, it can be seen that CCC has a negative relationship with ROA, which is in accordance with the studies of Uyar and Goddard et al. [18, 24] as well with the hypothesis 4 previously formulated.

Based on the results of **Table 7**, and comparing to **Table 5**, we observe that when CCC is used to the detriment of ACP, ASP, and APP, for the sample of large Portuguese companies, some differences arise in both models.

	Coefficient	STD error	Z	P value
Const	−7.099776	7.344084	−0.97	0.334
CCC	−0.0259253	0.0133265	−1.95	0.052*
CR	1.080459	0.6132817	1.76	0.078*
Lev	−19.94105	2.433001	−8.20	0.000***
Size	1.425786	0.5076238	2.81	0.005***
Tang	9.064535	5.727313	1.58	0.113
Sargan			24.78524(19)	0.1677
Wald			286.37(6)	0.0000
AR (1)			−3.7405	0.0002
AR (2)			0.1766	0.8598

*The regression is performed using an unbalanced data panel consisting of 68 companies and 440 observations. The variables are duly defined in the data, variables, and methodology section. It should also be noted that: (i) *, **, and *** indicates significance levels at 10%, 5%, and 1% respectively; (ii) the Sargan test with a p value greater than 5% shows that the instruments are valid, and the values in parentheses of the test represent degrees of freedom; (ii) the Wald test has a p value less than 5% which means that the joint significance and the coefficients are significant distributed asymptotically as χ^2 under a null hypothesis without significance, with degrees of freedom in parentheses.*

Table 6.
Results of the model (2) for Spain.

	Coefficient	STD error	Z	P value
Const	−12.67382	1.805622	−7.02	0.000
CCC	0.0117469	0.005131	2.29	0.022**
CR	−0.4680455	0.2460254	−1.90	0.057**
Lev	1.82428	2.700528	0.68	0.499
Size	1.045946	0.1348222	7.76	0.000***
Tang	−4.035826	2.027262	−1.99	0.047**
Sargan			24.01575(19)	0.1955
Wald			538.09(6)	538.09
AR (1)			−1.6114	0.1071
AR (2)			0.9166	0.3594

*The regression is performed using an unbalanced data panel consisting of 37 companies and 220 observations. The variables are duly defined in the data, variables, and methodology section. It should also be noted that: (i) *, **, and *** indicates significance levels at 10%, 5%, and 1% respectively; (ii) the Sargan test with a p value greater than 5% shows that the instruments are valid, and the values in parentheses of the test represent degrees of freedom; (iii) the Wald test has a p value less than 5% which means that the joint significance and the coefficients are significant distributed asymptotically as χ^2 under a null hypothesis without significance, with degrees of freedom in parentheses.*

Table 7.
Results of the model (2) for Portugal.

Thus, when estimating model 2, we highlight the negative relationship between the current ratio and ROA, with a significance level of 1%. This relationship was not observed when model 1 was estimated. However, in the estimation of model 1, one of the variables that was positively related to ROA was leverage. Regarding model 2 leverage ceases to be one of the significant variables.

Table 7 demonstrates a positive relationship between CCC and ROA, differing from the relationship between these same variables for the sample of large Spanish companies.

4.4 Model 3: estimation

When the evaluation measure of performance used is ROE, only leverage presents significance with the dependent variable used (see **Table 8**).

Thus, one can accept hypothesis 6, and corroborate the results of Muritala et al. [29]. The more leveraged companies present higher financial costs, which will contribute to the decrease of ROE [46].

Considering the results presented in **Table 9**, it is possible to verify that when the sample of the Portuguese companies is used with the ROE as a measure of performance, the number of significant variables increases considerably.

Consistent with hypothesis 1, there is a significant relationship between ACP and ROE, which also corroborates the results of García-Teruel et al. [5], emphasizing the fact that companies increase their ACP to increase their volume of sales, but in their study, the authors concluded that this would not lead to an increase in profitability.

Our results show that a decrease in ASP will lead to an increase in ROE. This inverse relationship between the two variables corroborates hypothesis 2, following Deloof and Pais et al. [9, 10].

According to Sensini et al. [47], when a company experiences a sudden drop in sales aligned with poor stock management, this will increase its losses, and it will decrease its profitability.

	Coefficient	STD.Error	Z	P value
Const	202.2626	135.8283	1.49	0.136
ACP	0.0019397	0.0480458	0.04	0.968
ASP	0.065436	0.0948203	0.69	0.490
APP	−0.0787663	0.0574182	−1.37	0.170
CR	−2.471852	2.949592	−0.84	0.402
Lev	−103.8548	21.68979	−4.79	0.000***
Size	−8.859585	9.892428	−0.90	0.370
Tang	−3.245457	44.93885	−0.07	0.942
Sargan			15.86487(19)	0.6663
Wald			344.60(8)	0.0000
AR (1)			−23.773	0.0174
AR (2)			0.42828	0.6684

*The regression is performed using an unbalanced data panel consisting of 68 companies and 440 observations. The variables are duly defined in the data, variables, and methodology section. It should also be noted that: (i) *, **, and *** indicates significance levels at 10%, 5%, and 1% respectively; (ii) the Sargan test with a p value greater than 5% shows that the instruments are valid, and the values in parentheses of the test represent degrees of freedom; (iii) the Wald test has a p value less than 5% which means that the joint significance and the coefficients are significant distributed asymptotically as χ^2 under a null hypothesis without significance, with degrees of freedom in parentheses.*

Table 8.
Results of the model (3) for Spain.

	Coefficient	STD.Error	Z	P value
Const	21.00624	11.56728	1.82	0.069
ACP	0.0287025	0.0125454	2.29	0.022**
ASP	−0.0574698	0.026982	−2.13	0.033**
APP	−0.0026771	0.0144353	−0.19	0.853
CR	0.2714,366	1.361008	0.20	0.842
Lev	−17.87054	9.814491	−1.82	0.069*
Size	−0.1942952	0.6833794	−0.28	0.776
Tang	−11.12407	3.209237	−3.47	0.001***
Sargan			15.74634(19)	0.6741
Wald			5048.52(8)	0.0000
AR (1)			−1.594	0.1109
AR (2)			−0.1939	0.8463

*The regression is performed using an unbalanced data panel consisting of 37 companies and 220 observations. The variables are duly defined in the data, variables, and methodology section. It should also be noted that: (i) *, **, and *** indicates significance levels at 10%, 5%, and 1% respectively; (ii) the Sargan test with a p value greater than 5% shows that the instruments are valid, and the values in parentheses of the test represent degrees of freedom; (iii) the Wald test has a p value less than 5% which means that the joint significance and the coefficients are significant distributed asymptotically as χ^2 under a null hypothesis without significance, with degrees of freedom in parentheses.*

Table 9.
Results of the model (3) for Portugal.

It should also be pointed out that leverage is negatively related to ROE, following Muritala and Pouraghajan et al. [29, 46] conclusions and validating our hypothesis 6.

Regarding the tangible fixed assets, it is possible to verify the existence of an inverse relation with ROE, thus agreeing with Maina et al. [38] and confirming our hypothesis 8.

4.5 Model 4: estimation

Model 4 for the Spain sample demonstrates that leverage is the only variable that has significance with ROE. The same happens in model 3 estimation, so when ACP, ASP, and APP are compiled in a single variable, the CCC, the significant variables do not change as it is possible to see through **Table 10**.

In the specific case of the Portuguese companies' sample, there are a substantial number of significant variables when estimating model 3, however, when the ACP, ASP, and APP are combined into a single variable, the CCC, we see a reduction in the number of significant variables. The differences between the estimation of model 3 and model 4 are due to the loss of significance of ACP and APP, which were excluded from the model to detriment of the CCC, keeping only the leverage and tangible fixed assets as significant variables (**Table 11**).

4.6 Model 5: estimation

When the Spanish companies were tested, considering Tobin's Q as an evaluation measure of performance, it is possible to verify that ASP shows a positive relationship with Tobin's Q. This result supports hypothesis 2 and corroborates

DOI: http://dx.doi.org/10.5772/intechopen.103009

	Coefficient	STD error	Z	P value
Const	171.305	127.4064	1.34	0.179
CCC	0.0455601	0.0484981	0.94	0.348
CR	−3.187983	2.992249	−1.07	0.287
Lev	−101.9112	19.84812	−5.13	0.000***
Size	−6.852814	9.211602	−0.74	0.457
Tang	−14.43055	43.51256	−0.33	0.740
Sargan			13.15944(19)	0.8303
Wald			316.58(6)	0.0000
AR (1)			−2.4392	0.0147
AR (2)			0.51475	0.6067

*The regression is performed using an unbalanced data panel consisting of 68 companies and 440 observations. The variables are duly defined in the data, variables, and methodology section. It should also be noted that: (i) *, **, and *** indicates significance levels at 10%, 5%, and 1% respectively; (ii) the Sargan test with a p value greater than 5% shows that the instruments are valid, and the values in parentheses of the test represent degrees of freedom; (iii) the Wald test has a p value less than 5% which means that the joint significance and the coefficients are significant distributed asymptotically as χ^2 under a null hypothesis without significance, with degrees of freedom in parentheses.*

Table 10.
Results of the model (4) for Spain.

	Coefficient	STD error	Z	P value
Const	25.46671	9.392254	2.71	0.007
CCC	−0.0117968	0.0074828	−1.58	0.115
CR	−0.2680787	1.27324	−0.21	0.833
Lev	−18.51862	8.295154	−2.23	0.026**
Size	−0.4120154	0.5681481	−0.73	0.468
Tang	−11.43038	2.21616	−5.16	0.000***
Sargan			15.15382(19)	0.7128
Wald			584.67(6)	0.000
AR (1)			−1.7892	0.0736
AR (2)			0.06376	0.9492

*The regression is performed using an unbalanced data panel consisting of 37 companies and 220 observations. The variables are duly defined in the data, variables, and methodology section. It should also be noted that: (i) *, **, and *** indicates significance levels at 10%, 5%, and 1% respectively; (ii) the Sargan test with a p value greater than 5% shows that the instruments are valid, and the values in parentheses of the test represent degrees of freedom; (iii) the Wald test has a p value less than 5% which means that the joint significance and the coefficients are significant distributed asymptotically as χ^2 under a null hypothesis without significance, with degrees of freedom in parentheses.*

Table 11.
Results of the model (4) for Portugal.

Nurein et al. [14] remarks. Kim et al. [13] argues that high levels of stocks lead to a reduction in the cost of possible disruptions to the productive process of companies and also means that companies do not run the risk of losing customers due to lack of products.

	Coefficient	STD error	Z	P value
Const	2.205,876	0.5459458	4.04	0.000
ACP	−0.0008001	0.0005406	−1.48	0.139
ASP	0.0042012	0.0006628	6.34	0.000***
APP	−0.0016697	0.0007991	−2.09	0.037**
CR	0.018317	0.0243078	0.75	0.451
Lev	0.5877777	0.2383076	2.47	0.014**
Size	−0.15792	0.0398748	−3.96	0.000***
Tang	−0.3054478	0.3264499	−0.94	0.349
Sargan			22.02086(19)	0.2832
Wald			7054.32(8)	0.0000
AR (1)			−1.6874	0.0915
AR (2)			0.19382	0.8463

*The regression is performed using an unbalanced data panel consisting of 68 companies and 379 observations. The variables are duly defined in the data, variables, and methodology section. It should also be noted that: (i) *, **, and *** indicates significance levels at 10%, 5%, and 1% respectively; (ii) the Sargan test with a p value greater than 5% shows that the instruments are valid, and the values in parentheses of the test represent degrees of freedom; (iii) the Wald test has a p value less than 5% which means that the joint significance and the coefficients are significant distributed asymptotically as χ^2 under a null hypothesis without significance, with degrees of freedom in parentheses.*

Table 12.
Results of the model (5) for Spain.

Based on **Table 12**, we verify a negative relationship between APP and Tobin's Q, which can be explained by the fact that the companies with the lowest profitability in certain cases are not able to settle the accounts payable [9]. The present relationship thus corroborates hypothesis 3.

In line with hypothesis 6, we are faced with a positive relationship between leverage and Tobin's Q, supported by Olokoyo et al. [30], who argues that high levels of debt are associated with higher performance.

As it is possible to verify in the Spanish companies' sample, there is a negative relationship between firm size and Tobin's Q. Therefore, the results support hypothesis 7 and are still compatible with the previous studies of Goddard, Yoon and Rogers et al. [24, 36, 48].

Consistent with hypothesis 1, if companies increase the ACP this will lead to a decrease in performance, especially for less profitable companies, since these companies are more reliant on receiving money from their customers to pay their short-term obligations. This evidence is in accordance with the Deloof, Pais and Mathuva et al. [9, 10, 13] studies, which also indicate that an increase in the ACP will lead to a decrease in performance. From the point of view of García-Teruel et al. [5] firms tend to increase their ACP, since they intend to increase their sales volume, but according to the authors, even if this happens the companies end up suffering a decrease in performance, resulting from the increase in the ACP.

Based on **Table 13**, it is possible to verify a positive relationship between ASP and Tobin's Q. These results corroborate hypothesis 2 previously formulated, and according to Nurein et al. [14], a possible justification for the fact that the variables relate positively depends on the inventory presented by the companies, that is, the

	Coefficient	STD.Error	Z	P value
Const	1.188477	0.2428485	4.89	0.000
ACP	−0.0014553	0.0002968	−4.90	0.000***
ASP	0.0010618	0.0000975	10.89	0.000***
APP	−0.0002919	0.000472	−0.62	0.536
CR	0.0769384	0.0088425	8.70	0.000***
Lev	0.0764171	0.0564738	1.35	0.176
Size	−0.0887998	0.0182623	−4.86	0.000***
Tang	0.1715389	0.0518692	3.31	0.001***
Sargan			17.97856(19)	0.5239
Wald			12.35619(8)	0.0000
AR (1)			−2.7775	0.0055
AR (2)			−0.96287	0.3356

*The regression is performed using an unbalanced data panel consisting of 37 companies and 203 observations. The variables are duly defined in the data, variables, and methodology section. It should also be noted that: (i) *, **, and *** indicates significance levels at 10%, 5%, and 1% respectively; (ii) the Sargan test with a p value greater than 5% shows that the instruments are valid, and the values in parentheses of the test represent degrees of freedom; (iii) the Wald test has a p value less than 5% which means that the joint significance and the coefficients are significant distributed asymptotically as χ^2 under a null hypothesis without significance, with degrees of freedom in parentheses.*

Table 13.
Results of the model (5) for Portugal.

larger the inventory of a company the greater the possibility of growth and valuation, since it presents a greater capacity for increase your sales.

The positive relationship between the current ratio and Tobin's Q is a relevant result found. What drives companies with higher levels of liquidity to increase their corporate performance comes from the ability of these companies in reducing potential risks [28]. The evidence found thus supports hypothesis 5, in addition to corroborating the study of Du et al. [27].

4.7 Model 6: estimation

Based on the observation of **Tables 12** and **14**, we observed that the number of significant variables was maintained both in the estimation of model 5 and in the estimation of model 6, although some of the significant variables were not the same in the two estimates.

Based on **Table 14**, it can be verified that CCC and leverage variables show a positive relationship with Tobin's Q. On the other hand, the variables firm size and asset tangibility show a negative relationship with the performance measure Tobin's Q. In this way, it can be concluded that the difference between the two estimates is that the CCC and asset tangibility become significant variables with Tobin's Q. In contrast, the ASP and APP are no longer significant variables.

There are some perceptible differences between models 5 and 6 regarding the significant variables. The highlight in model 6's estimation was the loss of significance of the tangible fixed assets variable, which was positively related to Tobin's Q for a significance level of 1%. The ACP and the ASP also cease to be significant when they are replaced by a single variable, namely the CCC.

	Coefficient	STD error	Z	P value
Const	1.689084	0.4446862	3.80	0.000
CCC	0.0005962	0.0002504	2.38	0.017**
CR	0.0310001	0.0216701	1.43	0.153
Lev	0.7807595	0.2457192	3.18	0.001***
Size	−0.1406512	0.0340643	−4.13	0.000***
Tang	−0.4621222	0.2600277	−1.78	0.076*
Sargan			23.6413(19)	0.2103
Wald			3994.30(6)	0.0000
AR (1)			−1.6663	0.0957
AR (2)			0.33507	0.7376

*The regression is performed using an unbalanced data panel consisting of 68 companies and 379 observations. The variables are duly defined in the data, variables, and methodology section. It should also be noted that: (i) *, **, and *** indicates significance levels at 10%, 5%, and 1% respectively; (ii) the Sargan test with a p value greater than 5% shows that the instruments are valid, and the values in parentheses of the test represent degrees of freedom; (iii) the Wald test has a p value less than 5% which means that the joint significance and the coefficients are significant distributed asymptotically as χ^2 under a null hypothesis without significance, with degrees of freedom in parentheses.*

Table 14.
Results of the model (6) for Spain.

As already seen in both samples, the results found between leverage and Tobin's Q reveal a positive relation. Although in many cases the use of external financing is associated with a decrease in corporate performance, this is not always so linear, as it can be seen in (**Table 15**) [30–32].

	Coefficient	STD error	Z	P value
Const	1.30377	0.1241634	10.50	0.000
CCC	−0.000054	0.0000774	−0.70	0.486
CR	0.0806346	0.0069785	11.55	0.000***
Lev	0.0955987	0.0568119	1.68	0.092*
Size	−0.1054368	0.0081945	−12.87	0.000***
Tang	0.0778192	0.1008745	0.77	0.440
Sargan			21.10506(19)	0.3310
Wald			22582.62(6)	0.0000
AR (1)			−2.4825	0.0130
AR (2)			−0.60043	0.5482

*The regression is performed using an unbalanced data panel consisting of 37 companies and 203 observations. The variables are duly defined in the data, variables, and methodology section. It should also be noted that: (i) *, **, and *** indicates significance levels at 10%, 5%, and 1% respectively; (ii) the Sargan test with a p value greater than 5% shows that the instruments are valid, and the values in parentheses of the test represent degrees of freedom; (iii) the Wald test has a p value less than 5% which means that the joint significance and the coefficients are significant distributed asymptotically as χ^2 under a null hypothesis without significance, with degrees of freedom in parentheses.*

Table 15.
Results of the model (6) for Portugal.

The results presented throughout this study show that short-term management variables that have an impact on corporate performance vary according to the dependent variable used to measure corporate performance and also vary across countries.

Between the two samples analyzed, some differences were evident, which may be justified by the way companies are managed. Thus, our results suggest that Portuguese companies are still in a phase of large external financing needs, and therefore probably more exposed to the market and to "external" variables.

On the other hand, Spanish companies already express some preference for the internal management and attitude of the manager, who probably has incentives to act in accordance with the interests of shareholders. Although our results do not test macroeconomic variables and institutional factors, they suggest that Portuguese companies may be facing more agency problems than Spanish ones.

Considering the results obtained, it should be pointed out that the ROE did not present many significant variables, highlighting only leverage, since it is the only significant variable with ROE, for the sample from Spain. This can be justified by the fact that ROE encompasses a wide range of decisions, such as operational, financial, and tax decisions. In spite of all this, it is still worth noting the increase of the significant variables with ROE for the Portuguese sample, this can be justified by the fact that the Portuguese companies need investors. That said, this will be a great measure of evaluation for a future investor.

Finally, when the valuation measure is Tobin's Q, it is possible to verify that almost all independent variables are significant, especially for the sample of Portuguese firms. In this way, it is possible to affirm that Tobin's Q is one of the best dependent variables to evaluate corporate performance. This is a variable that shows interest for all internal and external elements of the company.

5. Conclusions

Although short-term management is not the focus of corporate finance, it proves to be an extremely useful and important tool for the efficient functioning of companies, since it facilitates the decision-making of their managers.

The present study aimed to contribute to the increase of the literature since it is a subject that has only taken on a leading role in recent years [11]. It was intended to observe the short-term management's impact on the Iberian Peninsula's corporate performance, for which three performance evaluation measures were used, namely ROA, ROE, and Tobin's Q. As such, a panel of 106 large Iberian companies was used for the period from 2010 to 2016.

Using the panel data methodology, the relevance of some results is emphasized. It is worth noting that companies need to reduce the ACP to increase corporate performance.

It is also highlighted the negative relationship between leverage and ROE, which by the way is the only significant relation for this measure when considering the Spanish sample.

Concerning the interest in using alternative performance variables, this study reveals that the ROA and Tobin's Q are the variables that best reflect the corporate performance when studying determinants based on short-term management. This result is even more interesting insofar as the ROA is considered a company/accounting variable and Tobin's Q is a market variable and therefore considers the investor's perception. Additionally, ROE proves to be the worst measure of performance evaluation.

The main limitations encountered were related to the fact that not all the companies presented in the sample offered all the necessary information for the period under analysis. Moreover, the number of scientific publications on this subject is still scarce, in particular regarding European countries, for example. For this reason, it is intended that this study contributes in a positive way to the increase of existing studies not only in Portugal and Spain but also for studies on this subject in Europe.

In future research, it would be interesting to add more European countries to the sample to conduct a comparative study, but also to introduce countries with different tax systems, common law vs. civil law, to see if the determinants of performance would change. In addition, it would be useful to see whether the determinants vary according to the different economic cycles, bull vs. bear markets, introducing sectoral, macroeconomic, and investor sentiment variables.

Acknowledgements

This work is supported by national funds, through the FCT—Portuguese Foundation for Science and Technology under the project UIDB/04011/2020.

Author details

Carmem Leal[1*], Diogo Rocha[2] and Elisabete Neves[3]

1 CETRAD—University of Trás-os-Montes e Alto Douro, Vila Real, Portugal

2 University of Trás-os-Montes e Alto Douro, Vila Real, Portugal

3 ISCAC|Coimbra Business School, Coimbra, Portugal

*Address all correspondence to: cleal@utad.pt

References

[1] Weill P. The relationship between investment in information technology and firm performance: A study of the valve manufacturing sector. Information Systems Research. 1992;**3**(4):307-333

[2] Berger AN, Di Patti EB. Capital structure and firm performance: A new approach to testing agency theory and an application to the banking industry. Journal of Banking & Finance. 2006; **30**(4):1065-1102

[3] Amidu M. How does dividend policy affect performance of the firm on Ghana stock exchange. Investment Management and Financial Innovations. 2007;**4**(2):103-112

[4] Konar S, Cohen MA. Does the market value environmental performance? Review of Economics and Statistics. 2001;**83**(2):281-289

[5] García-Teruel PJ, Martínez-Solano P. Effects of working capital management on SME profitability. International Journal of Managerial Finance. 2007;**3**:164-177

[6] Lamberson M. Changes in working capital of small firms in relation to changes in economic activity. American Journal of Business. 1995;**10**(2):45-50

[7] Jose ML, Lancaster C, Stevens JL. Corporate returns and cash conversion cycles. Journal of Economics and Finance. 1996;**20**(1):33-46

[8] Banos-Caballero S, Garcia-Teruel PJ, Martinez-Solano P. How does working capital management affect the profitability of Spanish SMEs? Small Business Economics. 2012;**39**(2):517-529. DOI: 10.1007/s11187-011-9317-8

[9] Deloof M. Does working capital management affect profitability of Belgian firms? Journal of Business Finance & Accounting. 2003;**30**(3-4):573-588

[10] Pais MA, Gama PM. Working capital management and SMEs profitability: Portuguese evidence. International Journal of Managerial Finance. 2015; **11**(3):341-358

[11] Singh HP, Kumar S, Colombage S. Working capital management and firm profitability: A meta-analysis. Qualitative Research In Financial Markets. 2017;**9**(1):34-47. DOI: 10.1108/QRFM-06-2016-0018

[12] Zeitun R, Tian GG. Capital structure and corporate performance: Evidence from Jordan. Australasian Accounting Business & Finance Journal. 2014; **1**:40-53

[13] Mathuva DM. Influence of working capital management components on corporate profitability: A survey on Kenyan listed firms. Research Journal of Business Management. 2010;**3**(1):1-11

[14] Nurein SA, Din MS, Mohd Rus R. Nonlinear relationship between investment in working capital and performance: Innovative evidence from food and beverages industry. European Journal of Economics, Finance and Administrative Sciences. 2015;**77**: 63-72

[15] Kim YH, Chung KH. An integrated evaluation of investment in inventory and credit: A cash flow approach. Journal of Business Finance & Accounting. 1990; **17**(3):381-389

[16] Richards VD, Laughlin EJ. A cash conversion cycle approach to liquidity analysis. Financial Management. 1980; **9**(1):32-38

[17] Sathyamoorthi CR, Wally-Dima LB. Working capital management: The case of listed retail domestic companies in Botswana. The Icfaian Journal of Management Research. 2008;7(5):7-24

[18] Uyar A. The relationship of cash conversion cycle with firm size and profitability: An empirical investigation in Turkey. International Research Journal of Finance and Economics. 2009; **24**(2):186-193

[19] Vural G, Sökmen AG, Çetenak EH. Affects of working capital management on firm's performance: Evidence from Turkey. International Journal of Economics and Financial Issues. 2012; **2**(4):488

[20] Mohamad NEAB, Saad NBM. Working capital management: The effect of market valuation and profitability in Malaysia. International Journal of Business and Management. 2010;**5**(11): 140

[21] Husna A, Satria I. Effects of return on asset, debt to asset ratio, current ratio, firm size, and dividend payout ratio on firm value. International Journal of Economics and Financial Issues. 2019; **9**(5):50

[22] Raheman A, Nasr M. Working capital management and profitability–case of Pakistani firms. International Review of Business Research Papers. 2007;**3**(1):279-300

[23] Eljelly AMA. Liquidity-profitability tradeoff: An empirical investigation in an emerging market. International Journal of Commerce and Management. 2004; **14**(2):48-61

[24] Goddard J, Tavakoli M, Wilson JOS. Determinants of profitability in European manufacturing and services: Evidence from a dynamic panel model. Applied Financial Economics. 2005; **15**(18):1269-1282

[25] Fagiolo G, Luzzi A. Do liquidity constraints matter in explaining firm size and growth? Some evidence from the Italian manufacturing industry. Industrial and Corporate Change. 2006; **15**(1):1-39

[26] Safdar MZ, Awan MZ, Ahmed Z, Qureshi MI, Hasnain T. What does matter? Liquidity or profitability: A case of sugar industry in Pakistan. International Journal of Economics and Financial Issues. 2016;**6**(3S):144-152

[27] Du J, Wu F, Liang X. In: SHS Web of Conferences. Vol. 24. 2016. p. 1013

[28] Holmström B, Tirole J. Liquidity and risk management. Journal of Money, Credit and Banking. 2000;**32**:295-319

[29] Muritala TA. An empirical analysis of capital structure on firm's performance in Nigeria. International Journal of Advances in Management and Economics. 2012;**1**(5):116-124

[30] Olokoyo FO. Capital structure and corporate performance of Nigerian quoted firms: A panel data approach. African Development Review. 2013; **25**(3):358-369

[31] Berger AN, Herring RJ, Szegö GP. The role of capital in financial institutions. Journal of Banking & Finance. 1995;**19**(3-4):393-430

[32] Adams M. Investment earnings and the characteristics of life insurance firms: New Zealand evidence. Australian Journal of Management. 1996;**21**(1): 41-55

[33] Kedzior M, Grabinska B, Grabinski K, Kedzior D. Capital structure choices in technology firms:

Empirical results from Polish listed companies. Journal of Risk and Financial Management. 2020;**13**(9):221

[34] Serrasqueiro ZS, Nunes PM. Performance and size: Empirical evidence from Portuguese SMEs. Small Business Economics. 2008;**31**(2):195-217

[35] Lee J. Does size matter in firm performance? Evidence from US public firms. International Journal of the Economics of Business. 2009;**16**(2): 189-203

[36] Yoon S. A note on the market structure and performance in Korean manufacturing industries. Journal of Policy Modeling. 2004;**26**(6):733-746

[37] Griliches Z, Lichtenberg FR. R&D and productivity growth at the industry level: Is there still a relationship? In: R&D, Patents, and Productivity. Chicago: University of Chicago Press; 1984. pp. 465-502

[38] Maina L, Ishmail M. Capital structure and financial performance in Kenya: Evidence from firms listed at the Nairobi Securities Exchange. International Journal of Social Sciences and Entrepreneurship. 2014;**1**(11): 209-223

[39] Nucci F, Pozzolo A, Schivardi F, others. Is firm's productivity related to its financial structure? Evidence from microeconomic data. Rivista Di Politica Economica. 2005;**95**(1):269-290

[40] Fahlenbrach R, Stulz RM. Bank CEO incentives and the credit crisis. Journal of Financial Economics. 2011;**99**(1): 11-26

[41] Sá TM, Neves ED, Góis CG. The influence of corporate governance on changes in risk following the global financial crisis: Evidence from the Portuguese stock market. Journal of Management & Governance. 2017;**21**(4): 841-878

[42] Arellano M, Bond S. Some tests of specification for panel data: Monte Carlo evidence and an application to employment equations. The Review of Economic Studies. 1991;**58**(2):277-297

[43] Neves MED. Payout and firm's catering. International Journal of Economics & Business Administration (IJEBA). 2017;**4**:104-132

[44] Blundell R, Bond S. Initial conditions and moment restrictions in dynamic panel data models. Journal of Econometrics. 1998;**87**(1):115-143

[45] Yazdanfar D, Öhman P. The impact of cash conversion cycle on firm profitability: An empirical study based on Swedish data. International Journal of Managerial Finance. 2014;**10**(4):442-452

[46] Pouraghajan A, Malekian E, Emamgholipour M, Lotfollahpour V, Bagheri MM. The relationship between capital structure and firm performance evaluation measures: Evidence from the Tehran Stock Exchange. International Journal of Business and Commerce. 2012;**1**(9):166-181

[47] Sensini L. Working capital management and performance: Evidence from Italian SME's. International Journal of Business Management and Economic Research (IJBMER). 2020;**11**(2): 1749-1755

[48] Rogers M. Networks, firm size and innovation. Small Business Economics. 2004;**22**(2):141-153

Section 7

Accounting Policy and IFRS

Chapter 9

National Adoptions of IFRS: Accounting Perspectives

Maria Bengtsson

Abstract

In the past few decades, there has been a global trend of international harmonization of accounting standards. The intended goal is to remove the barriers that hinder investors when comparing the accounting information of companies from different nations, while simultaneously reducing the transaction costs for firms. However, research has shown that countries adopt IFRS unequally, ranging from resistance, partial adoption to full adoption. If the IFRS are not adopted to the same extent around the world, the central purpose of international standards can be compromised. This chapter aims to explain some key terms essential in understanding current development in international accounting and lay out the development and progress of IFRS diffusion.

Keywords: IFRS, national adoption, convergence, divergence

1. Introduction

National accounting standards have historically been developed by each nation or by a cluster of nations for the entities that reside within their accounting judiciaries [1, 2]. These standards are typically designed to meet specific national needs [3]. However, in the past few decades, there has been a global trend of international harmonization of accounting standards, with many countries having either partially or completely replaced their national accounting standards with the International Financial Reporting Standards (IFRS) [4, 5]. As profiled by the International Accounting Standards Board (IASB) in 2019, over 140 jurisdictions in all major regions in the world (**Figure 1**) have either required or permitted IFRS usage for their domestic publicly accountable entities [6]. Such a massive adoption of a single set of accounting standards worldwide may represent the most significant accounting regulatory change in recent years [7].

The IFRS can be defined as a single set of accounting standards that are intended to be consistently and globally applied—that is, to be used by developed, transitional, and emerging economies alike [8]. The IFRS are intended to provide investors and other users of financial statements with the ability to compare the financial performance of publicly listed companies on a like-for-like basis with the companies' international peers. Conceptually speaking, adopting a single set of global accounting standards is undeniably appealing. In theory, global standards would remove the barriers that hinder investors when comparing the accounting information of companies from different nations, while simultaneously reducing the transaction costs for firms [9–11]. Empirical

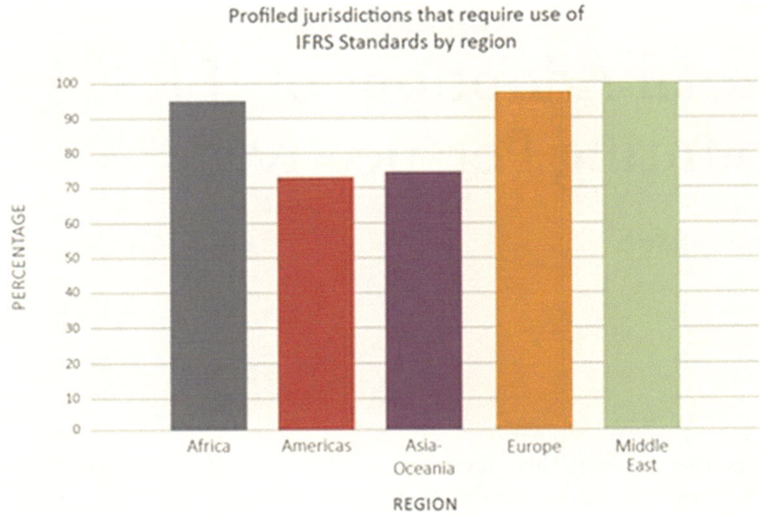

Figure 1.
IFRS adoption by region. Source: IFRS Foundation 2019.

studies have confirmed that IFRS adoption has (to a certain degree) increased the compatibility of financial statements across national borders, and that the IFRS have achieved many of the goals they were intended to reach [1, 7, 12, 13].

However, despite the economic benefits of the IFRS and their apparent support by the great majority of countries, research has shown that national IFRS adoptions are difficult and problematic [14–16]. One major issue is that countries do not adopt IFRS to the same extent. Nobes and Zeff [17] show that some countries adopt the IFRS as issued by the IASB, while others claim that their own national GAAP are "based on" or "similar to" the IFRS—when, in fact, large differences remain. According to an extensive report compiled by Deloitte [18], it is also common for countries to claim that they have "adopted" the IFRS while choosing to deviate or not to include certain provisions from the IFRS as issued by the IASB. In addition, despite the great number of countries that have adopted IFRS, the three largest economies in the world—the United States, China, and Japan—have not yet fully accepted the IFRS into their national reporting standards, even for listed companies [6].

Thus, it is debatable whether international accounting harmonization is indeed as successful as it seems to be [19]; in fact, it may be just a veneer over continued national differences [15, 20]. Users of financial information should be aware that IFRS do not necessarily carry the same implications throughout the world [16], despite the IASB's intentions. Some scholars warn that, if the IFRS are not adopted to the same extent around the world, the central purpose of international standards will be compromised, as foreign investors will be unable to be confident when reading financial statements [15, 17]. Uneven IFRS adoption could even be harmful to investors who believe that accounting standards have been converged worldwide—when, in fact, financial reporting differences continue to exist across national borders while being covered under the façade of the IFRS.

1.1 The IFRS adoption process

IFRS adoption is a complex and multi-level governance process (**Figure 2**) [2, 21]. After being promulgated by the IASB, IFRS adoption occurs at both the *de jure* level

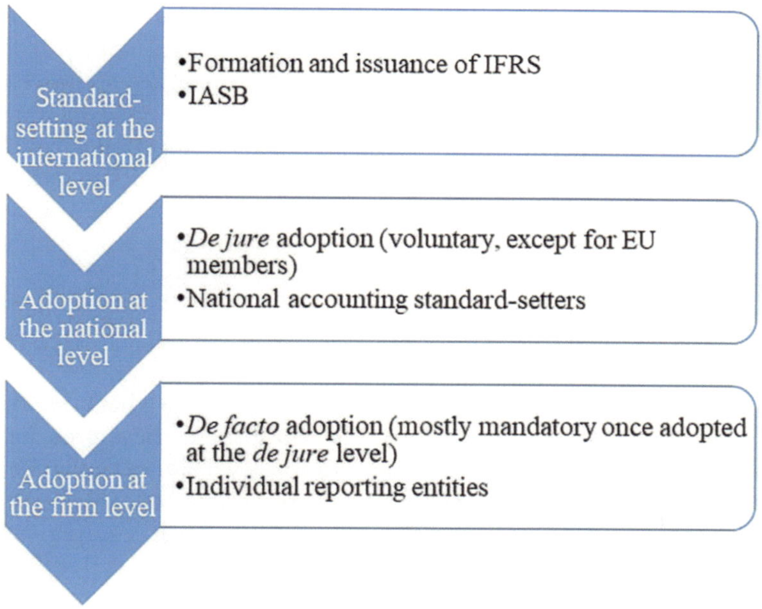

Figure 2.
Multi-tier IFRS adoption.

(e.g., recognizing the IFRS as part of a nation's law) and the *de facto* level (e.g., annual and quarterly reporting by the nation's entities). That is, a country may choose to adopt the IFRS as issued by the IASB, include it as part of its mandatory regulations [22], and require some or all of the entities within its jurisdiction to comply with the IFRS. On the other hand, when allowed by national regulation, firms may also choose to adopt IFRS before the country's official IFRS adoption [10]. These two level of adoption are interrelated, although differences must be acknowledged [23]. National accounting standard-setters are likely to take domestic firms' needs into consideration when deciding whether or not to adopt IFRS. By the same token, firms need to comply with the national requirements to either mandatorily adopt or voluntarily adopt IFRS. **Figure 2** depicts the multi-level diffusion and adoption of IFRS.

It is important to recognize that firm-level IFRS adoption is conditional on countries' decisions to allow or mandate IFRS in an adoption process [23]. Many countries first voluntarily adopt IFRS at the national level, and then write the standards into the local GAAP, which then become mandatory at the firm level. It has been shown that countries have adopted IFRS unevenly [18], so differences in countries' IFRS adoptions already exist at the national level before trickling down to the firm level [5, 24, 25]. As most domestically listed firms must comply with the national GAAP or regulations, instead of directly complying with IFRS, they may have no choice but to deviate from the IFRS, as issued by the IASB [7, 26–28].

1.2 Some key terms

Financial accounting research is often loaded with special concepts, both technical and theoretical, that bear specific meanings that either clarify for or further confuse readers. This issue is manifested in international accounting due to the scope of diversity in accounting traditions. Some of the important concepts in this field have been unclearly used or defined. Many employ these concepts, but few define them. In addition, certain concepts are often treated as interchangeable, even though they do not represent precisely the same thing. This is perhaps inevitable for a subject as complex as IFRS. Nevertheless, to better understand international accounting harmonization, it is necessary to clarify these embedded meanings, since different usages may tilt discussions in somewhat different directions. It is also important to note that there is no strict "right" or "wrong" definitions of these terms, as important and evolving concepts can hardly be expected to have clear-cut definitions. Rather, the purpose of the effort is to note blurred or unclear definitions and introduce some clarity to the extent that has been identified in IFRS literature.

1.2.1 International accounting system

A dichotomy exists in the accounting literature in regard to what is meant by the term "international accounting system" and how it should be approached. One approach defines "accounting system" at the national level. For example, Gray [29] states that a country's accounting system constitutes various national characteristics, such as the structure and development of capital markets, legal requirements, professional accounting standards, and tax law. Similarly, Doupnik and Salter [30] believe that the international accounting system resides in national legislature. By contrast, other authors regard an accounting system as a firm-level practice. For instance, Nobes [31] defines an accounting system as "a set of practices used in a published annual report." Commenting on the difference in the two approaches, Nobes [31] argues that, although there is a formal set of rules or systems at the legislature level, companies sometimes choose to depart from these rules. According to Nobes, the advantage of using the firm-level definition, although it is admittedly narrow, is that this definition can actually have wider empirical implications.

1.2.2 De jure harmonization versus de facto harmonization

An important conceptual distinction must be understood between the *de jure* and *de facto* harmonization. *De jure* harmonization of international accounting standards involves the formal harmonization of regulations at the country level, while *de facto* harmonization refers to the material harmonization of the financial reporting practices performed at the firm level [22]. In the accounting literature, both Tay and Parker [32] and Canibano and Mora [33] refer to *de jure* harmonization as the harmonization of accounting regulations and to *de facto* harmonization as the increase in comparability that arises from greater conformity in practice. Qu and Zhang [22] argue that *de jure* harmonization is the basis for achieving *de facto* harmonization. In fact, *de jure* harmonization can but does not necessarily lead to *de facto* harmonization, if the standards allow for more options for companies [33]. Nevertheless, *de facto* accounting harmonization cannot be achieved without first achieving *de jure* accounting harmonization [33]. The decision to adopt IFRS can be made both at the *de jure* level (if the IFRS are mandated to be followed as nation-wide reporting standards) and at the *de facto* level (if the IFRS are one of the reporting standards firms are allowed to choose from) [34].

1.2.3 Convergence versus adoption

The terms "convergence" and "adoption" have recently come into use as nations attempt to narrow the gap between their national accounting standards and the

IFRS. It is important to note that convergence is not equivalent to adoption [5, 15]. The differences between these two concepts have set off a great deal of debate within the field of international accounting research. Nobes [35] argues that, in order to be called adoption, relevant entities must state that their financial statements are in full compliance with the IFRS as issued by the IASB. Thus, at the country level, "adoption" should mean that the national set of accounting standards is directly replaced by the IFRS as issued by the IASB. This position is taken by the Member States of the EU, which have fully applied the IFRS since 2005. By comparison, "convergence" is the gradual mechanism of changing local accounting standards into IFRS. Although it does not mean full adoption, convergence can indicate only a minimal difference between a nation's standards and the IFRS [36]. According to the IASB's position, convergence will not, by definition, lead to a common set of global standards. Nevertheless, convergence has been and will likely remain a useful process to facilitate adoption by narrowing differences. Thus, convergence should be a means of making the transition to the full adoption of IFRS standards, and not an end in itself [37]. By the same token, Zeff and Nobes [38] emphasize that convergence is a dynamic process of consistency with IFRS in accounting principles and substance, which is neither a direct adoption of IFRS nor a word-for-word translation of IFRS. Rather, convergence is the act of moving towards uniformity. Zeff and Nobes use China and Venezuela as examples of countries that use the IFRS as a starting point for drafting national standards, but then diverge significantly from the IFRS as issued by the IASB. Some countries that have "converged" with the IFRS are nonetheless counted by the IFRS Foundation and by others as adopters of the IFRS, which—according to Zeff and Nobes [38]—is misleading.

In the same vein, Ball [15] notes that convergence is "the process of narrowing the differences between IFRS and the accounting standards of countries that retain their own standards." Convergence is a modified version of adoption in which multiple sets of rules or practices are the same [5]. Therefore, the relation between convergence and adoption is not dichotomous. These two concepts represent the subtleties of the development and diffusion of IFRS at various stages. Following this logic, Nobes [35] states that the word "convergence" is more correct when applied to the joint program of the IASB and the United States' Financial Accounting Standards Board (FASB), because both have changed particular standards to match each other's, and the IASB and FASB have run many joint projects. In the case of other countries, however, convergence with the IFRS is a euphemism for the piecemeal adoption of IFRS [35].

1.2.4 Standardization versus harmonization

Standardization and harmonization are often used interchangeably in IFRS studies. However, the difference between them should not be ignored [39]. Standardization implies a movement towards uniformity, whereas harmonization is a movement away from total diversity [32]. In the context of International Accounting Standards (IAS), McLeay et al. [39] suggest that "whilst international standardization implies a movement towards global uniformity, harmonization implies a movement towards similarity in the choice between alternative accounting treatments." They define international standardization as a process that constrains choice, ultimately resulting in the adoption of the same accounting method by all firms and all countries. International accounting harmonization, on the other hand, is a process that results in a systematic choice between accounting methods across national borders [39]. Such choices are dependent upon the nature of the nation or firm and its operating environment, but are otherwise independent of the location in which the nation or firm happens to be registered [39]. Similarly, Canibano and Mora [33] argue that harmonization is a more realistic and conciliatory approach than standardization, and is also more attainable and less rigid. However, other scholars disagree. For instance, Arnold [40] believes that harmonization is equivalent to standardization. That is, according to Arnold, accounting harmonization equates to the standardization of financial reporting standards, auditing standards, and/or other accounting-related rules and regulations such as licensing and qualification requirements or ethics rules.

2. The history and legitimacy of IFRS

It has been argued that the international harmonization of accounting standards is a result of the economic integration and increasing trading between national borders [41]. In addition, corporate economic scandals have shaken investors' trust in financial reporting. To regain both inventors' trust and economic order, it has become necessary to strengthen the comparability and transparency of financial reporting across national borders [8].

2.1 Background of IFRS diffusion: economic integration and global financial crisis

Economic globalization and integration form an important context in which national IFRS adoption has become not only necessary, but also urgent [9, 42]. Economic globalization has created a new common ground for businesses to engage in trade and transactions across national borders [41]. In this new "game," certain common rules must be understood and followed by all participants to ensure a functional trading place. As the vice chairman of IASB, Ian Mackintosh comments:

It is increasingly difficult to see different and often incompatible national accounting standards as anything other than a legacy of a bygone era. They add cost, complexity and translation risk to companies and investors operating in today's global marketplace [43].

According to the IASB, about one third of all financial investments in the world are international transactions. It is essential for differences in national accounting standards to be eliminated, or at least understood by all players. Thus, it is necessary for national accounting standard-setters to change their existing national accounting systems in order to facilitate international economic changes, assuming that a growing economy is part of the national plan. Global standards are achievable and an inevitable consequence of continued economic globalization. As stated on the IASB website:

This [globalization] evidence indicates that global standards are both desirable, achievable and inevitable. As economic globalization continues apace, so too will the force of the arguments in favor of IFRS adoption within those remaining jurisdictions [44].

In addition to global economic integration, the accounting scandals in the early 2000s that brought down large multinational corporations (MNCs) such as Enron and Arthur Anderson have increased investors' awareness of the importance of trustworthy accounting standards. Furthermore, in the summer of 2007, accumulating losses on U.S. subprime mortgages triggered widespread disruption to the global financial system. In less than a year, the situation developed into an international financial crisis and eventually resulted in a global economic downturn that further shook investors' confidence in the stock market. As stated on the IASB website:

Post-crisis, policymakers are all too aware of how every national capital market in the world, even the largest, functions as little more than a satellite of the global financial system [43, 44].

To reestablish confidence in the soundness of markets and financial institutions, as well as to prevent further crises, the G20[1] summit in Washington on November 15, 2008, produced a thorough analysis and summary of the root causes of these crises and put forward action plans that included improving the IASB's governance and supporting the IFRS as the single set of high-quality global accounting standards. Both national and international organizations developed recommendations and resources aimed at promoting the IFRS. The G20 called on the IASB and the Financial Accounting Standards Board (FASB) in the US to improve standards on valuation and provisioning and to achieve a single set of accounting standards. The G20 summit in London in April 2009 further required proactive collaboration from member countries on convergence with the IFRS in order to prevent similar financial crises. In the same year, the G20 formed the special Financial Crisis Advisory Group (FCAG). The FCAG supports the IASB in promoting the IFRS to be the single set of global accounting standards in order to reestablish investors' confidence in accounting information.

However, the G20 has never required countries to fully adopt the IFRS. Instead, it encourages its members to converge with the IFRS. The IASB does not agree with this position and has expressed on multiple occasions that only full adoption of IFRS, not convergence with IFRS, can ensure global financial stability and prevent similar financial crises. According to the IASB, the G20 and its various committees, while pushing the diffusion of IFRS, have frequently focused on national interests, which can create barriers and impediments to economic growth and jeopardize global financial stability. As the chairman of the IASB remarked:

This inability to deliver compatible outcomes with the FASB clearly demonstrates the inherent instability of convergence as a means to achieve a single set of global accounting standards. For this reason, our Trustees wisely concluded that convergence can never be a substitute for adoption of IFRS. Thankfully, throughout the financial crisis, the momentum towards adoption has continued unabated in many countries [44].

Despite this disagreement from the IASB, the G20—which promoted the IFRS in the past due to the financial crisis—has recently been less enthusiastic. Support for the work of the IASB has been decreasing. For example, in the past, the communiqués had always included a paragraph such as this:

We underline the importance of continuing work on accounting standards convergence in order to enhance the resilience of the financial system. We urge the International Accounting Standards Board and the US Financial Accounting Standards Board to complete by the end of 2013 their work on key outstanding projects for achieving a single set of high-quality accounting standards [45].

However, the newest communiqués issued after the meeting of the G20 in 2014 and thereafter no longer contain a call for converged accounting standards.

---

[1] The G20 consists of the finance ministers and central banks from 19 countries and the EU.

2.2 The history and development of the IASB

The formal history of the IASB began with the International Accounting Standards Committee (IASC). In 1973, the IASC was jointly established by professional accounting bodies in Australia, Canada, France, Germany, Japan, Mexico, the Netherlands, the United Kingdom, Ireland, and the United States. Between 1973 and 2001, the IASC issued IAS. The IASC was essentially a structure, rather than a committee in the traditional sense of a group of people. The IASC originally had a goal of "harmonization" by reducing differences between accounting standards in major capital markets. By the 1990s, however, the IASC reshaped its goal into "convergence," which, according to the organization, is a step above harmonization. The convergence concept is to develop a "single set of high-quality, international accounting standards that would be used in at least all major capital markets." In 1995, The IASC and the International Organization of Securities Commissions (IOSCO) agreed on what constituted a comprehensive set of core standards. The IASC undertook a project to complete those core standards by 1999. The IOSCO agreed that, if it found these core standards acceptable, it would recommend the endorsement of IASC standards for cross-border capital and listing purposes in all capital markets [46]. In May 2000, the IOSCO completed its assessment and accepted the IASC's core standards. Members of the IOSCO were encouraged to use the IASC standards to prepare their financial reporting for international offerings and listings, supplemented where necessary to address outstanding substantive issues at a national or regional level, or to use waivers of particular aspects of the IASC standards without requiring further reconciliation under exceptional circumstances [47].

In 1997, after nearly 25 years of existence, the IASC concluded that, in order to continue to bring about convergence between national accounting standards and practices and high-quality global accounting standards, it had to find a better way to perform its role effectively. To do so, the IASC saw a need to change its structure. The standard-setting body was thus renamed as the IASB. Formally, the IASB is a private standard-setting organization based in London. It operates under the IASC Foundation, which is more widely known as the IFRS Foundation. The IASB is primarily funded by fundraising activities, which are the responsibility of the IFRS Foundation. The governance, oversight, and standard-setting processes of the IASB are similar to those of the FASB in the United States. The IASB has 14 board members (including a chair and a vice chair) with a variety of functional backgrounds and from different continents. The currently sitting IASB Chair is Andreas Barckow. The primary purpose of the IASB is to promulgate IFRS. It is committed to the mission of developing a single set of high-quality, understandable, and enforceable global accounting standards and working with national standard-setters to achieve accounting standards convergence. The IASB has inherited 25 standards issued by the IASC, covering various issues. Because the IAS standards were essentially distillations of existing accounting practices used around the world, they often allowed alternative treatments for the same transactions. The IASB decided to undertake a comparability and improvement project to reduce the number of allowable alternatives and make the IFRS standards more prescriptive than descriptive [48].

2.3 The development and adoption of IFRS around the world

Although IFRS have now been accepted by the majority of countries around the world, their initial acceptance by national accounting standard-setters and firms was not as smooth as many might think. The process began in the 1970s, and it took a long time for the IFRS to gain worldwide recognition.

2.3.1 Initial hesitations and uncertainties regarding adoption

Prior to the first major wave of IFRS adoption among the European countries in 2005, there was a great deal of debate about the relevance and feasibility of implementing a single set of accounting standards worldwide. During this time, national and international standard-setters tried to understand how the globalization of the economy had influenced countries' acceptance of IFRS; they also tried to identify key factors or obstacles that could affect a nation's capacity for adoption and willingness to adopt. In this process, there were concerns that, even if countries or firms chose or were required to adopt IFRS, they might not be ready and might apply IFRS differently, creating a bigger problem than before. The KPMG issued a survey of 149 accounting professionals showing that there was general concern that uncertainty over the applicability of IFRS among EU companies had delayed the voluntary IFRS adoption of many [49]. Similarly, the Institute of Chartered Accountants in England and Wales (ICAEW) raised concerns regarding the lack of preparation for the introduction of IFRS. The ICAEW conducted a survey among its members asking whether they would, if given the choice, move to IAS. Only over a third of the businesses said that they would be likely to move to IAS. The ICAEW concluded that tardy preparation for IFRS adoption by some firms could cause them to receive qualified audit opinions upon IFRS adoption [50].

Another concern was the feasibility of implementing an Anglo-Saxon accounting model into other social contexts. Some observers have regarded international accounting harmonization as predominantly implying compliance with an Anglo-Saxon accounting model [51], and contend that the international accounting standards agenda of the IASB is a means of imposing an Anglo-American hegemony. Such a contention was somewhat evident in the 1990s, when the staffing complement of the IASB was dominated by Anglo-Americans. For example, even though the ASEAN Federation of Accountants (AFA) had sought a greater level of representation and participation by Asian nations in the deliberations of the IASC, prior to 1995, only Malaysia and Singapore out of the ASEAN AFA member countries had been represented on working committees. Setting aside the achievability of global standardization, Dye and Sunder [52] also question whether having a single global set of accounting standards is even desirable. They argue that there were several benefits in allowing firms to follow either IFRS or the U.S. GAAP, and contend that competitions among standard-setters can help to meet the needs of globalization and increase the efficiency of accounting standards.

2.3.2 Major waves of IFRS adoption around the world

Despite the skepticism in the early stage of IFRS harmonization, during the push for the internationalization of accounting standards, the accounting differences between IFRS and other major national accounting standards, such as the U.S. GAAP, were narrowing [53]. In the late 1990s, some countries began to allow voluntary adoption of IFRS. For example, in 1998, the law §292a HGB was passed in Germany, permitting German listed companies to prepare consolidated accounts in accordance with the IFRS. In the meantime, many major stock exchanges around the world, including the London, Frankfurt, Zurich, Luxembourg, Bangkok, Hong Kong,

Amsterdam, Rome, and Kuala Lumpur stock exchanges, began to accept financial statements from foreign listed companies prepared under the IFRS without reconciliation. In the United States, the SEC also began to allow disclosures based on IFRS. As stated by the SEC, the reasons for accepting such standards in the U.S stock changes were as follows:

Our decision to adopt the International Disclosure Standards was based on our conclusion that the standards were of high quality and that their adoption would provide information comparable to the amount and quality of information that U.S. investors receive today [54].

The FASB decided that the need for international standards was strong enough to warrant more focused activity on its part. The then FASB Chairman, Dennis Beresford, expressed his support for "superior international standards" that would gradually replace national standards, and identified new initiatives to get the FASB more directly involved in the drive to improve international standards [55]. The FASB and the IASC began to undertake concurrent projects to improve their earnings per share standards with the specific objective of eliminating the differences between them.

The large listed European companies that chose early voluntary adoption of IFRS did so because they believed that the use of international standards would enable better communication with information users, especially international investors. For example, KPMG [49] reported in a survey that the reasons for European companies to switch from national standards to international standards included (1) the possibility of increasing the availability of capital and lowering its cost; (2) the perceived high quality of the IFRS; and (3) the preferences of institutional investors and analysts.

Then, in the early 2000s, efforts to internationally harmonize accounting standards finally evolved into a broad worldwide convergence effort at the national level. In 2002, the EU adopted legislation requiring all listed companies to prepare their consolidated financial statements using IFRS starting in 2005, which represented the first major capital market to require IFRS. The regulation states that IFRS adoption is intended to achieve "a high degree of transparency and comparability of financial statements and hence an efficient functioning of the (EU) Community capital market and of the Internal Market." In the same year, the FASB and the IASB embarked on a partnership to improve and converge the U.S. GAAP and international accounting standards. That partnership is described in the Norwalk Agreement, which was issued after the joint meeting. The Norwalk Agreement set out the shared goal of developing compatible, high-quality accounting standards that could be used for both domestic and cross-border financial reporting [56]. Beginning in November 15, 2007, the U.S. SEC allowed the listing of foreign companies using the IFRS on the NYSE without having to first reconcile their financial statements with the U.S. GAAP. In the meantime, several other jurisdictions such as Hong Kong and Australia also chose to adopt IFRS. Japan and China also formed convergence plans with the IASB. In 2007, China achieved major convergence between the Chinese GAAP and the IFRS.

In addition, there was a continuation of the worldwide planning efforts at the international level. For example, in response to the international financial crisis, the G20 summit in Washington on November 15, 2008 produced a profound analysis and summary of the root causes of the crisis and put forward action plans that included improving the IASB's governance and establishing a single set of high-quality global accounting standards [57]. The G20 summit in London in April 2009 required proactive collaboration from member countries in converging accounting standards [58]. The IMF routinely provided foreign aid to developing countries or countries in financial trouble with the demand that reform be enacted in the public and private sectors. Such demands were often tied to the demand that IFRS accounting standards be adopted. After the few rounds of major waves of IFRS adoption around the world, the success of IFRS convergence is now apparent. According to the recent IASB report, more than 140 jurisdictions have adopted IFRS with very few modifications, and the few jurisdictions that have made modifications are generally regarded as taking temporary steps in their plans to adopt IFRS.

2.3.3 Recent slowdown and increased skepticism

In more recent years, despite the momentum of IFRS adoption by nations, there have been renewed concerns over the success and legitimacy of IFRS. Notwithstanding the claims by the IASB that modifications to the IFRS are rare, some academic research has shown continued major differences among national financial reporting [15, 59–61]. Of course, as Nobes and Zeff [17] point out, the most obvious limitation to the scope of the mandatory use of IFRS is that the phrase "all the major countries" does not include the world's three largest economies: the United States, China, and Japan. They argue that, with the great increase in adoptions of IFRS, warnings about the vague claims are even more relevant, because the population of adopters is now much larger yet still shows considerable variety.

In addition, the speed of IFRS adoption has begun to slow down as the initial enthusiasm fades away. The Chinese GAAP, for example, have remained in a convergence but non-adoption status since 2006. The Chinese Ministry of Finance (MOF) originally set 2011 as the target year for the continuing and full convergence program of the ASBE, making 2010–2011 a critical period for China's convergence. The MOF planned to initiate the overhaul of its ASBE system in 2010 and finish by 2011. All large and medium-sized enterprises would be required to use the revised standards as of 2012 [62]. This goal, as of 2019, remains in the planning stage without further movement. In the United States, in January 2008, participants in an FASB roundtable predicted that it would take about 5 years to complete the full adoption of IFRS by the United States. More than 12 years have passed since then, yet the United States has not only not adopted the IFRS, but also started to actively resist them.

Even if IFRS could achieve global convergence in the short term, observers have questioned whether these benefits are sustainable. By adopting IFRS, a country essentially allows a foreign entity with no local accountability to dictate its reporting laws and thereby control the economic incentives and activities of its people and businesses [63]. The former chairman of the SEC, Cox, points to this concern as a reason why a full-scale adoption of IFRS is unlikely to occur in the United States. He expressed his frustration and the downgrading of his trust in the IFRS in a keynote speech addressing the SEC:

...when I was SEC Chairman, I worked to ensure that the United States was doing everything necessary to make financial information from companies in different countries both comparable and reliable. But that was several years ago. And a great deal has changed since then. Today, I come to bury IFRS, not to praise them [63].

Cox further argued that the full adoption of IFRS by the United States might once have been possible, but is no longer so [63]. Some of the IFRS-adopting economies have also been requiring a national standard-setter to review and, if needed, modify the IFRS before they become the law of the land. This cherry-picking approach may lead each national regulator to adopt certain standards while rejecting others, thereby causing countries to diverge again in their accounting standards in the long run. On the other side, the IASB, which is facing increasing resistance, has emphasized that it remains committed to the long-term goal of the global adoption of IFRS as developed by the IASB, in their entirety and without modification. The IASB believes that convergence may be an appropriate short-term solution for a particular jurisdiction and may facilitate adoption over a transitional period. Convergence, however, should not be a substitute for adoption. Adoption mechanisms may differ among nations and may require a period of time to implement, but they should enable and require relevant entities to state that their financial statements are in full compliance with IFRS as issued by the IASB [64]. As stated on the IASB's website:

There is a natural temptation for countries (and stakeholders within those countries) to argue against full adoption of IFRSs, to call for convergence of national standards and IFRSs rather than adoption, or to introduce national exceptions to IFRS rules. The temptation to pursue convergence rather than adoption should be resisted. Full adoption of IFRSs must be the end goal...Having once achieved convergence, standards could well diverge again [64].

To summarize, the most important reasons for the speedy and wide diffusion of IFRS are the growing integration of the world's economy and a series of financial crises. This combination has increased the demand from international investors for better quality and comparability of financial reporting. As a result, the mission of the IASB has evolved over time. After initial hesitation on the part of nations, followed by fast adoption in many parts of the world, IFRS harmonization has begun to slow down in recent years.

3. Chapter summary

This chapter has provided clarifications of some seemingly exchangeable but different terminologies when examining the complex topic of IFRS. The development and diffusion of IFRS have led a winding road characterized by initial doubts, fast adoption and recent slowdown. This chapter brought forward important insights regarding current development on international accounting harmonization by pointing out the trend of massive adoption of IFRS by country and the simultaneous variations that continue to hinder the efforts by the IASB. After 20 years of diffusion around the world, the IFRS have been widely recognized as high-quality accounting standards that can make it possible for financial information to be compared across national borders [8]. However, this success can only be sustained if the IFRS are adopted and applied properly in practice [20, 60].

DOI: http://dx.doi.org/10.5772/intechopen.103679

Author details

Maria Bengtsson
Kristianstad University, Sweden

*Address all correspondence to: maria.bengtsson@hkr.se

References

[1] Camfferman K, Zeff SA. The challenge of setting standards for a worldwide constituency: Research implications from the IASB's early history. The European Accounting Review. 2018;**27**:289-312

[2] Judge W, Li S, Pinsker R. National adoption of international accounting standards: An institutional perspective. Corporate Governance: An International Review. 2010;**18**:161-174

[3] Roberts A. The very idea of classification in international accounting. Accounting, Organizations and Society. 1995;**20**:639-664

[4] El-Helaly M, Ntim CG, Al-Gazzar M. Diffusion theory, national corruption and IFRS adoption around the world. Journal of International Accounting, Auditing and Taxation. 2020;**38**:100305

[5] Camfferman K, Zeff SA. Nobes, Parker. Comparative International Accounting (11 Uppl.). *Gosport: Ashford Colour Press Ltd.*; 2012

[6] IASB. *Use of IFRS Standards by Jurisdiction* [Online]. 2019. ifrs.org: IFRS Foundation. Available from: https://www.ifrs.org/use-around-the-world/use-of-ifrs-standards-by-jurisdiction/#profiles [Accessed: February 2, 2022]

[7] Byard D, Li Y, Yu Y. The effect of mandatory IFRS adoption on financial analysts' information environment. Journal of Accounting Research. 2011;**49**:69-96

[8] IASB. *Why Global Accounting Standards?* [Online]. 2020. Available from: https://www.ifrs.org/use-around-the-world/why-global-accounting-standards/ [Accessed: February 2, 2022]

[9] Alon A, Dwyer PD. Early adoption of IFRS as a strategic response to transnational and local influences. The International Journal of Accounting. 2014;**49**:348-370

[10] Guerreiro MS, Rodrigues LL, Craig R. Voluntary adoption of international financial reporting standards by large unlisted companies in Portugal–institutional logics and strategic responses. Accounting, Organizations and Society. 2012;**37**:482-499

[11] Riahi O, Khoufi W. Understanding IFRS adoption. Journal of Applied Accounting Research. 2019;**20**:543-570

[12] Aisbitt S. Assessing the effect of the transition to IFRS on equity: The case of the FTSE 100. Accounting in Europe. 2006;**3**:117-133

[13] Ye Q, Gao J, Zheng W. Accounting standards, earnings transparency and audit fees: Convergence with IFRS in China. Australian Accounting Review. 2018;**28**:525-537

[14] Albu CN, Albu N, Alexander D. When global accounting standards meet the local context—Insights from an emerging economy. Critical Perspectives on Accounting. 2014;**25**:489-510

[15] Ball R. International financial reporting standards (IFRS): Pros and cons for investors. Accounting and Business Research. 2006;**36**:5-27

[16] Cieslewicz JK. Relationships between national economic culture, institutions, and accounting: Implications for IFRS. Critical Perspectives on Accounting. 2014;**25**:511-528

[17] Nobes CW, Zeff SA. Have Canada, Japan and Switzerland adopted IFRS? Australian Accounting Review. 2016;**26**:284-290

[18] Deloitte 2014. Use of IFRS by Jurisdiction. London: IAS PLUS

[19] Kvaal E, Nobes C. IFRS policy changes and the continuation of national patterns of IFRS practice. The European Accounting Review. 2012;**21**:343-371

[20] Ball R. IFRS–10 years later. Accounting and Business Research. 2016;**46**:545-571

[21] Richardson AJ. Regulatory networks for accounting and auditing standards: A social network analysis of Canadian and international standard-setting. Accounting, Organizations and Society. 2009;**34**:571-588

[22] Qu X, Zhang G. Measuring the convergence of national accounting standards with international financial reporting standards: The application of fuzzy clustering analysis. The International Journal of Accounting. 2010;**45**:334-355

[23] Ramanna K, Sletten E. Why Do Countries Adopt International Financial Reporting Standards? *Harvard Business School Accounting & Management Unit Working Paper*. 2009. pp. 9-102

[24] Chen CJ, Gul FA, Su X. A comparison of reported earnings under Chinese GAAP vs. IAS: Evidence from the Shanghai stock exchange. Accounting Horizons. 1999;**13**:91-111

[25] Ding Y, Su X. Implementation of IFRS in a regulated market. Journal of Accounting and Public Policy. 2008;**27**:474-479

[26] Brandau M, Endenich C, Trapp R, Hoffjan A. Institutional drivers of conformity–evidence for management accounting from Brazil and Germany. International Business Review. 2013;**22**:466-479

[27] Daske H, Hail L, Leuz C, Verdi R. Mandatory IFRS reporting around the world: Early evidence on the economic consequences. Journal of Accounting Research. 2008;**46**:1085-1142

[28] Holthausen RW. Accounting standards, financial reporting outcomes, and enforcement. Journal of Accounting Research. 2009;**47**:447-458

[29] Gray SJ. The impact of international accounting differences from a security-analysis perspective: Some European evidence. In: *International Accounting and Transnational Decisions*. Butterworth-Heinemann: Elsevier; 1983. pp. 95-107

[30] Doupnik TS, Salter SB. External environment, culture, and accounting practices: A preliminary test of a general model of international accounting development. The International Journal of Accounting. 1995;**3**:189-207

[31] Nobes C. Towards a general model of the reasons for international differences in financial reporting. Abacus. 1998;**34**:162-187

[32] Tay JS, Parker RH. Measuring international harmonization and standardization. Abacus. 1990;**26**:71-88

[33] Canibano L, Mora A. Evaluating the statistical significance of de facto accounting harmonization: A study of European global players. The European Accounting Review. 2000;**9**:349-369

[34] Hope O-K, Jin J, Kang T. Empirical evidence on jurisdictions that adopt IFRS. Journal of International Accounting Research. 2006;**5**:1-20

[35] Nobes C. Accounting classification in the IFRS era. Australian Accounting Review. 2008;**18**:191-198

[36] Mita AF, Husnah N. An empirical examination of factors contributing to the adoption of IFRS in developing countries. Journal of Economics, Business, & Accountancy Ventura. 2015;**18**:427-438

[37] IASB. Method of Adoption. London: IFRS Foundation; 2017

[38] Zeff SA, Nobes CW. Commentary: Has Australia (or any other jurisdiction)'Adopted'IFRS? 1. Australian Accounting Review. 2010;**20**:178-184

[39] Mcleay S, Neal D, Tollington T. International standardisation and harmonisation: A new measurement technique. Journal of International Financial Management & Accounting. 1999;**10**:42-70

[40] Arnold PJ. The political economy of financial harmonization: The east Asian financial crisis and the rise of international accounting standards. Accounting, Organizations and Society. 2012;**37**:361-381

[41] Campbell JL. *Institutional Change and Globalization*. New Jersey: Princeton University Press; 2004

[42] AL-Htaybat K. IFRS adoption in emerging markets: The case of Jordan. Australian Accounting Review. 2018;**28**:28-47

[43] IASB. *Ian mackintosh discusses the challenges of global standardisation* [Online]. 2014b. Available from: https://www.iasplus.com/en/news/2014/05/mackintosh-speech [Accessed February 15, 2020]

[44] IASB. *Closing the Accounting Chapter of the Financial Crisis-Speech by Hans Hoogervorst, Chairman of the IASB*. New Delhi: IFRS Foundation; 2014a. Available from: https://www.ifrs.org/content/dam/ifrs/news/speeches/2014/hans-hoogervorst-march-2014.pdf [Accessed March 10, 2018]

[45] G20. *Communiqué of Meeting of G20 Finance Ministers and Central Bank Governors*. Moscow; 2013. Available from: http://www.g20.utoronto.ca/2013/2013-0216-finance.html [Accessed February 10, 2020]

[46] IOSCO. *1995 Press Release and Work Program*. Paris: IFRS Foundation; 1995. Available from: https://www.iosco.org/library/pubdocs/pdf/IOSCOPD109.pdf [Accessed February 2, 2022]

[47] IOSCO. 2000. *IASC Standards-Assessment Report*. Available from: https://www.iosco.org/library/pubdocs/pdf/IOSCOPD109.pdf [Accessed February 2, 2022]

[48] IASB. *Progress towards Global Standards* [Online]. Paris: IFRS Foundation; 2021. Available from: https://www.ifrs.org/about-us/who-we-are/#history [Accessed: February 3, 2022]

[49] KPMG. Global Financial Reporting, IAS or US GAAP? A European Survey. London: KPMG; 2000

[50] ICAEW. Tardy IFRS prep will lead to audit qualifications. 2004

[51] Hoarau C. International accounting harmonization: American hegemony or mutual recognition with benchmarks? The European Accounting Review. 1995;**4**:217-233

[52] Dye RA, Sunder S. Why not allow FASB and IASB standards to compete in the US? Accounting Horizons. 2001;**15**:257-271

[53] Street DL, Nichols NB, Gray SJ. Assessing the acceptability of international accounting standards in the US: An empirical study of the materiality of US GAAP reconciliations by non-US companies complying with IASC standards. The International Journal of Accounting. 2000;**35**:27-63

[54] SEC. *International Accounting Standards* [Online]. 2000. Available from: https://www.sec.gov/rules/concept/34-42430.htm [Accessed: February 2, 2022]

[55] FASB. *Comparability in international accounting standards-a brief history* [Online]. 2013. Available from: https://www.fasb.org/jsp/FASB/Page/SectionPage&cid=1176156304264 [Accessed March 10, 2018]

[56] IASB. The Norwalk Agreement [Online]. 2002. Available from: https://www.ifrs.org/content/dam/ifrs/around-the-world/mous/norwalk-agreement-2002.pdf [Accessed March 10, 2018]

[57] The World Bank. *Thoughts on Globalization and the Global Financial Crisis-Speech by Graeme Wheeler* [Online]. Washington, D.C: The World Bank; 2008. Available from: https://www.worldbank.org/en/news/speech/2008/11/13/thoughts-on-globalization-and-the-global-financial-crisis [Accessed March 10, 2018]

[58] IMF. *London Summit – Leaders' Statement*. London: The IMF; 2009. Available from: https://www.imf.org/external/np/sec/pr/2009/pdf/g20_040209.pdf [Accessed]

[59] Jeanjean T, Stolowy H. Do accounting standards matter? An exploratory analysis of earnings management before and after IFRS adoption. Journal of Accounting and Public Policy. 2008;**27**:480-494

[60] Kvaal E, Nobes C. International Differences in IFRS Policy Choice: A Research Note. Accounting and Business Research. 2010;**40**(2):173-187

[61] Tarca A, Morris RD, Moy M. An investigation of the relationship between use of international accounting standards and source of company finance in G ermany. Abacus. 2013;**49**:74-98

[62] MOF. Chinese Accounting System for Business Enterprises. Beijing, China: Ministry of Finance; 2006

[63] Cox C. How America's participation in international financial reporting standards was lost. In: *Keynote Address to the 33rd Annual SEC and Financial Reporting Institute Conference*. California: SEC and Financial Reporting Institute; 2014

[64] IASB. *Speech by Hans Hoogervorst in Beijing: China and IFRS – An Opportunity for Leadership in Global Financial Reporting*. IFRS Foundation; 2011 [Accessed March 10, 2018]

Chapter 10

Monitoring of the Entrenchment of Managers through Board Characteristics: Insights from Gender Diversity, Background and Independence Director's

Nadia Ben Farhat-Toumi, Nouha Ben Arfa and Rim Khemiri

Abstract

The purpose of this study is to investigate the relationship between the entrenchment managerial and board characteristics in publicly traded French firms. These two concepts are at the intersection of corporate finance and accounting, as managerial entrenchment and board characteristics may affect earnings management, which would make investors reluctant to invest in a firm. Using data on listed firms belonging to the SBF120, over the period 2011–2018, we mainly find that: the entrenchment managerial is impacted by (1) gender diversity, (2) educational background (3) and independence directors.

Keywords: managerial entrenchment, board diversity, educational background, board independence

1. Introduction

The literature on both opportunistic and autocratic behavior of executives has bent the debates on the composition and functioning of the board of directors (BOD) to better protect the interests of shareholders, as well as the stakeholders of the company [1–3]. Recently, the resurgence of scandals of financial malpractice by CEOs, such as Bernard Maddof for the Ponzi pyramid in 2009, Jeffrey Skilling for the Enron affair in 2006 and recently Carlos Ghosn for the Renault-Nissan alliance in 2018, have furthermore oriented studies towards the analysis of the impact of certain characteristics of the BoD on the managerial latitude of executives. In France, the law of May 15, 2001 on the New Economic Regulations (NER) concerning the powers and functioning of governing bodies, has highlighted the dissociation of the functions of chairman and chief executive officer as well as the limitation on the accumulation of mandates.

A board of directors is effective when management and control functions are exercised by two different people [4–7], to establish checks and balances and to avoid any personal misappropriation that is harmful to the company and its shareholders. In practice, this rule remains uncommon, even though it allows for real separation of decision-making and control functions, thus distributing responsibilities while guaranteeing a clarified separation of powers. The accumulation of functions thus allows the manager to adopt an autocratic management style to appropriate power in his or her interest and, moreover, to extend the duration of his or her mandate. This is the phenomenon of entrenchment as defined by Shleifer & Vishny [8]. According to entrenchment theory, this behavior allows the executive to entrench himself and anesthetize the boards [9]. This phenomenon has been the subject of several questions, especially about the effectiveness of the board. The board, which must monitor and advise the executive, is composed of directors with different demographic, individual and social characteristics. Several research studies emphasize the importance of the diversity of profiles within a board. Wirtz [3] and Maati & Maati-Sauvez [2], emphasize that a diverse board reduces the opportunism of managers. In this work, we are interested in certain characteristics of the board of directors, namely the independence of board members, gender diversity and the education of directors. The choice of these variables is explained on the one hand by the importance given to the feminization of boards in France through the Copé/Zimmerman law of 2011. On the other hand, the social ties between directors and executives from the Grandes Écoles such as École Nationale d'Administration (ENA) and Polytechnique, is favorable to the entrenchment of executives [2, 10, 11].

Moreover, the results of studies examining the relationship between the board and executive entrenchment appear to be controversial. In particular, studies of the relationship between the social ties between executives and directors are controversial, as these relationships can both hinder and contribute to the effectiveness of boards. Another debate on the issue of the entrenchment of managers is that of the presence of women on boards. Can this presence call into question the autocratic behavior of the CEO? Is this presence a reason for legitimacy in the face of the quota imposed by the law or can the woman face an entrenched CEO?

Thus, these questions and the lack of consensus on the link between the composition of boards of directors and the entrenchment strategies of managers call into question past studies. In this article, we propose to analyze the impact of women directors, education of directors, and board independence on executive entrenchment strategies.

Our research makes both theoretical and managerial contributions. First, for the relationship between the presence of women and the presence of a rooted CEO, few studies have examined this relationship in the French context. Thus, our article contributes to the governance literature by explaining the relationship between gender diversity and executive behavior. We provide some support for the hypothesis that the presence of women can change the strategies implemented by CEOs.

Then, we apprehend the means of entrenchment of the CEO by integrating the three strategies from the literature namely the age of the CEO, the duration of his mandate and the accumulation of functions. Indeed, studies have mainly focused on the entrenchment of CEOs through his network or his mandate [2, 11].

We quantify our work using a sample of 83 listed companies comprising the SBF 120 index and observed over a period from 2011 to 2018. In this framework, we show that women can both control and be impartial to the autocratic behavior of executives and this is a function of the rooting strategy. We also identify a negative and significant impact between directors from the Grandes Écoles (ENA/Polytechnique) and executive tenure, whereas the literature has only highlighted a positive link between these directors and executive tenure. Finally, we show that an independent board can limit the discretionary power of managers. Our results may have a managerial effect if we focus on the dissociation of the executive's functions. The presence of a woman as well as directors who are enarques or polytechnicians seems to be useful when the manager combines the two functions of chairman and director.

The remainder of the paper is organized as follows. Section 2 reviews the literature and develops our hypotheses. Section 3 describes the methodological aspects. Empirical results are presented and discussed in Section 4. Finally, in Section 5, we conclude with implications for further research and practice.

2. Board diversity

In this section, we present the review of the literature on the relationship between gender diversity, education of directors, board independence, and management entrenchment, while developing our research hypotheses.

2.1 Gender diversity

Since the constitution and implementation of the policy on quotas for women's representation on boards, several European countries such as Spain, Norway, Belgium and Italy have adopted legislative measures for the implementation of this policy in companies. Since 2011, France has introduced a law requiring listed companies to increase the number of women on their boards. This law sets a mandatory quota of 40% of the underrepresented gender on boards of directors by January 1, 2017 in listed companies. It also requires companies that do not have any women on their Boards at the time of its enactment to appoint women within the following 6 months.

The activism that has focused on the gender balance in corporate governance bodies bears witness to the pitfalls of the feminization of boards. Beyond the regulatory and institutional framework, several researchers have stressed the importance of increasing the appointment of women to boards of directors. The arguments put forward for increasing the number of women on boards of directors are numerous [12, 13]. Two perspectives can be mobilized.

First, consistent with Fama & Jensen's agency theory [14], board members should monitor managers to minimize agency costs and maximize firm value for shareholders. Researchers have investigated the relationship between board feminization and firm financial performance [15–19]. Other empirical studies highlight the importance of the latter in strengthening governance practices, including the board of directors. Harford et al. [20] and Wang et al. [21], specify that firms with an effective board reduce managerial opportunism and authority. In addition, Adams and Ferreira [15], show that board feminization impacts CEO departure rates at the head of the lowest-performing firms.

Second, the other stream of literature on gender diversity, which focuses on women's human capital, has shown a positive relationship between the feminization of boards and the quality of governance. Huse & Solberg [22] as well as Spell & Bezrukova [23] find a positive and significant relationship between the human factor of women (skills, attitudes, behavior...) and managerial manipulation (financial fraud).

In the same spirit, another group of researchers highlights the importance of appointing women to boards [24, 25]. They argue that a board with one or more women is less prone to manipulation by managers. However, the Maati and

Maati-Sauvez [2] study find that executives are more influential in the presence of increased board feminization.

Given the conflicting results on the relationship between women's presence and CEOship manipulation, we propose the following hypothesis:

Hypothesis 1: CEO is less entrenched when the percentage of women present on the board is high.

2.2 Education of directors

As suggested by some authors such as Hambrick & Mason [26] and Barro & Lee [27], human capital is the body of knowledge and skills that each individual has been able to acquire through education and training. The human capital theory assumes that individuals' knowledge and skills enable them to be productive in their assignments [28]. A highly educated board will be better able to advise and monitor the CEO [21]. Several research studies highlight the importance of the level of director education on the effectiveness of the board and strategic choices. Rosenkopf & Nerkar [29], highlight a significant and positive relationship between the quality of director education and organizational decision making.

Gales & Kesner [30] as well as other researchers point out that a board with scientific directors allows for more innovative strategies, and can advise and monitor a research project [21]. Other work has examined the relationship between board member education and firm performance. The results reveal that the level of education of directors is positively associated with financial performance and enhances the monitoring role of the board [31, 32]. Thus, an educated board improves corporate governance. These ideas could therefore lead us to assume that good corporate governance requires an effective board composition.

The education of its members is a decisive criterion in the composition of the latter, thus reducing the opportunism of the CEOs. Hence the following hypothesis:

Hypothesis 2: The nature of the education of directors reduces the entrenchment of CEO.

Several empirical studies define the quality of education by the prestige of the schools attended [33, 34]. Despite the importance of educational background in the recruitment of directors, the prestige of the institution they attend, as well as the networks developed within that school, have a very important impact on the selection of board members. The social capital built up within these prestigious institutions contributes not only to the development of human capital but also to the company's social network [35, 36]. Work on the sociology of education and the elite has highlighted the importance of schools in the construction of elite identity [37]. Most empirical studies emphasize that administrators from elite schools possess a social network that allows them easy access to even government resources [38] and possesses greater control to monitor CEOs [39].

In France, the Grandes Écoles (GÉ), notably ENA and Polytechnique play a similar role as Ivy Leagues in the US or Cambridge and Oxford in the UK [40]. Several research studies argue that this elite network, which allows easier access to the board of directors, weakens the latter's monitoring role [41, 42].

However, the existence of these social relationships can also be a key factor in the governance structure. For Kramarz & Thesmar [41], CEOs may use their social networks to make advice and monitoring more effective. Examining these results does not provide a general framework, which leads us to test the following hypothesis:

Hypothesis 3: A predominantly elitist board of directors impacts executive entrenchment.

2.3 Board independence

For the proponents of the agency theory, the presence of independent directors on the board of directors makes it possible to restrict the opportunistic behavior of the managers. Fama & Jensen [14] emphasize that these independent members must work in the interest of the shareholders.

Several empirical studies have tested the relationship between board independence and management entrenchment. The results obtained are not conclusive and do not show a consensus concerning this relationship. Indeed, Chen & Jaggi [43] and Ben Ali [44], show that boards dominated by independent members are likely to better monitor the executive and protect shareholders' interests. In this sense, Jensen [6] and Patelli & Prencipe [45] emphasize that independent directors must fulfill their oversight role to build their reputation. The results of Chen [46], show that an independent board reduces agency conflicts. According to the same authors, investment opportunities are higher in firms with a more independent board. Thus, managerial incentives are better controlled in the presence of independent members [47–49]. The results of Ma & Khanna [48] show that reputation strongly motivates independent directors, who for their own interest must disapprove of executive strategies and decisions that may lead to a bad decision. However, Parrat [50] does not confirm the monitoring role of independent directors. Indeed, the author explains that the latter are chosen by the manager according to personal criteria. Therefore, they cannot oppose the decisions of the latter [51].

The analysis of this research does not allow for a consensus due to the diversity of the results, which leads us to formulate the following hypothesis:

Hypothesis 4: Board independence impacts CEO entrenchment.

3. Research methodology

3.1 Sample and data

The initial sample is composed of French companies belonging to the SBF120 index over the 2011–2018 period[1]. The choice of this period for our empirical study is justified by the entry of the Copé-Zimmerman law adopted in 2011.

The data was collected from several sources. Data on the education of directors was collected manually from the companies' annual reports. When not available, we used the Who's Who database[2]. We used Bloomberg for data on corporate governance and executives and Datastream for accounting and financial data.

To create our sample, we first excluded firms belonging to the finance sector. Then, we selected firms for which annual reports and data on directors and officers

[1] Our starting sample is composed of all companies belonging to the SBF120 index as of December 31, 2018. We have removed companies that have disappeared from the SBF120 index (for example, Dexia and Areva were removed from the index in 2012).

[2] Directors are also officers of other companies. Who's is a database that provides information on directors.

are available. After applying these selection criteria, the final sample was reduced to 82 companies.

3.2 Measures

Dependent variables: these are the three following variables.

- AGEDIR: is measured by a binary variable equal to 1 if the age of the manager is close to retirement, 0 otherwise.
- ANCDIR: since the average seniority of managers is 4 years, we have retained 4 as the binarization threshold.
- CUMDIR: is measured by a binary variable equal to 1 if the manager has been at the head of the company for 8 years or more, 0 otherwise.

Explanatory variables: to test our models, we retain the following explanatory variables that constitute governance variables.

- INDEP: is measured by the proportion of independent directors on the Board.
- WEF: measured by the proportion of women on the Board.
- STRP: is measured by directors with a management background.
- ING: is measured by directors with an engineering background (all schools combined).
- JUR: measured by directors with a legal background.
- GE: measured by directors coming from ENA or Polytechnique.

Control variables: our models include control variables that may influence executive entrenchment. As a result, we included variables controlling for the effects of industrý (ICB) [52], firm size (CA), firm performance (ROA). Listing seniority (ANCOT) is likely to influence managerial entrenchment [8, 53]. We also used ownership concentration (CONCAC), which is measured by the percentage of voting rights of the largest shareholder.

3.3 Descriptive statistics

Descriptive statistics for the period 2011–2018 are presented in **Table 1**. It can be seen that, on average, 21% of the French managers in our sample are over the legal retirement age (60 years). We observe that 27% of firms have an executive with more than 8 years of service. About 53% of firms have an executive who combines the two functions of executive and chairman of the board. A separation is implemented by 46% of listed companies[3]. This observation can be explained by the opening of the

[3] In 2017, 32.7% of SBF120 companies opted for a board with separation of functions. https://hcge.fr/wp-content/uploads/2018/10/Rapport_HCGE_octobre2018.pdf.

Variables	Measures	Frequencies
AGLEGDIR	0	79.02
	1	20.98
ANCDIR	0	72.84
	1	27.16
CUMDIR	0	46.70
	1	53.30
ICB	1	86.25
	2	5.00
	3	2.50
	6	6.25
CONCAC	0	14.94
	1	85.06

Table 1.
Descriptive statistics of the dichotomous explanatory variables.

market to foreign investors, who are in favor of the separation of functions. About 93.75% of the companies in our sample belong to the industrial sector and 6.25% to the technological sector. We find that 85% of the companies have a concentrated shareholding structure[4].

Table 2 also shows that on average 19%[5] of women hold a position on the board of directors, an average that has risen slightly according to the study by Hollandts et al. [54]. This tiny increase can be explained by the quota requirement introduced

Variables	Means
FEM	0.194
GEST	0.347
JURI	0.359
ING	0.234
GE	0.361
INDEP	0.521
ANCOT	3.394
CA	8.548
ROA	5.071

Table 2.
Descriptive statistics for continuous explanatory variables.

[4] Shareholder concentration: measured by the percentage of voting rights of the main shareholder. If this percentage reaches 50% the variable equals 1, 0 otherwise.
[5] A figure that does not reach the quota set by Copé-Zimmerman, i.e., 40%.

Variables	(1)	(2)	(3)	(4)	(5)	(6)	(7)	(8)	(9)	(10)	(11)	(12)	(13)	(14)	(15)
(1) AGDIR	1.000														
(2) ANCDIR	0.122	1.000													
(3) CUMDIR	0.142	0.581	1.000												
(4) FEM	0.119	0.007	−0.032	1.000											
(5) GEST	0.046	0.000	−0.007	0.225	1.000										
(6) JURI	−0.061	−0.017	−0.035	−0.240	−0.479	1.000									
(7) ING	−0.011	−0.002	0.067	0.077	−0.265	−0.376	1.000								
(8) GE	−0.085	−0.049	−0.145	0.063	0.197	−0.100	0.176	1.000							
(9) INDEP	−0.075	0.011	0.016	0.098	0.050	−0.123	0.055	0.051	1.000						
(10) MANADM	0.074	−0.043	0.019	−0.072	−0.155	0.130	0.196	0.093	−0.098	1.000					
(11) ANCOT	0.108	0.086	0.118	0.063	0.240	−0.040	−0.088	0.043	0.211	−0.174	1.000				
(12) ICB	−0.048	−0.056	0.058	−0.003	−0.325	0.122	0.036	−0.236	−0.087	−0.033	−0.134	1.000			
(13) CA	−0.031	0.223	0.138	0.131	0.231	−0.285	0.262	0.359	0.171	−0.043	0.304	−0.334	1.000		
(14) ROA	0.003	−0.037	−0.078	0.021	−0.085	0.083	−0.117	−0.042	−0.037	0.030	−0.081	−0.059	−0.196	1.000	
(15) CONCAC	−0.071	0.163	−0.034	0.019	0.149	−0.097	0.037	0.216	0.029	−0.018	0.062	−0.306	0.342	0.094	1.000

Table 3.
Pearson correlation matrix.

by Copé Zimmerman in 2011[6]. On average, 52% of directors are independent, which refers to the recommendation made by the AFEP-MDEF code. Directors with a background in higher education occupy an average of 36.06% of board positions, followed closely by legal experts with an average of 35.9%, then managers with an average of 34.6%[7] and finally, engineers who occupy 23% of board positions.

Before starting the logistic regression in panel data, it is necessary to check for the possible presence of multicollinearity between the variables retained in our model. Multicollinearity can distort the accuracy of the estimation of the regression coefficients by making it sensitive to small fluctuations in the data. Therefore, we use the Pearson correlation matrix presented in **Table 3**. The study of the Pearson correlation matrix reveals the non-existence of multicollinearity problems between the selected variables.

3.4 Models

In line with the work cited in the second section, we use the following models to test our hypotheses and analyze the effect of the composition of the board of directors on executive entrenchment:

$$\begin{aligned} \mathrm{AGEDIR}_{it} = {} & \beta_0 + \beta_1 \mathrm{FEM}_{it} + \beta_2 \mathrm{INDEP}_{it} + \beta_3 \mathrm{GEST}_{it} + \beta_4 \mathrm{JURI}_{it} + \beta_5 \mathrm{ING}_{it} + \beta_6 \mathrm{GE}_{it} \\ & + \alpha_1 \mathrm{ANCOT}_{it} + \alpha_2 \mathrm{ICB}_{it} + \alpha_3 \mathrm{CA}_{it} + \alpha_4 \mathrm{ROA}_{it} + \alpha_5 \mathrm{CONCAC}_{it} + \varepsilon_{it} \end{aligned} \tag{1}$$

The first equation of our study links the age of the executive (AGEDIR) and the characteristics of boards of directors, namely gender diversity (FEM), the percentage of independent directors (INDEP), the education of directors: (GEST) for managers, (JURI) for legal experts, (ING) for engineers, as well as the attendance of top schools (GE)[8].

Indeed, several empirical studies emphasize that the age of the CEO and the proximity of retirement are factors that favor his or her entrenchment [56, 57]. The age of the CEO reflects his or her experience in leading the company and his or her ability to become entrenched. CEOs close to retirement have a strong legitimacy that allows them to take root [58–60]. In the same vein, Krause [61], Hollandts et al. [54] as well as Raheja [62] show that the entrenchment strategies of CEOs are related to their retention until retirement. In our study, the legal retirement age is set at 60 years [54, 61].

$$\begin{aligned} \mathrm{ANCDIR}_{it} = {} & \beta_0 + \beta_1 \mathrm{FEM}_{it} + \beta_2 \mathrm{INDEP}_{it} + \beta_3 \mathrm{GEST}_{it} + \beta_4 \mathrm{JURI}_{it} + \beta_5 \mathrm{ING}_{it} + \beta_6 \mathrm{GE}_{it} \\ & + \alpha_1 \mathrm{ANCOT}_{it} + \alpha_2 \mathrm{ICB}_{it} + \alpha_3 \mathrm{CA}_{it} + \alpha_4 \mathrm{ROA}_{it} + \alpha_5 \mathrm{CONCAC}_{it} + \varepsilon_{it} \end{aligned} \tag{2}$$

The second equation of our study links the seniority of the executive (ANCDIR) and the characteristics of the boards of directors, namely gender diversity (FEM), the percentage of independent directors (INDEP), the education of directors: (GEST) for managers, (JURI) for legal experts, (ING) for engineers, as well as the attendance of top schools (GE). Previous studies argue that the CEO's rootedness is related to his seniority in the company [63, 64]. The seniority of the CEO allows him to strengthen his bargaining power against shareholders and therefore to become entrenched [60].

[6] The percentage of women on boards according to the study by Hollandts et al. [54] is 13% with a study period from 2002 to 2014. Our period is from 2011 to 2018.

[7] Managers outside ENA/Polytechnique.

[8] In our study, we define the Grandes Écoles by the institutions: ENA and Polytechnique, institutions that reflect the ties of friendship between the CEOs and an elite [55].

$$\text{CUMDIR}_{it} = \beta_0 + \beta_1\text{FEM}_{it} + \beta_2\text{INDEP}_{it} + \beta_3\text{GEST}_{it} + \beta_4\text{JURI}_{it} + \beta_5\text{ING}_{it} + \beta_6\text{GE}_{it} + \alpha_1\text{ANCOT}_{it} + \alpha_2\text{ICB}_{it} + \alpha_3\text{CA}_{it} + \alpha_4\text{ROA}_{it} + \alpha_5\,\text{CONCAC}_{it} + \varepsilon_{it} \quad (3)$$

The third model of our study links the duality of the CEO (CUMDIR) and the characteristics of boards of directors, namely gender diversity (FEM), the percentage of independent directors (INDEP), the education of directors: (GEST) for managers, (JURI) for legal experts, (ING) for engineers, as well as the attendance of top schools (GE). Proponents of agency theory emphasize the importance of separating the roles of CEO and chairman of the board [65]. Indeed, this duality encourages the entrenchment of the CEO [66–68].

We performed the Hausman test, which is the standard test for specifying individual effects in a panel. It is used to discriminate between fixed and random effects, otherwise to control for individual and time-specific effects. We find that in almost all equations, the p-value of the Hausman test is below the 5% threshold. Thus, the fixed effects models are the most appropriate. The fixed-effects model assumes that the influence of the independent variables on the dependent variable is identical over any period for all individuals.

4. Results and discussion

The results of the different estimates are presented in **Table 4**. The association between gender diversity and the rootedness of managers is represented by a double effect, which may be related to the observation period, which includes the

Model 1							
AGDIR	**Coef.**	**St. err.**	**t-value**	**p-value**	**95% conf**	**Interval**	**Sig**
FEM	4.765	1.620	2.94	0.003	1.591	7.940	***
GEST	2.174	2.573	0.84	0.398	−2.870	7.217	
JURI	−3.698	2.548	−1.45	0.147	−8.693	1.296	
ING	−6.656	2.857	−2.33	0.020	−12.255	−1.056	**
GE	−0.800	1.677	−0.48	0.633	−4.088	2.488	
INDEP	−4.854	1.576	−3.08	0.002	−7.943	−1.765	***
ANCOT	0.701	0.718	0.98	0.329	−0.706	2.109	
ICB	−0.112	0.462	−0.24	0.808	−1.017	0.793	
CA	0.568	0.389	1.46	0.145	−0.195	1.331	
ROA	0.012	0.050	0.24	0.812	−0.086	0.110	
CONCAC	−2.408	1.465	−1.64	0.100	−5.280	0.463	
Constant	−4.711	4.139	−1.14	0.255	−12.823	3.402	
Constant	2.630	0.372	.b	.b	1.901	3.359	

Mean dependent var	0.202	SD dependent var.	0.402
Number of obs	639.000	Chi-square	29.934
Prob > chi^2	0.002	Akaike crit. (AIC)	478.126

Model 2							
ANCDIR	**Coef.**	**St. err.**	**t-value**	**p-value**	**95% conf**	**Interval**	**Sig**
FEM	2.821	2.068	1.36	0.172	−1.232	6.874	
GEST	−1.168	4.590	−0.25	0.799	−10.165	7.829	
JURI	5.916	4.207	1.41	0.160	−2.330	14.163	
ING	−8.018	5.628	−1.43	0.154	−19.048	3.012	
GE	−7.050	4.415	−1.60	0.110	−15.702	1.603	
INDEP	1.201	2.057	0.58	0.559	−2.831	5.233	
ANCOT	−0.877	2.243	−0.39	0.696	−5.274	3.519	
ICB	0.439	0.661	0.66	0.507	−0.857	1.734	
CA	3.762	0.938	4.01	0.000	1.924	5.600	***
ROA	0.020	0.055	0.35	0.723	−0.089	0.128	
CONCAC	3.381	2.579	1.31	0.190	−1.673	8.434	
Constant	−38.452	10.828	−3.55	0.000	−59.674	−17.229	***
Constant	4.510	0.515	.b	.b	3.501	5.519	
Mean dependent var			0.272		SD dependent var.		0.445
Number of obs			639.000		Chi-square		34.160
Prob > chi^2			0.000		Akaike crit. (AIC)		357.068
Model 3							
CUMDIR	**Coef.**	**St. err.**	**t-value**	**p-value**	**95% conf**	**Interval**	**Sig**
FEM	−4.483	1.764	−2.54	0.011	−7.940	−1.026	**
GEST	−0.653	3.147	−0.21	0.835	−6.821	5.514	
JURI	4.419	3.365	1.31	0.189	−2.178	11.015	
ING	0.098	3.480	0.03	0.977	−6.722	6.919	
GE	−10.697	3.025	−3.54	0.000	−16.626	−4.768	***
INDEP	−1.348	0.902	−1.49	0.135	−3.117	0.420	
ANCOT	1.384	1.688	0.82	0.412	−1.924	4.691	
ICB	0.470	0.724	0.65	0.516	−0.949	1.889	
CA	2.668	0.841	3.17	0.002	1.020	4.316	***
ROA	−0.033	0.038	−0.87	0.386	−0.108	0.042	
CONCAC	−1.945	2.596	−0.75	0.454	−7.033	3.144	
Constant	−21.192	6.589	−3.22	0.001	−34.107	−8.277	***
Constant	4.021	0.371	.b	.b	3.295	4.747	
Mean dependent var			0.526		SD dependent var.		0.500
Number of obs			639.000		Chi-square		36.741
Prob > chi^2			0.000		Akaike crit. (AIC)		466.219

$^{***}p < 0.01$, $^{**}p < 0.05$, $^{*}p < 0.1$.

Table 4.
Regression results.

introduction and application of the Copé-Zimmerman Act. The first Model 1 presented below shows the positive and significant effect of the gender diversity variable on the age variable (AGEDIR), at the 1% threshold, which partially refutes hypothesis 1. Model 3 reveals a negative and significant effect of the gender diversity variable on multiple job titles (CUMDIR), at the 5% threshold, which partially confirms hypothesis 1. This overall effect may be linked to the increase in the number of women on boards following the Copé-Zimmerman Act (2011, 2014). The presence of women thus reinforces the retention of the executive until the legal retirement age. However, this presence also allows dissociation of the manager's functions.

The first result could be explained by the pressure on women directors to conform to the choices of an entrenched CEO and therefore with some discretionary power. Our results are in line with the findings of Eagly and Carli [69] who point out that women face discriminatory barriers mainly in male-dominated environments. These include her exclusion from the executive's networks and moreover from the board of directors [70]. Our finding also corroborates the conclusions of Pigé [60] who considers that an executive with a high level of seniority, especially those beyond retirement age, benefits from an external legitimacy that gives him significant weight in front of the different members of the board.

This limits women's access to information and board decisions and negatively biases judgments about their performance as directors. However, this discriminatory disadvantage may give the appearance of a female competence advantage [71], and these barriers encourage women to be more competent and overcome prejudice. According to Eagly et al. [72], Yoder [73] and Fortier [74], this effect plays an important role in women's access and development within high responsibility positions. This may explain the result of Model 3 concerning the accumulation of the manager's functions. Indeed, our tests show the influence of women in the entrenchment of the CEO especially in the separation between the functions of chairman and CEO. This result is consistent with the agency theory. The presence of women thus constitutes a disciplinary lever in the control of entrenched CEOs [15].

Regarding the independence of the board of directors, our results show a negative and significant relationship between the presence of independent directors and the age of the managers, which confirms hypothesis 4. This result is consistent with agency theory, which assumes that the board of directors must be sufficiently independent to best supervise the manager [14]. Our results corroborate those of Hermalin and Weisbach [47] who point out that the effectiveness of control increases with the level of independence of the board. On the one hand, companies apply to the letter the new recommendations concerning the independence and control of the board. The academic literature has often criticized the proximity between managers and directors. By avoiding appointing directors who are close to management, companies gain a certain legitimacy with investors. Our results thus contradict these previous studies [42]. On the other hand, independent directors become opportunistic by seeking to enhance and improve their reputation [50]. They put aside their feelings towards the executive and carry out their monitoring mission objectively, thus avoiding a bad image of their status in the director market. This can explain our results and confirms the agency theory [14].

Concerning the social network of directors, a negative and significant influence of a curriculum at ENA/Polytechnique on the rooting of executives is highlighted (H3 validated). Contrary to the studies of Nguyen [42] and Kramarz and Thesmar [41], the network of Grandes Écoles does not favor the rooting of executives. A possible explanation for this result is possible concealment of the proximity between managers and directors. Indeed, to avoid any suspicion of elitism between the CEO, the director, the latter may control the decision-making and management functions of the BOD to take over the function itself. In the literature, the CEO can be replaced by a successor but cannot be ousted [75]. Indeed, **Table 4** shows that the variable (GE) negatively and significantly influences Model 3 (Cumulative tenure), but does not influence the age of the CEO (Model 1). This effect can be explained by the possibility of a succession of the same polytechnician or enarque. Elite directors do not oppose executives who are close to retirement and intervene when they hold multiple directorships to obtain a potential succession.

Our results also show that directors with an engineering background have a significant and negative impact on the age of managers. This result is consistent with the results of Johnson et al. [76] who suggest that directors with technical qualities and higher-level are likely to control the strategic decisions of a board. Their level and cognitive experience give them certain personal importance within the board [77, 78]. This gives them the power to reduce the CEO's entrenchment strategies, particularly by preventing him or her from maintaining the position until retirement. For our control variables, our results show a positive and significant relationship between firm size and managerial tenure and multiple job titles. A possible interpretation of this result is that the manager's anchoring is associated with turnover. Specifically, the executive has an interest in making profits to legitimize his position and maintain his tenure. This finding is consistent with the entrenchment theory. Indeed, by improving the performance of the company, the CEO acquires a capital of reputation that allows him to be irreplaceable and to acquire an important latitude within the company [79].

5. Conclusion

The purpose of this article is to examine the impact of women directors, director training, and board independence on the entrenchment of managers. First, the presence of women is significantly and negatively related to the age of the director. Women seem to favor the retention of the executive until retirement. But secondly, their presence reduces the number of functions they hold. Thus, women are more assiduous in applying the law concerning the dissociation of functions, but when it comes to their seniority through their legal retirement age, they do not have an impact, probably because of the age limit set by the law for managers, which remains flexible.

Our results also demonstrate the positive and significant impact of independent members as well as directors coming from top schools such as ENA and Polytechnique on executive entrenchment. From a theoretical point of view, our results corroborate those of previous research arguing that a diversified board contributes to the control of executive strategies. From a managerial point of view, our results should encourage companies to take more into account the recommendations of the AFEP-MEDEF regarding the diversity of the organization of management and control powers and the diversity of boards to guarantee certain objectivity in decision-making.

Our findings also highlight that the diversity of boards is an important governance mechanism that can limit the manipulation of managers. Moreover, this study is in line with the recommendations of the High Council for Equality between Women and Men on the need to have more diversity on boards of directors.

In particular, it might be interesting to include other characteristics, such as the education of women directors and the presence of foreign directors, in future studies to explain executive entrenchment.

Author details

Nadia Ben Farhat-Toumi[1], Nouha Ben Arfa[2*] and Rim Khemiri[3]

1 Université Evry Val Essonne, France

2 ESTA School of Business and Technology, France

3 Université Polytechnique Hauts-de-France, France

*Address all correspondence to: nbenarfa@esta-groupe.fr

References

[1] Anderson R, Reeb D, Upadhyay A, Zhao W. The economics of director heterogeneity. Financial Management. 2011;**40**(1):5-38

[2] Maati J, Maati-Sauvez C. L'hétérogénéité des administrateurs des entreprises cotées en France: Influence de la complexité de la firme et de la latitude managériale et conséquences sur la performance financière. Finance, Contrôle, Stratégie. 2016;**19**(4):53-79

[3] Wirtz P. Compétences, conflits et création de valeur: Vers une approche intégrée de la gouvernance. Finance Contrôle Stratégie. 2006;**9**(2):187-201

[4] Abad D, Lucas-Pérez ME, Vera A, Yagüe J. Does gender diversity on corporate boards reduce information asymmetry in equity markets? Business Research Quarterly. 2017;**20**(3):192-205

[5] Godard L, Schatt A. Caractéristiques et Fonctionnements des conseils d'Administration Français: Un état des lieux. Revue Française de Gestion. 2005;**31**(158):69-87

[6] Jensen MC. The modern industrial revolution, exit, and the failure of internal control systems. The Journal of Finance. 1993;**48**(3):831-880

[7] Mfouapon GK, Feudjo JR. Les déterminants de l'efficacité du conseil d'administration (CA): Une exploration à partir des caractéristiques du président du CA? Recherches en Sciences de Gestion. 2015;**106**(1):25-44

[8] Shleifer A, Vishny RW. Management Entrenchment: The case of managers' specific investments. Journal of Financial Economics. 1989;**25**:123-139

[9] Mard Y, Marsat S, Roux F. Structure de l'actionnariat et performance financière de l'entreprise:le cas français. Finance Contrôle Stratégie. 2014;**17**(4):59-83

[10] Pan Y, Wang TY, Weisbach MS. CEO investment cycles. Review of Financial Studies. 2016;**29**(11):2955-2999

[11] Vanappelghem C, Blum V, Nguyen P. La proximité entre dirigeant et administrateurs peut-elle favoriser la performance de l'entreprise Can CEO-directors ties enhance firm performance? Finance Contrôle Stratégie. 2018;**20**(4):27-68. Available from: revues.org

[12] Huse M, Nielsen S, Hagen I. Women and employee-elected board members, and their contributions to board control tasks. Journal of Business Ethics. 2009;**89**(4):581-597

[13] Hillman AJ, Shropshire C, Cannella Jr AA. Organizational predictors of women on corporate boards. Academy of Management Journal. 2007;**50**(4):941-952

[14] Fama E, Jensen M. Separation of ownership and control. Journal of Law and Economics. 1983;**26**(2):301-325

[15] Adams RB, Ferreira D. Women in the boardroom and their impact on governance and performance. Journal of Financial Economics. 2009;**94**(2):291-309

[16] Toumi N, Ben KR, HamrouniI A. Board director disciplinary and cognitive influence on corporate value creation. Corporate Governance: The International Journal of Business in Society. 2016;**16**(3):564-578

[17] Campbell K, Minguez-Vera A. Gender diversity in the boardroom and firm financial performance. Journal of Business Ethics. 2008;**83**(3):435-451

[18] Ferrary M. Les femmes influencent-elles la performance des entreprises ? Une étude des entreprises du CAC 40 sur la période 2002-2006. Travail, genre et sociétés. 2010;**23**:181-190

[19] Francoeur C, Labelle R, Sinclair-Desgagné B. Gender diversity in corporate governance and top management. Journal of Business Ethics. 2008;**81**(1):83-95

[20] Harford J, Li K, Zhao X. Corporate boards and the leverage and debt maturity choices. International Journal of Corporate Governance. 2008;**1**(1):3-27

[21] Wang MJ, Su XQ, Wanh HD, Chen YS. Directors' education and corporate liquidity: Evidence from boards in Taiwan. Review of Quantitative Finance and Accounting. 2017;**49**(2):463-485

[22] Huse M, Solberg AG. Gender related boardroom dynamics: How women make and can make contributions on corporate boards. Women in Management Review. 2006;**22**(2):113-130

[23] Spell CS, Bezrukova K. Genre, prise de décision et performance. Travail, genre et sociétés. 2010;**23**:191-199

[24] Nielsen S, Huse M. The contribution of women on boards of directors: Going beyond the surface. Corporate Governance: An International Review. 2010;**18**(2):136-148

[25] Srinidhi B, Gul FA, Tsui J. Female directors and earnings quality. Contemporary Accounting Research. 2011;**28**(5):1610-1644

[26] Hambrick DC, Mason PA. The organisation as a reflection of its top managers. Academy of Management Review. 1984;**9**(2):193-206

[27] Barro RJ, Lee JW. A new data set of educational attainment in the world, 1950-2010. Journal of Development Economics. 2013;**104**(1):184-198

[28] Becker GS. Human Capital. 3rd ed. Chicago: University of Chicago Press; 1993

[29] Rosenkopf L, Nerkar A. Beyond local search: Boundary-spanning, exploration, and impact in the optical disk industry. Strategic Management Journal. 2001;**22**(4):287-306

[30] Gales LM, Kesner IF. An analysis of board of director size and composition in bankrupt organizations. Journal of Business Research. 1994;**30**(3):271-282

[31] Akpan EO, Amran NA. Board characteristics and company performance: Evidence from Nigeria. Journal Finance Accounting. 2014;**2**(3):81-89

[32] Haniffa RM, Cooke TE. Culture, corporate governance and disclosure in Malaysian corporations. Abacus. 2002;**38**:317-349

[33] Gottesman AA, Morey MR. Does a Better Education Make for Better Managers? An Empirical Examination of CEO Educational Quality and Firm Performance. April 21, 2006. Pace University Finance Research Paper No. 2004/03. DOI: 10.2139/ssrn.564443. Available at SSRN: https://ssrn.com/abstract=564443

[34] Terrence J, Rao R, Jalbert M. Does school matter? An empirical analysis of CEO education, compensation and firm performance. International Business & Economics Research Journal. 2002;**1**(1):83-98

[35] Belliveau MA, O'Reilly CA, Wade JB. Social capital at the top: Effects of social similarity and status on CEO compensation. Academy of Management Journal. 1996;**39**(6):1568-1593

[36] Burt RS. Structural Holes. Cambridge: Cambridge University Press; 1992

[37] Van Zanten A. Promoting equality and reproducing privilege in elite educational tracks in France. In: Maxwell C, Aggleton P, editors. Elite Education. International Perspectives. London/New York: Routledge; 2015

[38] Goldman E, Jörg R, So J. Do politically connected boards affect firm value. Review of Financial Studies. 2009;**22**(1):2331-2360

[39] Dass N, Kini O, Nanda V, Onal B, Wang J. Board expertise: Do directors from related industries help bridge the information gap? Review of Financial Studies. 2014;**27**(5):1533-1159

[40] Brezis ES, Crouzet F. The Role of Higher Education Institutions: Recruitment of Elites and Economic Growth. December 2004. DOI: 10.2139/ssrn.641302. Available at SSRN: https://ssrn.com/abstract=641302

[41] Kramarz F, Thesmar D. Social networks in the boardroom. Journal of the European Economic Association. 2013;**11**:780-807

[42] Nguyen-Dang B. Does the rolodex matter? Corporate elite's small world and the effectiveness of boards of directors. Management Science. 2012;**58**(2):236-252

[43] Chen C, Jaggi B. Association between independent non-executive directors, family control and financial disclosures in Hong Kong. Journal of Accounting and Public Policy. 2000;**19**(4-5):285-310

[44] Ben Ali C. Qualité de la publication financière et mécanismes de gouvernance en France. Management & Avenir. 2013;**3**(61):109-128

[45] Patelli L, Prencipe A. The relationship between voluntary disclosure and independent directors in the presence of a dominant shareholder. European Accounting Review. 2007;**16**(1):5-3

[46] Chen HL. Does board independence influence the topmanagement team? Evidence from strategic decisions toward internationalization. Corporate Governance; An International Review. 2011;**19**(4):334-350

[47] Hermalin BE, Weisbach MS. The determinants of board composition. RAND Journal of Economics. 1988;**19**:589-606

[48] Ma J, Khanna T. Independent directors' dissent on boards: Evidence from listed companies in China. Strategic Management Journal. 2016;**37**:1547-1557

[49] Liu Y, Miletkov Mihail K, Wei Z, Yang T. Board independence and firm performance in China. Journal of Corporate Finance. 2015;**30**(C):223-244

[50] Parrat F. Théories et pratiques de la gouvernance d'entreprise: Pour les conseils d'administration et les administrateurs. France: Maxima; 2015

[51] Caby J, Koehl J. La gouvernance d'entreprise après la crise financière: Soft Law ou Hard Law. Post-Print halshs-02024651. France: HAL; 2009

[52] Bebchuk LAM, Fried J. Executive compensation as an agency problem. Journal of Economic Perspectives. 2003;**17**(3):71-92

[53] D'Arcimoles C-H, Trebucq S. Etude de l'influence de la performance sociétale sur la performance financière et le risque des sociétés françaises cotées (1995-2002); Colloque interdisciplinaire Audencia Nantes, Ecole de Management Nantes. France; 16-17 octobre 2003

[54] Hollandts X, Borodak D, Tichit A. La dynamique de changement des

formes de gouvernance: Le cas français (2000-2014). Finance, Contrôle et Stratégie. 2018;**21**(3):129-158

[55] Kadushin C. Friendship among the French financial elite. American Sociological Review. 1995;**60**(2):202-221

[56] Davidson WN, Xie B, Xu W, Ning Y. The influences of executive age, career horizon and incentives on pre- turnover earnings management. Journal of Management Science. 2007;**11**:45-60

[57] Matta E, Beamisch PW. The accentuated CEO career horizon problem: Evidence from international acquisitions. Strategic Management Journal. 2008;**29**(7):683-700

[58] Hill C, Phan PH. CEO tenure as a determinant of CEO pay. Academy of Management Journal. 1991;**34**(3):21-23

[59] Paquerot M. Stratégies d'enracinement des dirigeants, performance de la firme et structure de contrôle. In: Le gouvernement des entreprises. France: Economica; 1997

[60] Pigé B. Enracinement des Dirigeants et Richesse des Actionnaires. Finance Contrôle Stratégie. 1998;**1**(3):131-158

[61] Krause R. Being the CEO's boss: An examination of board chair orientations. Strategic Management Journal. 2017;**38**(3):697-713

[62] Raheja CG. Determinants of board size and composition: A theory of corporate boards. Journal of Financial and Quantitative Analysis. 2005;**40**(02):283-306

[63] Di Meo F, García Lara JM, Surroca J. Managerial entrenchment and earnings management. Journal of Accounting and Public Policy. 2017;**36**(5):399-414

[64] Hambrick DC, Geletkanycz MA, Fredrickson JW. Top executive commitment to the status quo: Some tests of its determinants. Strategic Management Journal. 1993;**14**:401-418

[65] Mallette P, Fowler KL. Effects of board composition and stock ownership on the adoption of "poison pills". Academy of Management Journal. 1992;**35**:1010-1035

[66] Booth JR, Millon C, Tehranian H. Boards of directors, ownership, and regulation. Journal of Banking and Finance. 2002;**26**:1973-1996

[67] Kang E, Zardhoohi A. Board CEOship structure and firm performance. Corporate Governance An International Review. 2005;**13**(6):785-799

[68] Lee SK, Lam TY. CEO duality and firm performance: Evidence from Hong Kong. Corporate Governance International Journal of Business in Society. 2008;**8**(3):299-316

[69] Eagly AH, Carli LL. The female CEOship advantage: An evaluation of the evidence. The CEOship Quarterly. 2003;**14**(6):807-834

[70] Fitzsimmons SR. Women on boards of directors: Why skirts in seats aren't enough. Business Horizons. 2012;**55**(6):557-566

[71] Sharpe R. As Leaders, Women Rule: New Studies Find That Female Managers Outshine Their Male Counterparts in Almost Every Measure. Business Week, p. 74. Available from: http://www.businessweek.com/commonframes/ca.htm?/2000/0047/b3708145.htm [Accessed December 15, 2000]

[72] Eagly AH, Wood W, Diekman AB. Social role theory of sex differences and similarities: A current appraisal. In: Eckes T, Trautner HM, editors. The Developmental Social Psychology of Gender. Mahwah, NJ: Erlbaum; 2000. pp. 123-174

[73] Yoder JD. Making CEOship work more effectively for women. Journal of Social Issues. 2001;**57**:815-828

[74] Fortier I. Les femmes et le CEOship. Gestion. 2008;**3**(33):61-67

[75] Chikh S, Filbien J. Acquisitions and CEO power: Evidence from French networks. Journal of Corporate Finance. 2011;**17**(5):1221-1236

[76] Johnson RA, Hoskisson RE, Hitt MA. Board of director involvement in restructuring: The effects of board versus managerial controls and characteristics. Strategic Management Journal. 1993;**14**:33-50

[77] D'Aveni RA. Top managerial prestige and organizational bankruptcy. Organization Science. 1990;**1**(2):121-142

[78] Finkelstein S. Power in top management teams: Dimensions, measurement, and validation. Academy of Management Journal. 1992;**35**:505-538

[79] Finet A. Chapitre 1. Pourquoi le gouvernement d'entreprise? Introduction et mise en place d'un cadre théorique d'analyse Dans Gouvernement d'entreprise. De Boeck Supérieur. France; 2005. pp. 15-38